The Hanoverian Army of the Napoleonic Wars

Text by PETER HOFSCHRÖER

Colour plates by BRYAN FOSTEN

MEN-AT-ARMS SERIES

EDITOR: MARTIN WINDROW

The Hanoverian Army of the Napoleonic Wars

Text *by* PETER HOFSCHRÖER

Colour plates by BRYAN FOSTEN

OSPREY PUBLISHING LONDON

Published in 1989 by
Osprey Publishing Ltd
59 Grosvenor Street, London, W1X 9DA
© Copyright 1989 Osprey Publishing Ltd

British Library Cataloguing in Publication Data
Hofschröer, Peter
    The Hanoverian Army of the Napoleonic Wars,
    1789–1816.—(Men-at-arms series)
    1. Hanover, Army, 1789–1816
    I. Title   II. Series
    335´.00943´59

    ISBN 0-85045-887-0

Filmset in Great Britain
Printed through Bookbuilders Ltd, Hong Kong

Artist's Note
Readers may care to note that the original paintings
from which the colour plates in this book were
prepared are available for private sale. All
reproduction copyright whatsoever is retained by the
publisher. All enquiries should be addressed to:
    Bryan Fosten
    5 Ross Close
    Nyetimber
    Nr. Bognor Regis
    Sussex PO21 3JW
The publishers regret that they can enter into no
correspondence upon this matter.

Acknowledgements
The author and publisher wish to record their
gratitude to Digby Smith for assistance in assembling
illustrations for this book; and to D. S. V. Fosten for
his invaluable advice during preparation of the colour
plates.

The Hanoverian Army of the Napoleonic Wars

Introduction

Of all the armies of the German States, that of Hanover remains of greatest interest to the British reader due to the close links between the crowns of the two states. One of the great 'ifs' of recent history is the question of the succession to the British throne in 1837. Had the British crown, like that of Hanover, been exclusively the property of the males of the line, then the century-old link between these two crowns would have been maintained. Prussia could not then have seized Hanover in 1866 without risking war with Britain, and Germany could not have been united under Bismarck's Prussia. Where, then, would Britain have stood on the eve of the Great War? Hanover is the symbol of the close relationship of the British and German peoples. Hanoverian regiments went to war in 1914 with cuffbands and helmet badges bearing battle-honours won alongside their British comrades— Gibraltar, the Peninsula and Waterloo.

Hanover's geographical position made her vulnerable to conquest by her predatory neighbours. She had been occupied during the Seven Years' War (1759–1763), was annexed by Prussia in 1806, became part of the Napoleonic satellite 'Kingdom of Westphalia' in 1807, and parts even became absorbed by France in 1810. Refugees from Hanover remained loyal to their legitimate ruler and fled to Britain, participating in the formation of the famous King's German Legion. The state of Hanover was restored after the Battle of Leipzig (October 1813), and became a kingdom in 1814. Throughout this period, Britain and Hanover had the same head of state, George III. He was Prince Elector of Hanover and King of Great Britain until 1820, although his son, who succeeded him as George IV, ruled Britain as Prince Regent from 1810.

The Hanoverian army wore uniforms and carried items of equipment largely similar to those used in the British Army. The King's German Legion, formed in 1803, was based more or less on an amalgam of Hanoverian and British military traditions. Not all redcoats armed with the Brown Bess could speak the 'King's English'—the king himself was perhaps not as proficient in the language as he should have been. Some of the most reliable troops Wellington had at Waterloo were red-coated Germans, veterans of the KGL.

Contemporary watercolour, from the series by Ronnenberg, showing an officer (left) and private of the 8th Infantry Regiment in c.1791; this unit had garrisons at Celle, Gifhorn, Burgdorf and Hildesheim. The red coat was faced white, and buttons and lace were silver and white. For general characteristics, cf. Plates A1, B3.

The Army of the Electorate of Hanover, 1792-1803

At this time, Germany was a federation of states with an elected emperor; this system, a legacy of Charlemagne, finally collapsed under the pressure of the expanding Napoleonic French Empire. The rulers of a selected number of German states formed the electoral college which chose the emperor, the rulers of Hanover being granted this privilege in 1692. Since the 16th century members of the house of Habsburg, the rulers of Austria, had been elected as emperor.

The Electorate of Hanover had met its obligations to the emperor and provided contingents for various wars in the 17th and 18th centuries. Once linked with the British crown, the Hanoverian army fought alongside Britain's armed forces in opposition to Austria and France in the Seven Years' War. After the Peace of Hubertusburg which ended the Seven Years' War, tension remained within Europe, particularly between Prussia and Austria, the rivals for hegemony in central Europe. The smaller German states attempted to form a third power bloc to protect their own interests, but this did not meet with success. The balance of power changed radically once the French Revolution broke out.

From the 1770s, the German states started to examine their administrative systems and some commenced a series of reforms. Karl August von Hardenberg, later a leading reformer in Prussia, attempted to reform the Hanoverian system, but his suggestions were rejected. The fact that George III never visited this part of his domain, leaving its administration to local appointees, did little to help the matter.

Without administrative reforms, there were insufficient moneys available to finance the army that Hanover needed to protect herself from her larger neighbours. Hanover had about 37,000 men in the field in 1762, but this was reduced to 14,000 at the end of the war. In 1785 the army had an establishment of 26,000 men, which continued to decline: in 1802, the Hanoverian army totalled a mere 17,000 men. The following year Hanover was occupied by the French, and the army disbanded.

Her territories became a pawn in the power struggles between Britain, France and Prussia.

The army, however, was not slow to modernise. The experience gained in the Seven Years' War was set out in new drill regulations; the infantry got theirs in 1784, the cavalry in 1787. The cavalry regulations were particularly good. The distances at which attacks were to be launched were restricted so that the commanding officer could maintain better control of his men. Of particular note is the fact that the light dragoons had the same regulations as the rest of the cavalry; the Hanoverian horse was thus becoming more like the 'all-purpose' cavalry of the 19th century than the 'specialist' cavalry of the 18th.

Officer and man of the 14th Infantry in c.1791, at about the time of its return from the Indies but before it (and the 15th) were disbanded and used to form the new 14th Light Infantry. The red coats are faced green; 'metal' and lace are silver and white. Unusually, the officer's lapels bear lace loops; both men seem to have lace-edged collars; and note the atypical lace trim around the tops of the cuffs—the right-hand man may represent an NCO? Plumes in this unit were yellow/white for officers and red/white/green for rankers. (Ronnenberg)

Bataillon zum Gefecht.

```
        K—O—O—O— UOU —O—K—O—K      Ao
pp      —   —   —   — FOF —   —   —   —    pp
 ┤ Dr  U--U—U—U—           —U—U—U—U  ├ Dr
        ΙΙΙΙ ΙΙΙΙ ΙΙΙΙ ΙΙΙΙ    ΙΙΙΙ ΙΙΙΙ ΙΙΙΙ ΙΙΙΙ
 ┬ Ka  O  O  O  O  K  O  O  O  O  ┬ Ka
                      Bt
AAAA Au U———         TTTTT      ———U AAAA Au
A    A   U———        TT TT      ———U A    A
ZZZZ    Schützen     TT TT    H So     ZZZZ
                     TT TT   Schützen
                  ₐKo
```

There was a great emphasis on proper training in the Hanoverian cavalry. In fact, the army command went as far as appointing regimental trainers (*Regimentsbereiter*) centrally, so that each regiment was trained to exactly the same standard. Furthermore, as the North German Plain is well-known for the quality of its horseflesh, the Hanoverian cavalry was particularly well mounted. Despite a lack of funding, Hanover's mounted arm was one of the best trained and mounted in Europe.

At around the same time Artillery and Engineer Schools were founded, and a high level of professionalism was encouraged; artillery NCOs attended for one year, officers for three. Scharnhorst, the famous reformer of the Prussian Army, taught at this school; he had joined Estorff's cavalry regiment as a cornet (*Faehnrich*) in 1787 after receiving instruction from Count William of Schaumburg-Lippe, himself one of the great military thinkers of this era. Scharnhorst soon became one of a group of officers devoted to the reform and modernisation of the Hanoverian army, including the then-Captain Friedrich von der

Hanoverian infantry battalion in battle formation, up to 1803; the key is as follows: *Ko* = commander, *M* = major, *A* = adjutant, *K* = captain, *O* = lieutenant or ensign, *Ao* = artillery officer, *So* = skirmishers' officer, *F* = colour, *U* = NCO, *Au* = artillery NCO, *H* = bugler, *T* = drummer or musician, *Z* = sapper, *A* = gunner, *Bt* = battalion drummer, *Ka* = cannon, *Pr* = limber, *P* = horse; long bars indicate ranks of men.

Decken, later an organiser of the King's German Legion. The regimental school of Estorff's cavalry was noted for the high standards of both practical and theoretical training. (In poor weather, Estorff took his officers indoors and had them practise manoeuvres with models on a sand table—one of the earliest recorded uses of a sand table in military training.)

The level of practical training in Hanover was equally advanced. From 1778, annual manoeuvres were held. These were not so much the 'grand parade' type of manoeuvre common in 18th century armies, but rather proper wargames with two opposing forces. However, despite the close co-operation of all three branches of the army—the infantry, cavalry and artillery—there was no

An infantry battalion in parade formation, pre-1803: the key is as in the previous diagram.

Bataillon zur Parade.

```
        K  O  O  O  K  O  O  O  FOF     O  O  K  O  O  O  KAMKo  Ao  So
                     TTTTTTTTT BT
  A  A                TTTT TTTT                              A  A
U———— A┤├ U—U—U—U—U—U—U—U—U—UUU—U—U—U—U—U—U—U—U A┤├        ———— U
 ‾‾‾  Au A  —  —  —  —  —  —  —  —  —  —  —  —  —  — Au A   ‾‾
Schützen  A ᴬ                                          A ᴬ  Schützen
           U        U      U        U      U      U      U
  pp    4. Kompanie   3. Kompanie   2. Kompanie   1. Kompanie    pp
  ┤ Dr                                         Grenadierkompanie ┤ Dr
 ⸝⸝⸝⸝                                                          ⸝⸝⸝⸝
```

5

Ronnenberg's watercolour of an officer and man of the Militia regiments, *c.*1791. The red coats are faced white; note absence of lace loops on the ranker's uniform. Despite the generally advanced attitude to military training, the Electorate suffered from dwindling manpower, and these ten *Landregimenter* were incorporated into the Line in 1794—a most unpopular decree.

unified command structure like that of the French divisions. This shortcoming became apparent during the Wars of the French Revolution, and Scharnhorst, as Quartermaster-General of the Hanoverian army complained bitterly about it. 'Nobody would ever believe', he remarked, 'that we campaigned for 18 months in the area around Moucron, Menin, Werwick and Courtrai without having a map of the area, and fought battles without precise knowledge of it, even though two engineer officers could have mapped it in a few days.'

From 1786, the regimental artillery was manned by selected men from each battalion of the infantry regiments, who received additional pay for their duties. Furthermore, a battery of horse artillery was

raised, with four 3 pdrs. and two 7 pounders. Two men were seated on the limber and two on the gun carriage; the NCO and four men were mounted. When firing, two men held the horses, so the actual gun crew consisted of an NCO and six men. The limbers of the 3 pdrs. held 76 rounds, those of the howitzers twenty. Each gun was pulled by six horses. During the 1794 campaign another horse battery was raised, and their size was increased to four 3 pdrs., three 6 pdrs. and two 7 pdr. howitzers.

There was a total of 16 regiments of infantry, the last two formed in 1781 for service in the East Indies. Each regiment consisted of one Light and eight Fusilier companies, a total of 1,035 men, including staff. The remnants of the East Indies regiments returned to Hanover in 1791/92 and were used, along with men selected from six other regiments, to form the new 14th Light Regiment: this was to consist of two battalions, each of four companies, and two companies of Jaeger, giving a total strength of 1,664 men. The rifle-armed Jaeger were paid the same rate as the artillery—more than the ordinary infantrymen—and were obliged to serve only two months a year in the army, the rest of their time being spent as gamekeepers. However, in 1801 the Jaeger Companies were disbanded as an economy measure.

The numbers of men in the infantry regiments continued to decline; so in 1794, in the face of considerable opposition and even mutiny, the ten *Landregimenter* or militia regiments were incorporated into the Line. The Electorate's financial plight did not improve. In 1798 the 9th and 12th Infantry Regiments were disbanded and their officers and men transferred to other regiments. In 1802 the regiments were renumbered: the former 10th became the 9th, the 11th the 10th, the 13th the 11th and the 14th the 12th.

It was apparent from experience gained in the campaigns of the Wars of the French Revolution that there was a lack of light infantry in the Hanoverian army. Although the 14th Regiment had performed well in that rôle, it was often outnumbered by the French *tirailleurs* and had to be supplemented by the Grenadiers of the Line regiments. Throughout Germany, as a result of experience gained in the Seven Years' War and American Revolutionary War, a theoretical debate was taking place over the rôle of light infantry and skirmishers. Some Hanoverian officers played an important part in this debate, including Wissel and Emmerich; however, a lack of finances prevented theory being put into practice.

In common with other German states, Hanover started to introduce a light infantry element into the line formations. Du Plat, the Inspector of Infantry, issued a Regulation in 1800 instructing his regiments to train one officer, four NCOs and 60 men per battalion as Sharpshooters (*Scharfschuetzen*), armed with the light Grenadier musket. Moreover, the third rank of each company was to be used as a 'Reserve Platoon' for the skirmish fight (in fact the Hanoverian army was disbanded before this Regulation was put into practice).

Organisation

Infantry

In 1789 the Infantry consisted of one Guard and 15 Line regiments, the last two of which were serving in the East Indies, returning in 1791/92. Each regiment consisted of two battalions each having one company of Grenadiers and five of Musketeers. The regimental staff consisted of one colonel, one lieutenant-colonel, two majors, one regimental surgeon, one regimental drummer, four oboists and the regimental driver.

The 12 companies contained a total of eight captains, two acting captains, 12 lieutenants, ten ensigns, 24 sergeants, 24 junior sergeants, 36 corporals, 28 musicians, 152 grenadiers and 480 musketeers.

Each infantry regiment had four 3 pdr. cannon served by six sergeants and 32 men. The regimental artillery was commanded by a trained artillery officer.

The regimental garrisons were as follows:
Guard Regiment: Hanover. *1st Inf.Regt.*: Muenden, Dransfeld, Hedemuenden, Uslar, Hardegsen. *2nd Inf.Regt.*: Einbeck, Moringen, Osnabrueck. *3rd Inf.Regt.*: Hamlin (Hameln). *4th Inf.Regt.*: Stade. *5th Inf.Regt.*: Verden, Hoya, Walsrode, Buecken, Rethem. *6th Inf.Regt.*: Nienburg, Neustadt, Stolzenau, Wunstorf. *7th Inf.Regt.*: Hamlin. *8th Inf.Regt.*: Celle, Gifhorn, Burgdorf, Hildesheim. *9th Inf.Regt.*: Northeim, Osterode, Goettingen. *10th Inf.Regt.*:

The second and fourth colours of the 10th Infantry Regiment; though not very clearly illustrated in these reproductions from Schirmer, they give an impression of the elaborate designs used in the pre-1803 army. Both were dark green, with a white central disc and blue scrolls, the motifs being painted in natural colours.

The second colour of the 12th Infantry Regiment; in this unit the colours, following the facings, were yellow. The Royal cyphers in the corners of these colours consisted of a crowned 'GR' over 'III'. (Schirmer)

Hanover. *11th Inf.Regt.*: Lueneburg. *12th Inf.Regt.*: Uelzen, Lueneburg, Harburg. *13th Inf.Regt.*: Ratzeburg, Moelln, Lauenburg, Bleckede, Hitzaker, Dannenberg, Luechow, Wulstrow. *14th Inf.Regt.*: East Indies (until 1791/2). *15th Inf.Regt.*: East Indies (until 1791/2).

The Hanoverian army contributed a contingent to the Allied army opposing the French advance into Holland. This Auxiliary Corps consisted of 12–13,000 men and was organised as follows:

General Staff: one general commanding, one lieutenant-general of cavalry, one lieutenant-general of infantry, two major-generals of cavalry, four major-generals of infantry, one major-general of artillery. The general commanding's personal staff consisted of one senior cavalry adjutant, one senior infantry adjutant, one adjutant general and one aide-de-camp. Each of the lieutenant-generals had two senior adjutants, each of the major-generals had one. There were also two brigade majors (cavalry and infantry), two brigade adjutants (cavalry and infantry), one quartermaster general, seven engineer officers, six guides, one staff secretary with one clerk, one auditor general with one clerk, one staff chaplain with one verger, one doctor, one surgeon, one waggon master general, one staff quartermaster. Finally, there were field post and medical personnel.

Infantry: The regiments used for this Corps were the Guard, 4th, 5th, 6th, 10th and 11th. Each regiment consisted of two battalions and was organised as follows:

Senior Staff: colonel, lieutenant-colonel, two majors.

Intermediate and Junior Staff: one regimental quartermaster, two adjutants, one field chaplain, one auditor, one regimental surgeon, one regimental drummer, eight oboists, two drivers, one armourer, one waggon master.

Regimental Artillery: one officer, two sergeants, four corporals, 32 gunners.

Eight Musketeer companies (formed into two battalions): each consisting of one captain, one first lieutenant, one second lieutenant, one ensign, one sergeant-major, four sergeants, five corporals, one company surgeon, three drummers, 14 junior corporals and 124 musketeers.

The Grenadier companies of the six regiments were combined into three Grenadier Battalions. The 1st Bn. consisted of the Grenadier companies of the Guard and 10th Infantry Regts., the 2nd from the 5th and 6th, the 3rd from the 4th and 11th. Each Grenadier battalion was organised as follows:

Staff: one commander, one adjutant, one farrier, one driver.

Company: Each of the four companies consisted of one captain, two first lieutenants, one second lieutenant, one sergeant-major, four NCOs, six corporals, one company surgeon, two fifers, three drummers, 16 junior corporals and 138 grenadiers.

The three battalions were formed into a brigade but were usually used individually. The 1st Grenadier Bn. was employed mainly as light troops.

Right at the beginning of the war, the 14th Infantry Regt. was converted into a light infantry regiment. It was supplied with lighter equipment and weapons and was to have two battalions each of four companies and two companies of Jaeger. The *Staff* consisted of one colonel, one lieutenant-colonel, two majors, one regimental quartermaster, two adjutants, one chaplain, one auditor, one regimental surgeon, one regimental drummer, two drivers, one armourer and one waggon master. Each company had one captain, two first lieutenants, two ensigns, one sergeant-major, four sergeants, six corporals, one company surgeon, two fifers, three drummers, 16 junior corporals and 138 privates. Each of the Jaeger companies consisted of one captain, one first lieutenant, two ensigns, two sergeants, one armourer, one farrier, four corporals, one company surgeon, two buglers and 85 jaeger. The *regimental artillery* consisted of six guns served by 43 men.

For the Campaign of 1794, each regiment received one acting captain, one lieutenant and two ensigns more than before. Furthermore, the Auxiliary Corps was joined by the 1st, 9th, and 14th (Light) Regt. and a 4th Grenadier Bn. formed from the Grenadiers of the 1st and 9th Regiments.

The regiments which remained in Hanover, the 2nd, 3rd, 7th, 8th, 12th and 13th were reinforced by men from the ten militia regiments. Instead of consisting of two battalions each of one Grenadier and five Musketeers companies, each regiment now consisted of two battalions each of one Grenadier and four Musketeer companies and one Depot company.

The Infantry Regiments, now 11 companies strong, were of the following establishment:
Staff: colonel, lieutenant-colonel, two majors, regimental chaplain, four company surgeons, regimental drummer, eight oboists, one driver. *Grenadier company*: one captain, two lieutenants, two sergeants, two junior sergeants, three corporals, two drummers, two fifers, 16 junior corporals and 70 grenadiers. *Musketeer and Depot companies*: one captain, one lieutenant, one ensign, two sergeants, two junior sergeants, three corporals, two drummers, 10 junior corporals and 78 privates. The *regimental artillery* was served by two sergeants, four corporals and 32 men taken from the line.

In 1796 Hanover provided a corps of 15,000 men which formed part of the Combined Prusso-Hanoverian Army of Observation. It consisted of five battalions of Grenadiers, six of Musketeers, and the Light Infantry Regiment with its two battalions and two companies of Jaeger. This Army of Observation was positioned in Westphalia and on the Rivers Hunte and Weser.

Four of the Hanoverian Grenadier battalions consisted of four companies, each with one captain, one lieutenant, two ensigns, one sergeant-major, two sergeants, one senior corporal, one farrier, five corporals, one company surgeon, three drummers, two fifers, 14 junior corporals and 124 grenadiers. The staff consisted of one commander, one adjutant, one battalion surgeon, one staff farrier, one waggon master, one armourer and one driver. The battalion artillery consisted of one sergeant, two corporals and 16 gunners. The artillery train was commanded by a corporal who had seven drivers under him. The battalion train consisted of one driver for the medical waggon, four drivers with the bread waggons and 16 with the pack horses.

The 5th Grenadier Bn. had the same staff, artillery and train as the other companies but had six companies each consisting of one captain, one lieutenant, one ensign, one chaplain, one sergeant,

Officer and man of the Cavalry Life Guard Regiment, c.1791: red coats faced with blue, lined white, with gold 'metal' and lace and white smallclothes; cf.Plate B1. (Ronnenberg)

9

one senior corporal, one farrier, two corporals, one company surgeon, two drummers, two fifers, 16 junior corporals and 74 grenadiers. All five battalions shared two artillery officers.

Each Musketeer battalion had four companies. The staff consisted of two staff officers, one regimental quartermaster, one adjutant, one regimental surgeon, one regimental drummer, one armourer, one waggon master and one driver. Each company consisted of one captain, one lieutenant, two ensigns, one sergeant-major, two sergeants, one senior corporal, one farrier, five corporals, one company surgeon, three drummers, 14 junior corporals and 124 privates. The battalion artillery consisted of one sergeant, two corporals and 16 gunners. The train consisted of one corporal and seven drivers. There were also 20 drivers with the baggage and bread waggons.

The Light Infantry Regiment was of the

following strength: *Staff*: four staff officers, two adjutants, one regimental quartermaster, one regimental surgeon, one battalion surgeon, one regimental drummer, one armourer, one waggon master, one driver. Each *company*: one captain, one lieutenant, two ensigns, one sergeant-major, two sergeants, one senior corporal, one farrier, four corporals, one company surgeon, two drummers, 10 junior corporals, 74 privates. Each *Jaeger company*: one captain, one lieutenant, two ensigns, one sergeant-major, two sergeants, one senior corporal, one farrier, four corporals, one company surgeon, two buglers, one armourer and 84 Jaeger. *Regimental artillery*: two 3 pdrs., two amusettes, one ensign (from the Artillery Regt.), two sergeants, four corporals and 28 gunners. *Artillery train*: two corporals, 15 drivers. *Baggage train*: two drivers with the pack waggon, eight drivers with the bread waggons, 20 drivers with the pack horses.

In 1798, as an economy measure, the 9th and 12th Infantry Regts. were disbanded and their officers and men transferred to the other regiments. Furthermore, every battalion was reduced in strength by one Musketeer company and the 14th Light lost both its Jaeger companies in 1801. From 1799 to 1801, the 9th and 12th Regts. did not exist; the other regiments were not renumbered until 1802.

The Guard Regiment was reorganised as follows: *Staff*: one colonel, one lieutenant-colonel, two majors, two adjutants, one regimental quartermaster, one artillery officer, one regimental surgeon, four company surgeons, one regimental drummer, eight oboists, one driver. *Regimental artillery*: one sergeant, three corporals, 24 gunners. *Grenadier company*: one captain, one first lieutenant, one second lieutenant, one ensign, one sergeant-major, one sergeant, one senior corporal, one farrier, four corporals, two drummers, two fifers, six junior corporals, 86 grenadiers. Three *Musketeer companies* were of the same strength as the Grenadiers except that they had no fifers.

The strength of an Infantry regiment was the same except that it only had one adjutant. The same applied to the Light regiment, except that each of the four companies had three musicians.

Recruits were normally volunteers, though occasionally, units were brought up to strength by forms of conscription, such as in 1793. Substitutes were not allowed. However, raising men in such a way proved too time-consuming and volunteers were taken from the jails—which, of course, led to a decline in disciplinary standards.

The commanders of the Infantry regiments were as follows:

Guard Regiment: 1789—Prince Adolph Friedrich, Duke of Cambridge.

1st Regiment: 1781—von Stockhausen, 1794—von Scheither.

2nd Regiment: 1792—von Issendorff, 1802—von Dincklage.

3rd Regiment: 1792—von Scheither, 1794—von Stedling.

4th Regiment: 1788—von Mutio, 1793—von Bothmer.

5th Regiment: 1788—von der Beck, 1793—von Hohorst, 1797—von Hugo, 1800—von Geyso, 1802—von Hassell.

6th Regiment: 1789—von Bessel, 1792—von Hammerstein.

7th Regiment: 1781—von der Bussche, 1794—du Plat.

8th Regiment: 1762—Prince Ernst of Mecklenburg, 1802—Prince of Schwarzburg-Sondershausen.

9th Regiment: 1792—von Quernheim, 1793—von Wangenheim, 1794—von Duering, 1796—von Hugo, 1798—disbanded.

10th Regiment: 1792—von Diepenbroick, 1796—von Saffe, 1801—von der Wense, 1802—renumbered 9th.

11th Regiment: 1783—Count Taube, 1795—von Diepenbroick, 1802—renumbered 10th.

12th Regiment: 1783—von Linsingen, 1795—von Walthausen, 1798—disbanded.

13th Regiment: 1792—von Bessel, 1795—von Scheither, 1802—renumbered 11th.

14th Regiment: 1793—von Wangenheim, 1794—von Diepenbroick, 1802—renumbered 12th.

Cavalry

In 1789 the Hanoverian Cavalry consisted of *Reiter* or 'Heavy' regiments and Dragoon regiments. Each regiment consisted of four squadrons, each of two companies.

The regimental staff consisted of one colonel, one lieutenant-colonel, one major, one regimental trainer, one surgeon, one regimental veterinary surgeon, one kettle-drummer, one staff trumpeter and one regimental driver.

The Life Guard regiment had five captains, three acting captains, five first lieutenants, eight second lieutenants, eight sergeants, eight quartermasters, eight trainers, 16 corporals, 8 trumpeters and 304 troopers. Each Heavy regiment was of a similar constitution except that it had only two acting captains, six first lieutenants and eight cornets.

The Dragoon regiments were also similar, but had five captains, two acting captains, six first lieutenants and eight ensigns. The staff of a Dragoon regiment consisted of three staff officers, one regimental trainer, one regimental surgeon, one regimental veterinary surgeon, one kettle-drummer, four oboists and one regimental driver. The Light Dragoon regiments had the same staff as the Dragoons and five captains, two acting captains, six first lieutenants and eight second lieutenants.

The headquarters of the regiments were as follows: *Life Guards*: Hanover *1st Cav. Regt.*:

The officer and trooper of the 9th Cavalry (Queen's Light Dragoons) in *c.*1791 display considerable uniform differences from the heavy regiments. The exact design of the jacked cap or hat is hard to make out; cf. our attempted reconstruction in Plate B2. (Ronnenberg)

Unknown artist's impression of an officer of a light company of a Line battalion of the King's German Legion, *c.*1815. (Bomann Museum, Celle)

captains, two first lieutenants, four second lieutenants or cornets, four sergeants, two quartermasters, two company trainers, eight corporals, one smith, three trumpeters, 123 troopers. (The Light Dragoon regiments had one additional armourer in their staffs.)

For the campaign of 1794, each of the Light Dragoon regiments was strengthened by two junior corporals and 52 troopers.

The Army of Observation of 1796 contained two squadrons of each of the following regiments: Life Guards, 4th, 5th, 8th, 9th and 10th. They were later joined by the 1st, 2nd and 3rd Regiments. Each of the regiments consisted of two squadrons as follows: *Staff*: two staff officers, one adjutant, one regimental quartermaster, one regimental surgeon, one regimental veterinary surgeon, two squadron surgeons, one smith, one staff trumpeter, one waggon master, one saddler, one driver. Each *Squadron*: two captains, two lieutenants, two cornets or ensigns, two sergeants, two quartermasters, six corporals, two company trainers, two trumpeters, 120 troopers. *Train*: one driver for the smithy, two drivers for the bread waggons, four drivers for the pack horses.

After the Revolutionary Wars, the 11 regiments were reduced to a strength of two squadrons or four companies. Each regiment was of the following strength:
Staff: two staff officers, one adjutant, one regimental quartermaster, one regimental trainer, one auditor (guard only), one regimental surgeon, one regimental veterinary surgeon, three squadron surgeons, one staff trumpeter, one kettle-drummer (guard only), two smiths. Each *Company*: one captain, one first lieutenant, two second lieutenants (the Heavy and Dragoon Regts. had one second lieutenant and one cornet or ensign), two sergeants, one quartermaster, one company trainer, four corporals, one trumpeter, 78 troopers (the Light Dragoons had six junior corporals and 72 troopers).

Artillery & Train
In 1789 the Artillery Regiment consisted of two battalions each of five companies. The staff consisted of one colonel, one lieutenant-colonel, two majors, one regimental surgeon, one secretary, one regimental drummer and seven oboists. In the 10

Lueneberg. *2nd Cav. Regt.*: Celle. *3rd Cav. Regt.*: Stade. *4th Cav. Regt.*: Harburg. *5th Cav. Regt.*: Verden. *6th Cav. Regt.*: Goettingen. *7th Cav. Regt.*: Nienburg. *8th Cav. Regt.*: Northeim. *9th Cav. Regt.*: Isernhagen. *10th Cav. Regt.*: Wunstorf.

The Auxiliary Corps which went to Holland in 1794 contained two squadrons from each of the following regiments: Life Guards, 1st, 2nd, 4th, 5th, 7th, 9th and 10th. These units were formed into Combined Regiments as follows: Life Guards and 2nd, 1st and 4th, 5th and 7th, 9th and 10th. Each of the Combined Regiments consisted of:
Staff: three staff officers, one regimental quartermaster, one adjutant, one regimental trainer, one chaplain, one auditor, one regimental surgeon, four squadron surgeons, one regimental veterinary surgeon, one staff trumpeter, four squadron trumpeters, one waggon master, one saddler, one driver. Each *Squadron* of two companies—two

companies, there was a total of six captains, three acting captains, seven lieutenants, ten ensigns, 32 sergeants, 52 corporals, 10 drummers, 64 bombardiers and 480 gunners. The regiment was garrisoned in Hanover, Hamlin, Ratzeburg, Stade and Harburg.

The Auxiliary Corps of 1793 was joined by three divisions of artillery, a total of 24 cannon and 14 howitzers. Two divisions each consisted of ten 6 pdrs., four 7 pdrs. and two 30 pdr. howitzers. Each division was divided into two batteries, each of the same constitution. The third division consisted of so-called 'Fast' or Horse Artillery, equipped with four 3 pdrs. and two 7 pdr. howitzers.

The manpower was allocated as follows: *Horse Artillery*: four officers, two sergeants, 12 corporals, one farrier, two assistant farriers, two drummers, 48 bombardiers and gunners, one armourer, one assistant, one company surgeon.

1st and 2nd Division: Each 12 (2nd 14) officers, seven sergeants, 24 corporals, three farriers, six assistant farriers, six drummers, 192 bombardiers and gunners, one armourer, one assistant, one surgeon (second division only), two company surgeons.

For each howitzer the Horse Artillery carried: 60 shells, 60 rounds of canister, 17 incendiaries; and for each cannon, 136 round and grapeshot. In reserve for each howitzer were 54 shells, 55 rounds of canister and three incendiaries; in reserve for each cannon were 128 roundshot and 192 rounds of grapeshot.

Each Division of heavy artillery carried, for each 30 pdr. howitzer, 90 shells, ten rounds of grapeshot, ten incendiaries; for each 7 pdr. howitzer—180 shells, 50 rounds of canister, 20 incendiaries; and for each cannon—210 round and grapeshot.

The Regimental Artillery had 136 roundshot and 84 grape for each gun; the Grenadier Battalions, however, carried 192 round and 128 grape.

The same amount of ammunition was carried in the Reserve Train as with the guns, as well as 192 rounds of ball and 128 of grape for each regimental cannon.

The Artillery had the following Train personnel: *Horse Artillery* one officer, 11 NCOs, one surgeon, one veterinary surgeon, 125 train soldiers, 309 horses. *Heavy Divisions* one captain, four officers, 46 NCOs, one surgeon, one veterinary surgeon, etc.,

totalling 432 men and 1,005 horses. *Reserve Ammunition Train* of the Heavy Guns one officer, eight NCOs, etc., totalling 189 men and 468 horses.

The Artillery Staff consisted of one commander, two majors, two regimental adjutants, one regimental quartermaster, one chaplain, one secretary, one auditor, one regimental surgeon, one chief armourer (Artillery), four armourers (Artillery), four assistants, four company surgeons, one regimental drummer, one armourer (small arms) with two apprentices, one cooper with one apprentice, one driver.

A 2nd Division of Horse Artillery was raised for the 1794 Campaign.

Surviving coatee of an officer of the 5th Line Battalion, KGL, c.1815. Of scarlet faced with dark blue, it is laced gold; the gilt buttons bear a crown over 'KGL' over '5'. On the white tail turnbacks are dark blue diamonds bearing a crown above 'KGL' above crossed branches. (Stadtmuseum Hannover)

King's Colour, 4th Line Bn., KGL, awarded by George III in 1806 and carried at Waterloo. Made of painted silk, the Union flag bears a crown and a wreath of mixed roses and thistles in natural colours, around a dark blue cartouche edged with gold stylised foliate bordering and bearing 'KING'S/GERMAN LEGION/IV BATTALION' in gold. (Stadtmuseum Hannover)

The Corps of Observation of 1796 had one company (battery) of Horse Artillery at the following strength: one captain, one first lieutenant, one second lieutenant, one ensign, three sergeants, 12 corporals, one farrier, two guards for the farrier, one bugler, 55 gunners. Its two batteries of Heavy Artillery each consisted of: two captains, two first lieutenants, four second lieutenants or ensigns, six sergeants, 12 corporals, two farriers, four guards, four drummers and 108 gunners. The Horse Battery had two 7 pdr. howitzers and four 3 pdrs.; each Heavy Battery had three 7 pdr. howitzers and six 6 pounders.

The Staff consisted of one lieutenant-colonel, one adjutant, one battalion surgeon, five company surgeons, one armourer, one assistant, two apprentices and one driver. The Staff of the Artillery Train consisted of one lieutenant-colonel, one regimental quartermaster, one adjutant and one quartermaster.

The Horse Artillery had a Train Company which consisted of one captain, one lieutenant, one ensign, one waggon master, four sergeants and quartermasters, seven corporals, one harnessmaker, one company surgeon, one veterinary surgeon, two apprentice smiths, two apprentice wheelwrights, two apprentice saddlers and 24 train soldiers. Each Heavy Battery had a Train Company at the following strength: one captain, one lieutenant, one ensign, one waggon master, five sergeants and quartermasters, nine corporals, one harnessmaker, one company surgeon, one veterinary surgeon, one master smith and three apprentices, one master wheelwright and two apprentices, one master saddler and two apprentices, 129 train soldiers.

The Staff consisted of one major, one adjutant, one regimental quartermaster, one secretary, one regimental surgeon, three company surgeons, one chief armourer, one assistant, four junior armourers, four assistants and the regimental drummer.

In 1795, the Horse Artillery was equipped with 6 pdrs. drawn by eight horses.

After the Revolutionary Wars were over, the artillery was reorganised as follows: two batteries of Horse Artillery attached to the Cavalry Divisions; three batteries of Line Artillery attached to the three Infantry Divisions; one battery of Heavy Artillery in the Reserve; and two batteries in the fortresses.

A Horse Battery consisted of two 7 pdr. howitzers, six 6 pdr. and four 3 pdr. cannon; a Line Battery consisted of two 7 pdr. howitzers and six 6 pdr. cannon; the Reserve Battery consisted of six 12 pounders.

Engineers

From 1789 the Miner and Sapper Company had its depot in Hamlin, the Pontoon and Pioneer Company in Hanover. The Auxiliary Corps of 1793 had a detachment of pioneers consisting of one sergeant, one corporal, one drummer and 15 pioneers. They had two mobile bridges.

The Auxiliary Corps of 1794 had a Pontoon Train of 24 pontoons with the necessary men, that is six engineer officers including the two with the Pontoon Company, one master pontooneer, one sergeant, two corporals, one surgeon, one drummer, 50 pontooneers and a Pontoon Train Company of one officer, one master harnessmaker, one train surgeon, one veterinary surgeon, one assistant, two train sergeants, six train corporals, 80 train soldiers and 242 horses.

After the Revolutionary Wars, the Engineer Corps consisted of one colonel, one lieutenant-colonel, one major, three captains, seven lieutenants, five ensigns and two conductors; a Miner Company of two sergeants, two corporals, two musicians and 30 miners; and a Pontoon Company of the same strength.

Uniforms to 1803

Generals and Staff

In 1791 generals wore a black felt tricorn hat decorated with gold lace, yellow silver tassels and a black rosette. The red frock coat had a dark blue collar, lapels and Swedish cuffs. The collar, lapels and cuffs were trimmed with gold lace; on the collar was a single bar of gold lace, on the lapels four pairs, and on the cuffs one pair. The tail turnbacks were white with a button. The waistcoat and jacket were white, the buttons gilt. The épée was carried in a black scabbard with silver fittings and a yellow silver sword knot.

General staff officers wore the same hat, a red frock coat without colouring on the collar, lapels and cuffs, a white waistcoat with gilt buttons and white trousers. The coat had 11 small bars of lace on each side and four chevrons on the lower part of the sleeves; the coat-tail turnbacks were white.

The epaulettes worn by generals and general staff officers were gold with fringes and two crossed marshal's batons. They also wore high black boots; and the sword carried by staff officers was similar to that of the generals.

Infantry

The black hats were trimmed with silver lace for Line officers and NCOs, with white for other ranks; tassels and cords were white for the rankers, silver for officers. The Guards Regiment had gold and yellow trim instead. Officers sported a black cockade, the men a white loop and button. The colours of the plumes distinguished the regiment (see chart below). The 14th and 15th Regts. had tall feather plumes, in red/white/green for rankers and yellow/white for officers. Grenadiers wore bearskin

caps with a silver plate bearing the leaping horse and crowned 'GR' cypher; some regiments, e.g. the 14th, also had their number on this plate. For the 1792 campaign the 1st Grenadier Bn. was issued with Corsican hats trimmed white, with white feather plumes; officers had yellow/white plumes.

The infantry coat was red, lined white; the Guard had gilt buttons, the Line silver. Cuffs, lapels, a single left shoulder strap, and a strap fastening the coat-tail turnbacks, were all coloured to distinguish the regiment (see chart below). NCOs had silver lace on their cuffs, and probably on the lapels and collars as well. Line officers had silver-fringed epaulettes, Guard officers gold. The men's lapels were decorated with bars of white lace and buttons (yellow in the Guard Regt.); officers' lapels bore silver (or gold) buttons only. There appear to have been two buttons beneath the tail pocket flap.

The waistcoat and trousers were white, the latter

Bugler of the Sharpshooter section of a KGL Line battalion, in field service marching order, c.1815. The shako tuft and cords are green, as are the bugle cords; the lace trimming on the coatee is blue on white, apparently musician's pattern. Note Sharpshooter's white waist belt with small 'expense' pouch. (Unknown artist: Bomann Museum, Celle)

in linen from 1 May to 1 November and in heavier cloth for the rest of the year. Boots and gaiters were black. The shirt collar showed over a black neckstock. Greatcoats were introduced for rankers in 1794, and were carried folded on top of the knapsack when not in use. Officers had always worn blue overcoats in foul weather, and boots instead of gaiters.

Grenadiers were armed with muskets, bayonets and infantry sabres; Line infantry (Fusiliers) with muskets and bayonets; light companies with rifles and bayonets; the slings were white. The rankers' sabre had a brass hilt and a brass-furnished brown scabbard. Officers' épées were silver-hilted, with yellow/silver knots, and brown leather scabbards. Grenadier officers wore sabres (they were also

Uniforms of the Hanoverian Infantry 1791 (After Ronnenberg)

Regt.	Lapels	Cuffs	Shoulder strap	Tail strap	Hat plume/pompon	Buttons
Guard	dk. blue	dk. blue	red	yellow	yellow & blue	gold
1st	green	green	green	green	white & green	silver
2nd	dk. blue	dk. blue	red	blue	white & blue	silver
3rd	black	black	white	white	white & black	silver
4th	sky blue	sky blue	sky blue	sky blue	white, red, sky blue	silver
5th	yellow	yellow	red	yellow	white & yellow	silver
6th	green	green	green, white trim	green	white & green	silver
7th	dk. green	dk. green	yellow, white trim	green	white & dk. green	silver
8th	white	white	red	white	white & red	silver
9th	white	white	white	white	white & red	silver
10th	dk. green	dk. green	red	green	white & dk. green	silver
11th	black	black	red	black	white, black & red	silver
12th	yellow	yellow	yellow	yellow	white, red & yellow	silver
13th	sky blue	sky blue	red	sky blue	white, sky blue, red	silver
14th	green	green	red, white trim	green, white trim	red, white & green	silver
15th	green	green	red, white trim	green, white trim	red, white & green	silver

NB: All regiments had eight bars of lace on their lapels; and the 14th and 15th had green collars.

Uniforms of the Hanoverian Cavalry (Schirmer, p. 183)

Regt.	Collar	Lapels	Cuffs	Tails	Tail strap	Waistcoat	Buttons
Life Gds.	dk. blue	dk. blue	dk. blue	white	blue & yellow	white	gold
1st	red	red	red	white	blue & yellow	white	gold
2nd	white	white	white	white	blue & yellow	white	gold
3rd	yellow	yellow	yellow	white	blue & white	white	silver
4th	white	white	white	white	blue & white	white	silver
5th Dr.	—	white	white	white	blue & white	white	silver
6th Dr.	—	yellow	yellow	white	blue & white	white	silver
7th Dr.	—	yellow	yellow	white	blue & white	white	silver
8th Dr.	—	white	white	white	blue & yellow	white	gold
9th Lt.Dr.	—	red	red	white	red & yellow	white	gold
10th Lt.Dr.	—	red	red	white	red & white	white	silver

permitted moustaches). Swords were carried from white baldrics; rankers' had oval brass plates, officers', silver plates with red enamel details.

In the 1792 campaign, the 1st Grenadier Bn., trained as light troops, fought in two ranks; regulations give them red musket slings, but contemporary illustrations show white. (They also had British wooden water bottles.)

The 14th Light Infantry had grey coats with grey lapels; brass buttons bearing the regimental number; green collars, cuffs and lining; and epaulettes for all ranks in yellow (?gold for officers). All rankers were armed with the light infantry musket; small cartridge boxes were carried and all belts were black. The regiment had no colours, and officers did not wear gorgets.

The Jaeger Companies had green coats with green lapels, and green jackets. Officers and NCOs had gold lace and epaulettes, rankers gold epaulettes but no lace. Buff leather trousers were worn with grey cloth gaiters. Headgear was the Corsican hat, folded up on the left side, with a green plume; officers and senior NCOs had a silver/yellow or white/yellow cord around the hat. Belts were black. NCOs and Jaegers (including buglers) were armed with rifles and *Hirschfaenger*—the traditional huntsman's sidearm. (Much of the above information comes from a contemporary source, the series of illustrations by Ronnenberg dated 1791.)

In 1800 a new type of infantry tunic was introduced, with high collars trimmed with white. The tunic was decorated with white lace 'loops' in much the same way as contemporary British infantry tunics. Shoulder straps were regimentally coloured, and piped white. The Grenadiers' fur cap had a white metal plate. The queue was now false, and pinned in place.

Like a number of other German states at this time, Hanover introduced sections of light *Scharfschuetzen* into its infantry battalions. When in the field each battalion was to have 60 of these Sharpshooters, led by one officer and four NCOs. They were armed with the light Grenadier musket and a short sidearm; NCOs had rifles, officers sabres. Their belts were black.

Colours

Each battalion of each infantry regiment carried two Colours. The 1st Colour of the 1st Battalion was

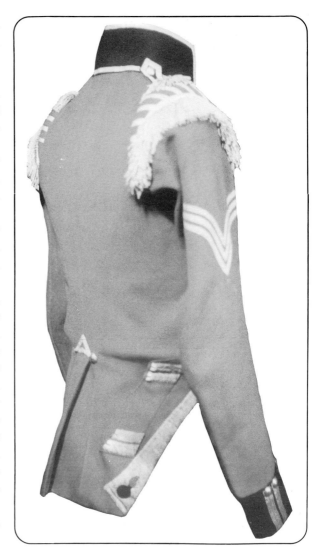

Coatee of a sergeant, grenadier company, Line battalion. The buttons are missing from the lace loops on the false pocket flaps; otherwise this important survival shows clearly the details of KGL coatees. The turnback ornament is interesting: a blue grenade with a red flame. (Bomann Museum, Celle)

known as the *Leibfahne* and was the same in nearly every regiment. The reverse of the *Leibfahne* displayed either the royal cypher or the leaping horse. During the French Revolutionary Wars, the following Infantry Colours were carried:

Guard Regt., 1st & 2nd Bns.
White field with the British Royal coat-of-arms, lion and unicorn. Underneath it, a blue scroll bearing the motto DIEU ET MON DROIT. Emblems of Royal Orders in each corner.

1st Regt.
Leibfahne: White field with the Royal coat-of-arms, lion and unicorn, garter of the Royal Order of the

Detail of the shoulder wing of a private's coatee, light company of a KGL Line battalion, or possibly of a Sharpshooter section: the small applied badge, in white embroidery on dark blue, shows a buglehorn. (Bomann Museum, Celle)

Garter with the motto HONI SOIT QUI MAL Y PENSE. Underneath that, a blue band bearing the motto DIEU ET MON DROIT. *2nd Colour*: Dark green field. A disc bearing a sword and wheel surrounded by a cloud and being approached by a lion. Above it, a scroll with the motto TU NE CEDE MALIS. *3rd Colour*: Prone, watchful lion under the inscription VIGILANTIA VINCIT. *4th Colour*: Unknown.

2nd Regt.

Leibfahne: As 1st Regt. *2nd Colour*: Dark blue field. Centre disc with a cloud coming down from it, an armoured hand holding a sword inscribed VICTORIA. Above this device, a scroll with the motto SI DEUS PRO NOBIS, QUIS CONTRA NOS. *3rd Colour*: Dark blue field with a lion. Motto: OFFENDO ET DEFENDO. *4th Colour*: Dark blue with a globe, the twelve signs of the Zodiac, sun, moon and stars. Motto: NON RETRORSUM.

3rd Regt.

Leibfahne: As 1st Regt. *2nd Colour*: Black 'Gibraltar' flag, blue band with the motto: MIT ELIOTT RUHM UND SIEG. Under the band, a grey rock inscribed GIBRALTAR and ten floating batteries surrounded by a laurel wreath. Below that, a blue band with the motto: DEN 14.SEPTEMBER IM JAHRE 1782. In the corners, the Royal cypher. *3rd Colour*: White field. A laurel wreath; inside it, a tower with the motto WACHSAMKEIT. In the corners, the Royal cypher. *4th Colour*: White field and centre. Laurel wreath. Two Germanic warriors shaking hands over a sacrificial altar. Over the top of this, a blue scroll with the motto DEUTSCHE FREYHEIT ODER TOT. In the corners, the Royal cypher.

4th Regt.

Leibfahne: As 1st Regt. *2nd Colour*: Light blue field. Device as 2nd Colour of 2nd Regt. Motto: DULCE ET DECORUM PRO PATRIA MORI. *3rd Colour*: Light blue. Mars sitting on trophies. Motto: PRO FIDE, REGE ET LEGE. *4th Colour*: Light blue. Man in armour with a lance pointing towards a pillar decorated with laurel wreaths. Motto: BELLICAE VIRTUTIS PRAEMIUM.

5th Regt.

Leibfahne: As 1st Regt. *2nd Colour*: Yellow 'Gibraltar' flag. *3rd Colour*: As the *Leibfahne*. *4th Colour*: Armoured Roman between two pillars joined together by a chain and decorated with three laurel wreaths which he is cutting with his sword. Motto: ANTIQUAE AVIDUS GLORIAE.

6th Regt.

Leibfahne: As 1st Regt. *2nd Colour*: Dark green 'Gibraltar' flag. *3rd Colour*: Possibly as the *Leibfahne*. *4th Colour*: Mars on trophies, a genius flying towards him. Motto: NULLI SINE MORTE TRIUMPHI.

7th Regt.

Leibfahne: As 1st Regt. *2nd Colour*: The Fama holding a sheet of paper bearing the words: EXTENDERE FACTIS. *3rd Colour*: Possibly as the *Leibfahne*. *4th Colour*: Light straw yellow. Pyramid with a snake winding its way up. Motto: PER ARDUA VIRTUS.

8th Regt.

1st Colour: Crimson field. White centre with lion. Over that, a blue scroll with the motto UT ALII DORMIANT. All surrounded by a laurel wreath. In the corners, the Royal cypher. *2nd Colour*: Crimson field. White centre surrounded by laurel wreath. In the centre, a Roman warrior drawing his sword. Above that, a blue scroll with the motto REGI ET PATRIAE. In the corners, the Royal cypher. *3rd Colour*: Crimson field. Armoured arm with a sword coming out of a grey cloud. The sword is wrapped in laurel leaves. Motto: RE NON VERBIS. *4th Colour*: As 1st.

9th Regt.

Leibfahne: As 1st Regt. *2nd Colour*: Green. A lion going to Wrath with a sword. Motto: PRO FIDE REGE ET LEGE. *3rd Colour*: As *Leibfahne*. *4th Colour*: Green. Armoured arm coming out of a cloud holding a sheet of paper; on it, the word JEHOVAH. Motto: QUIS CONTRA NOS.

10th Regt.

Leibfahne: As 1st Regt. *2nd Colour*: Dark green. Laurel wreath around white centre disc. Armoured arm coming out of cloud with sword. Above it, blue scroll with motto CUI VULT. In the corners, the Royal cypher. *3rd Colour*: Dark green. Red banner with Royal Monogram, surrounded by trophies. Motto: BEY DIESEN NAMEN ÜBERWINDEN ODER STERBEN. In the corners, the Royal cypher. *4th Colour*: Dark green. White centre disc surrounded by laurel wreath. Monument with trophies. Over

Sergeant-major of a KGL Line battalion, *c.*1815. The double-breasted coatee bears all gold lace; the shako cords and rank badge are also shown gold, as is the overall stripe. (Unknown artist: Bomann Museum, Celle)

that, a blue scroll with the motto DER TAPFERKEIT BELOHNUNG.

11th Regt.

Leibfahne: As 1st Regt. *2nd Colour*: Yellow. Lion with sword, leaning on tree stump. Motto: WER DARF ES MIR NEHMEN? *3rd Colour*: White. Ermine in front of a cavern surrounded by a laurel wreath. Motto: LIEBER STERBEN ALS BEFLECKT SEIN. *4th Colour*: White. As 3rd Colour except with trophies around the laurel wreath and two chained slaves under it.

12th Regt.

Leibfahne: As 1st Regt. *2nd Colour*: Yellow. Armoured warrior carrying sword. Motto: DECORI MISCETUR VIRTUS. *3rd Colour*: Yellow. Lion with sword. Motto: IN PACE AD BELLUM PARATUS. *4th Colour*: Yellow. Rocks in sea with winds, waves and lightning. Motto: TU NE CEDE MALIS.

13th Regt.

Leibfahne: As 1st Regt. *2nd Colour*: Dark blue. Four wreaths and crowns with the motto: PRAEMIA SPERATA. *3rd & 4th Colours*: Unknown.

14th Regt.

Leibfahne: Probably as 1st Regt. *2nd Colour*: White. Ermine surrounded by yellow scroll with the motto: MALO MORI QUAM FOEDARI. *3rd Colour*: White. Lion with sword in one paw, a death's head in the other. Motto: AUT MORI AUT VINCERE. *4th Colour*: Unknown.

15th Regt. Colours unknown.

Cavalry

The Life Guard Regiment wore red coats, while all other cavalry regiments had blue coats with white coat-tail turnbacks fastened together by means of a button. The coat lapels had four buttons, the Swedish cuffs two. There was also one button on the collar. The Dragoons had an additional button in the top corners of the lapels, and fringed epaulettes. The hat was trimmed with lace of the button colour and had a black cockade. It had a yellow and white plume. For the regimental distinctions, see charts.

Belts, cartridge boxes and other leatherwork were white. The greatcoat bag was dark blue faced white. The saddle cloth and holster covers were dark blue trimmed with lace in the button colour. In the corner of the cloth was the white leaping horse emblem in a red field surrounded by a yellow wreath and crown. The Life Guards had a red shabraque with a yellow trim, the corner emblem consisted of the cypher 'GR' surrounded by the garter with a crown above it. The holsters had only the letters and crown. This regiment's greatcoat bags were also red.

Artillery

Gunners wore a blue-grey coat with red facings and light blue shoulder strap. Buttons were yellow. The hat had a gold trim and tassel, a black cockade and gold clasp. The waistcoat and trousers were white. Belts were natural leather.

Tactics

Infantry

Mention has already been made of the Regulations of 1784. A closer look at the Regulations of 1802 would perhaps show how the tactics of the Hanoverian army developed in the light of the experience of the Revolutionary Wars.

The central point of these Regulations was the necessity to co-ordinate the Line and Light infantry. Each battalion consisted of four companies, a section of *Schuetzen* (light infantry) and two cannon. The line companies were formed into three ranks, and the primary functions of the front two ranks were to deliver controlled volleys and bayonet charges. The rôle of the light troops was to fight in broken terrain; to cover the movements of the Line companies, especially from enemy skirmishers; to protect the cannon; and to form van, rear and flank guard when on the march. The third rank of each company was formed into a reserve which was to be used where necessary, particularly to support the *Schuetzen*. This use of skirmishers and the combination of Line and Light troops was similar to the practices of other German states at this time; readers are referred to MAA 149, *Prussian Light Infantry, 1792–1815* for a fuller account of how skirmishers functioned at this time.

The battalion deployed into battle order as follows: On the order '*Batallion, zum Gefecht-rangiert!*', all officers and delegated NCOs took up their positions. The leading officer went to the front rank, the colour officer and two senior corporals stood in the second rank with the colour. The captain of the reserve stood behind the centre of the

Cap plate as worn on the 1812 Belgic shako by a soldier of the 7th Line Bn., KGL. (Bomann Museum, Celle)

battalion, his officers and NCOs behind their respective divisions. The cannon were placed on each flank, the gunners and sappers formed up with them. The light ammunition waggon was placed 100 paces behind the centre of the battalion. The *Schuetzen* stood in two ranks behind the flanks of the battalion. The musicians formed up behind the centre of the battalion.

There were two ways in which the Line infantry fired: by division or by battalion. Firing was by the front two ranks only, as the third rank was pulled out of the line and used as a reserve. Each company consisted of two divisions; firing by division was from right to left.

Bayonet charges were made as follows: a volley was fired, and the battalion advanced towards the enemy as quickly as possible. At ten paces from the enemy, the front rank would charge bayonets while the second would hold their muskets in one hand on the right side.

Square was formed as follows: the 3rd Coy. remained standing with the colour party behind it. The 2nd Coy. formed the right flank, the 4th the left and the 1st Coy. closed the square. The reserve formed the third rank, one cannon was placed at the corner formed by the 3rd and 2nd Coys, the other at the corner between the 1st and 4th. The *Schuetzen* covered the gaps around the guns and between the companies. The limbers and ammunition waggon were placed inside the square wherever possible.

Cavalry

The Regulations of 1787 remained in force throughout the Revolutionary Wars.

The squadron was formed as follows. The right flank company was formed from the right to left, the left flank company from the left to right. The biggest men on the best and fastest horses were placed in the front rank. Every effort was made to have uniformity of size in the front rank. On parade, the captain rode two paces in front of the centre, the lieutenant one pace in front of the second section of the right flank, and the cornet or ensign one pace in front of the second section of the left. The sergeant-major rode behind the front, one pace to the rear of the second rank with the senior company officer; the quartermaster rode with the junior company officer. The company trainer and two corporals rode on both flanks of the first rank and on the right of the second. The trumpeter rode on the right flank of the first rank.

Cavalry attacks were made by regiment in line, echelon and column. The signal to attack was given by trumpet. The standards fell back into the second rank and their place in the front rank was taken by another trooper. The squadron commanders remained in front of their squadrons. The regiment advanced at a walk, the second squadron giving the direction. When closer to the enemy, the walk became a trot; 200 paces from the enemy the order to gallop was given; and the charge was made when 120 paces from the enemy. When charging, the second rank was to double its distance from the first.

The object of an attack in echelon was to hit the enemy in the flank. The attack in column was made only when the terrain restricted deployment, otherwise the line was the preferred formation.

The King's German Legion

Sandwiched between an expanding French Empire and a greedy Prussia, the state of Hanover soon became a pawn in the struggles of the Great Powers. When war broke out again between France and Britain in May 1803, the French invaded Hanover and forced her army to adopt neutrality. A group of patriotic officers sponsored by the Duke of Cambridge set about recruiting a force of volunteers

Puzzling contemporary plate of an officer of the 1st Light Bn., KGL, 1812, by an unknown artist. It seems to incorporate known features of the uniforms of both Light battalions. The headgear could be either the shako of the 1st or the mirleton of the 2nd, but has the gold cords recorded for the 2nd. The jacket has the three rows of buttons recorded for the 2nd, but the pointed cuffs of the 1st, and white or silver piping rather than the black recorded for both. On balance, this looks closer to the 2nd Bn. than the 1st. (Bomann Museum, Celle)

Officer of the 1st Light Bn., KGL, by Schwertfeger. This follows the conventional versions of the uniform: green shako plume and cords; green jacket with two rows of silver buttons and silver shoulder-scales; black facings and braid trim.

In February 1806, the Legion consisted of the following:

1st Horse Bty.: Capt. Julius Hartmann
2nd Horse Bty.: Capt. August Roettiger
1st Foot Bty.: Capt. Heinrich Brueckmann
2nd Foot Bty.: Capt. Heinrich Kuhlmann
3rd Foot Bty.: Capt. Ludwig Heise
4th Foot Bty.: Capt. Friedrich Ruperti
1st Heavy Dragoon Regt.: Col. Georg von Bock
2nd Heavy Dragoon Regt.: Maj.-Gen. Otto von Schulte
1st Light Dragoon Regt.: Maj.-Gen. Karl von Linsingen
2nd Light Dragoon Regt.: Maj.-Gen. Victor von Alten
3rd Light Dragoon Regt.: Col. Georg von Reden
1st Light Bn.: Col. Karl von Alten
2nd Light Bn.: Lt.Col. Colin Halkett
1st Line Bn.: Col. Christian von Ompteda
2nd Line Bn.: Col. Adolf von Barsse
3rd Line Bn.: Col. Heinrich von Hinueber
4th Line Bn.: Col. Ernst von Langwerth
5th Line Bn.: Col. Georg von Drieberg
6th Line Bn.: Col. August von Honstedt
7th Line Bn.: Col. Friedrich von Drechsel
8th Line Bn.: Col. Peter du Plat

Organisation

As part of the British Forces, the KGL came under the command of the Duke of York. The Duke of Cambridge was Colonel-in-Chief of the Legion, and his Adjutant-General was Col. von der Decken. From 1806 the Legion's artillery was placed under the overall control of the Board of Ordnance.

There was no general staff as such in the Legion because its units tended to be used individually or in small groups. Brigades and divisions were temporary formations for use in the field only, and these larger formations tended to contain a mixture of troops from British, Portuguese and KGL units. Moreover, the Legion's generals often commanded such a formation rather than a purely KGL force. The Light Battalions and the Heavy Dragoons were never used separately, but the artillery was almost always attached to different formations.

The KGL's artillery was designated a 'regiment' after the formation of the 4th Foot Battery. This term, however, denoted only its administrative position and not its tactical use. The regimental staff

from Hanover to serve the British crown. After initial hesitation, recruits flooded to England. From 13 October, this corps was designated the 'King's German Regiment'; on 19 December, the designation became the 'King's German Legion', a force consisting of elements of all arms.

The Legion continued to grow. Two battalions of light infantry were formed, the favoured recruits coming from the Hanoverian Light Regiment. Hanoverian Guards were taken into the 1st Bn; and by February 1806 the Legion had a total of eight Line Battalions. Initially, one Heavy and one Light Dragoon Regiment were formed. A 2nd and then a 3rd Light Regt. were formed subsequently, along with a 2nd Heavy Regiment. The artillery grew in a similar fashion. Initially, one Horse and one Foot Battery was raised, followed by more as the manpower became available.

consisted of one colonel commander, one lieutenant-colonel, two majors, each with one adjutant, quartermaster and auditor, five surgeons, one veterinary surgeon, one sergeant-major, one quartermaster-sergeant and one auditor-sergeant.

Each horse battery consisted of one captain first class, one captain second class, two first, two second lieutenants, one sergeant-major, one quartermaster, three sergeants, four corporals, seven bombardiers, one trumpeter, 90 gunners, one farrier, two smiths, one collarmaker and two wheelers. The train consisted of one sergeant, two corporals, one trumpeter and 57 drivers. There were six guns in a battery, five 6 pdrs. and one $5\frac{1}{2}$ in. howitzer, the former with six-horse limbers, the latter with an eight-horse limber.

The foot batteries, of which some had 6 pdrs. and some 9 pdrs., likewise had six officers, but only three sergeants. When mounted, the musicians were trumpeters, when dismounted, drummers. The 6 pdr. batteries tended to have four cannon and two howitzers; the 9 pdr. batteries always had four cannon and two $5\frac{1}{2}$ in. howitzers. The latter were also three bombardiers, four gunners, 39 drivers and one smith stronger. Each battery had eight ammunition and two baggage waggons and one field smithy. These waggons were all drawn by six horses. The carriages were produced under the supervision of Capt. Roettiger and were lighter than those used by the British troops.

The staff of a cavalry regiment consisted of one colonel commander, two majors, one of which normally commanded the regiment with the rank of colonel or lieutenant-colonel, one adjutant, one auditor, three surgeons, one veterinary surgeon, one sergeant-major, one auditor-sergeant, one saddler, one armourer, one farrier. A troop consisted of one captain, one lieutenant, one cornet, one quartermaster, four sergeants, four corporals, one trumpeter and 76 privates. The troops were designated by letter, A, B, C, etc., and the squadrons were numbered.

The staff of an infantry battalion consisted of one colonel commander, one lieutenant-colonel, who, with the rank of colonel, normally commanded the battalion, two majors, one adjutant, one auditor, one quartermaster, three surgeons, one sergeant-major, one auditor-sergeant, one quartermaster-sergeant and one armourer. A company consisted of

Schwertfeger shows this soldier of the 1st Light Bn. in the conventional black shako with green tuft, silver badge and green cord; green jacket with one row of silver buttons, and black facings at collar, cuff, shoulder strap, with large black tufts and black lace trim.

one captain, two lieutenants, one ensign, five sergeants, five corporals, one musician (drummer in the Line battalions, bugler in the Light), 96 privates and one pioneer. The companies were distinguished by letter.

Drill and Training

Initially, the Hanoverian Regulations were used and orders were given in German. In contrast to the British Army, where drill was the responsibility of the NCOs, KGL officers drilled their men personally, and a high standard was thus maintained. The KGL was regarded as the equivalent of the Guards and crack Line formations of the British Army.

When the Legion's artillery fell under the jurisdiction of the Board of Ordnance on 1 August 1806 the British Regulations were introduced. The cavalry regulations introduced on 1 February 1807 had the orders in both German and English, although orders continued to be given in German. British Regulations were introduced to the infantry in 1807 but were never fully adopted. The Light infantry never used British Regulations but developed its own, based on Hanoverian and British Regulations as well as its experience of war. Orders were given in German even though its commander, Colin Halkett, was Scottish (he had served in the Dutch forces). These regulations were finally published in printed form in 1813. British Regulations were used for guard duty and parades, but when it came to real fighting the old Hanoverian Regulations were preferred.

The cavalry formed up in two ranks with a four foot gap between the ranks. Turns were made by threes. The senior captain of the two troops commanded the squadron, which was divided into four divisions. The two lieutenants each commanded a troop and rode on its outside flank, an NCO riding behind them, taking their place if necessary. The junior cornet rode in the centre of the squadron, an NCO behind him. The sergeants rode on the flanks of the centre divisions. The second captain and senior cornet rode behind the front, observing the second rank. All-out charges were made when 100 paces from the enemy: at this point, the sword was raised into the air. Flankers were sent out 300–400 paces to the front and spread

A recruiting handbill dated 1815: the use of the English phrase on a German-language document is interesting. It reads: 'Through the departure of those men who asked to be dismissed when peace came, there are vacancies in the King's German Legion [note old spelling 'Teutschen' for 'Deutschen'] which by order of his Royal Highness the Prince Regent of England are to be filled immediately by volunteers. Every free German man who has the inclination to serve in this corps is hereby requested to report without delay to make up the numbers of this corps as soon as possible. Each man is to receive four guineas bounty, and, from the day of his acceptance, free board and lodging. English pay and board are so well known that it is not necessary to say anything about them. Any soldier who is wounded when in service or becomes disabled by any illness will receive an English pension for life. Hanoverian subjects who are not liable for service in the militia will be accepted.'

GOD SAVE THE KING.

Durch die Entlassung derjenigen Mannschaft, welche nach eingetretenem Frieden um ihren Abschied nachgesucht haben, sind in der

Königlich Teutschen Legion

Vacanzen entstanden, welche auf Befehl Sr. Königl. Hoheit des Prinz-Regenten von England sofort durch freywillige Anwerbung ersetzt werden sollen. Es wird daher jeder freye teutsche Mann, welcher Neigung hat, in diesem so ausgezeichneten Corps Dienste zu nehmen, hiermit aufgefodert, sich unverzüglich zu melden, um baldmöglichst die noch fehlende Zahl zur Completirung dieses Corps ersetzt zu erhalten.

Jeder Mann erhält 4 Guinée Handgeld, und von dem Tage seiner Annahme an, freye Verpflegung und Quartier.

Die englische Bezahlung und Verpflegung ist zu gut bekannt, um nöthig zu haben, etwas darüber zu sagen. Der Soldat, der während seiner Dienstzeit durch Wunden, oder im Dienst zugezogene Krankheit unfähig wird, erhält die englische Pension Zeitlebens.

Hannoverische Unterthanen, die Nicht Landwehrpflichtig sind, werden angenommen.

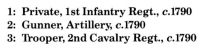

1: Private, 1st Infantry Regt., *c*.1790
2: Gunner, Artillery, *c*.1790
3: Trooper, 2nd Cavalry Regt., *c*.1790

3

2   1

A

1: Trooper, Life Guards, 1792
2: Trooper, 9th Dragoons, 1792
3: Officer, 12th Infantry Regt., 1792

B

1: Private, 14th Light Inf. Regt., 1794
2: Officer, 14th Light Inf. Regt., 1794
3: Trooper, 10th Light Dragoons, 1800

2   1   3

C

1: Grenadier, Line Bn. KGL, *c.*1812
2: Officer, 1st Hussars KGL, *c.*1813
3: Officer, 2nd Light Dragoons KGL, *c.*1814

3

2

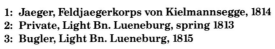

1: Jaeger, Feldjaegerkorps von Kielmannsegge, 1814
2: Private, Light Bn. Lueneburg, spring 1813
3: Bugler, Light Bn. Lueneburg, 1815

1   2   3

1: Private, Landwehr Bn. Osterode, 1814
2: Militia officer, winter walking-out dress, 1814
3: Gunner, Artillery, 1814

2   3   1

F

1: **Trumpeter, Estorff's Hussars, 1814**
2: **Hussar, Estorff's Hussars, 1813?**
3: **Hussar, Estorff's Hussars, 1814?**

1   3   2

G

1: Freikorps Czernischeff, spring 1813
2: Skirmisher, Field Bn. von Bennigsen, 1813-14
3: Corporal, Field Bn. Verden, 1814-15

2   3   1

H

out 20–25 paces apart, the men of the second rank ten paces behind them.

Infantry companies were divided into two platoons of two sections each. They formed up from the right to the left flank according to their captain's seniority, although this system was not rigidly adhered to. In 1812 the number of companies in a battalion was increased from six to ten; the Grenadier Coy. stood on the right flank, the Light Coy. on the left. The Sharpshooters were responsible for the skirmish fight; a battalion of eight companies had four sergeants, 52 men and one bugler under a subaltern officer. They stood in two ranks behind the flanks. Sometimes the Sharpshooters of a brigade were amalgamated under a captain. Sometimes the Light companies were similarly brigaded, the grenadiers only rarely.

From 1804, the battalion was formed in two ranks. The battalion commander and his adjutant were to the front of the battalion, the captains on the right flank of their divisions. All other officers stood three paces behind the second rank. The square was hollow and was three or four ranks deep. The first or first two ranks knelt, the other ranks stood firing. Bayonets were normally fixed, but the light troops fixed theirs only when ordered. Charges were normally made after firing a volley, the Line troops advancing at 75 paces per minute, the Lights at 108. The front rank charged bayonets, the second carried their muskets in the right hand. Manoeuvres were carried out in open columns of division.

Richard Knoetel's plate showing different ranks of the KGL 1st Light Bn. in 1808 may be compared, with advantage, with the figures and angles shown in Plate G, *Wellington's Infantry (2)'*, MAA 119.

Knoetel's contrasting plate showing the 2nd Light Bn.'s uniforms: again, cf. Plate G and commentary in MAA 119.

Uniforms & Equipment

The uniforms of the KGL were largely similar to those of the British Army.[1] There were, however, certain distinctions. Coats and tunics were, of course, mostly scarlet; dark blue was worn by the Light cavalry and artillery, and dark green by the Light infantry.

Generals, engineer and Line infantry officers wore long-tailed frock coats. In 1812, the latter received short-tailed coatees. Facings were white for generals, blue (or possibly white) for Line officers, and violet or black for engineer officers.

[1]See also MAA 119, *Wellington's Infantry (2)*, for further details and illustrations.

The Artillery wore dark blue coatees with red facings. Eventually, the Horse Artillery of the Legion received dolmans like those of the British horse gunners.

The Heavy Dragoons wore red long-tailed frock coats; the 1st Regt. had dark blue facings, the 2nd black. They were converted into Light Dragoons on 25 December 1813, and dark blue coatees with red facings were introduced. These were, however, not worn until the 1815 campaign.

The 1st Light Dragoons initially wore the uniform of the former Hanoverian 9th Cavalry Regt., that is blue coatees with red distinctions and yellow trim, but soon the British hussar uniform was introduced. That uniform was always worn by the other Light Dragoons. The 1st Regt. had scarlet acings, the 2nd white and the 3rd yellow; the 1st and 2nd had yellow frogging, the 3rd white; the 1st and 3rd had black fur, the 2nd white.

The Light infantry wore a uniform of its own choosing. Moreover, the green tunics of the 1st Bn. were lighter in colour than those of the 2nd. Collars and cuffs were black. The 1st had a short-tailed jacket, the 2nd wore dolmans. The officers of the 2nd had black silk frogging; their men did not have any frogging, but had three rows of buttons.

Buttons were yellow for generals, staff officers, engineers, Artillery, the Heavy and 1st Light Dragoons, the 1st and 2nd Hussars and the Line infantry; and white for the 3rd Hussars, the 2nd Light Dragoons and the Light Battalions. Officers with yellow buttons had gold embroidery on their coats. The men's tunics had a white trim which had a blue worm.

Officers tended to wear a black tricorn with a white-over-red feather plume and black cockade. From 1811, Foot Artillery officers started to wear the shako, Horse Artillery the crested helmet. Officers of the Line Battalions started to wear the shako from 1812. The Light Dragoons also wore a shako, as did the Hussars at first; a black busby with red bag was introduced later. The 1st Light Bn. wore a black shako, the 2nd a cap.

Generals and staff officers wore white trousers and black Hessian boots. Engineer officers wore grey overalls with gold stripes, foot artillery officers with red stripes. Gunners had grey trousers, black leather gaiters and shoes. The Horse Artillery had white trousers and Hessian boots. The Heavy Dragoons had white trousers and long boots. The Light Dragoons, 2nd and 3rd Hussars and the infantry had grey overalls. The 1st Hussars had dark blue overalls. Officers had silver or gold trim. The infantry wore black leather gaiters and shoes. Mounted troops had blue greatcoats with a cloak collar, foot troops grey.

Generals had aiguillettes, chevrons and embroidery on their coats, staff officers, except the Light infantry and Hussars, fringed epaulettes. Captains had a single epaulette on the right shoulder, subalterns had metal 'wings'. The men of the Heavy Dragoons, Line and Light infantry had woollen 'wings'. NCOs' distinctions were gold or silver chevrons on the upper right sleeve. The sergeant-major had four with a crown above them,

the sergeant three, farrier and cadet two, corporal one.

Officers wore a sash: that of the generals was gold and red silk. All other officers wore red silk. Sergeant-majors had red silk sashes, sergeants red wool. Hussars and the 2nd Light Bn. had barrel sashes, the Light Dragoons waist sashes.

Officers of the Horse Artillery were armed with a sabre worn with a gold and red silk *portépée*, a sabretache on a white belt or gold strap when on parade, and a pistol carried in a holster. Foot Artillery officers carried a sword, gunners a short sword on a white belt. Six carbines were carried on each limber.

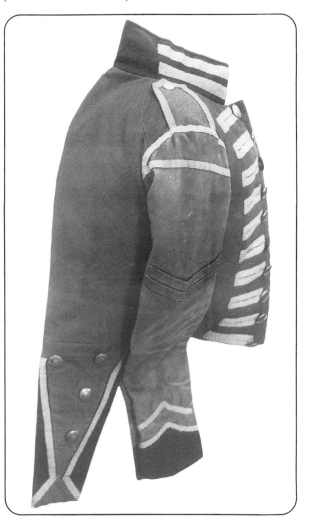

This surviving coatee, supposedly of a corporal of the 2nd Heavy Dragoons, KGL, and with the black (rather than blue) facings of that regiment, differs from Knoetel in details of the yellow lace trim—only one chevron appears above the cuff edge; and the collar is unbordered, but bears two loops. (Stadtmuseum Hannover)

Officers of the Heavy Dragoons carried a sword in a steel scabbard on a black belt. The troopers carried theirs on a white belt and were also armed with a carbine and pistol. The Light Dragoons and Hussars carried the curved sabre on a black belt. All cavalry troopers had black sabretaches and white belts. On parade, officers wore steel cartridge boxes on a gold or silver belt.

The infantry were armed partly with rifles, partly with muskets: one third of the Light infantry were armed with rifles, as were the Sharpshooters attached to the Line battalions. The remainder were armed with muskets. Officers of the Light Battalions were armed with hussar sabres worn with sabretaches. They had a whistle on their cross strap. Officers of the Line Battalions worn their épées on a white cross strap.

The 1st Heavy Dragoons had blue shabraques, the 2nd black trimmed red for men and gold for officers on parade. Harnesses were brown. Initially, the Hussars had shabraques but these were replaced by white sheepskins. All mounted troops, cavalry and artillery had blue greatcoat bags. Cleaning kit was carried in a leather bag on the left of the saddle,

Richard Knoetel's plate shows dragoons of (left) the 1st and (right) the 2nd Heavy Dragoon Regts., KGL, in 1806 field service marching order. The coatees are scarlet, faced blue and black, with yellow lace trim. Cf. Plate E, *Wellington's Heavy Cavalry*, MAA 130.

the pistol in a holster on the right. Each cavalryman also had a white linen bread bag and blue wooden canteen. On the left, a bag of oats was carried; on the right, the cooking gear.

The infantry had a waterproofed canvas backpack. The greatcoat was worn rolled on top of it and the mess tins on the back of it. A bread bag and canteen were also carried. The sappers also carried a shovel along with a saw or axe, and wore a white or brown apron.

Initially, the Legion wore their hair in a queue, but this gradually disappeared. The 3rd Hussars wore sidelocks weighted with lead. Only the Hussars were allowed to wear moustaches; the 2nd Light Bn. saw themselves as hussars, however, and also sported moustaches.

The Artillery, Hussars and Light battalions did not have any flags. Each of the Heavy Dragoon regiments had a regimental or King's standard, each squadron a guidon. The standards were rectangular and had a red field. In the centre under a crown were the rose, thistle and clover with the inscription HONI SOIT QUI MAL Y PENSE. Along the edge next to the pole were the regimental designation and white horse. The guidons were like large lance pennants, dark blue in the 1st Regt. and black in the 2nd. They were decorated in a similar fashion to the regimental colours. All standards were carried by the junior cornet.

Each line battalion carried two colours, the King's and the Battalion: the former was the Union flag, the latter blue. They were decorated in a similar fashion to the cavalry standards. They were carried by the junior ensign.

Conclusion

After the capture of Paris in 1814 and Napoleon's first abdication, the Legion was threatened with disbandment. However, the British government had enough foresight not to do away with such a good body of troops immediately. Reduced a little in strength, the Legion was given an extension. The Hundred Days came just in time to prolong its existence. In the meantime, around 200 officers and NCOs of the KGL had found their way back home, where they helped organise the Hanoverian militia, more of which is related below. With that, history had turned a full circle. After Waterloo, the Legion unit returned to their homeland and were eventually absorbed into the reconstituted Hanoverian army, although not without difficulties and frictions.

The New Army 1813-16

The destruction of the Grande Armée in Russia in 1812 left a power vacuum in Germany. The Russian Army was too weak to fill it immediately, and initially there was a degree of hesitation amongst Germany's rulers. In February 1813 the King of Prussia threw in his lot with the Czar, and other parts of northern Germany followed suit. Volunteer formations were raised in Hanover, part of which had been annexed by a voracious French Empire in 1810 and part of which was contained in the puppet Kingdom of Westphalia, ruled by a member of the Bonaparte dynasty.

Three battalions were formed in 1813: the Lauenburg, the Light Bremen-Verden and the Light Lueneburg. These were joined by a Feldjaegerkorps formed from gamekeepers and foresters, which was initially two, later four companies strong. These were joined later in that spring by two battalions earlier earmarked for the Russo-German Legion, namely Bennigsen and Roehl. In August 1813, the infantry was organised as follows:

1st Light Bn. Lueneburg:	Lt.Col. von Klencke
2nd Light Bn. Bremen-Verden:	Maj. de Vaux
3rd Bn. Lauenburg:	Maj. von Bennoit
4th Bn. Bennigsen:	Lt.Col. von Bennigsen
5th Bn. Roehl:	Maj. von Langrehr

At the beginning of 1814, these were joined by:

Light Bn. Grubenhagen:	Lt.Col. von Beaulieu
Light Bn. Osnabrueck:	Col. von Anderten
Field Bn. Calenberg:	Gen. von Hedemann

These battalions varied in strength. For instance, the establishment of Bremen-Verden was:

Staff—four officers, one surgeon, three NCOs, 17 privates.

Each of the eight companies—four officers, one surgeon, 12 NCOs, two drummers, 120 privates. This strength was never achieved in practice. On 23 April 1813 there were 519 men on the roll.

Training was based on the Regulations of 1802.

Every twelfth man in the Line battalions was trained as a skirmisher—ten men per company. They stood on the right flank and had a bugler.

In January 1814 30 militia battalions were formed, based on the provinces and districts of Hanover. All fit NCOs and men of the former Hanoverian army were required for duty in the militia. From 1 February 1814, the Hanoverians were no longer regarded as being part of the British Army and started to carry their own emblems on their flags.

On 4 February 1815 all field and militia battalions were combined into regiments. Bremen-Verden was renamed Bremen; Bennigsen, Verden; and Langrehr, Hoya. One field and three militia battalions formed a regiment—see the table at the bottom of this page.

At first there was little uniformity of dress: volunteers brought their old uniforms, and deliveries of new equipment were sporadic.

In spring 1813, *Light Battalion Lueneburg* wore a green peaked cap with a light blue band; and a long, dark green coat with a light blue collar and Swedish cuffs. Trousers were light grey with a broad light blue stripe. Belts were tan. During the armistice of summer 1813, Battalion Lueneburg received the old stores of the 1st and 2nd Light Battalions of the KGL; all tunics issued had the three rows of buttons characteristic of that unit. Collar, cuffs, wings, shoulder straps and belts were black; trousers and greatcoat grey. Headgear was the 'stovepipe' shako. The shako badge consisted of the leaping horse above a yellow band with the inscription NUNQUAM RETRORSUM. The rosette and cords were black, the plume green. The officers' uniform was a little different: the pointed cuffs were decorated with hussar lace, as was the back of the jacket, which also had black frogging. Trousers were grey with a green stripe. A red waist sash was worn. Another source shows the officers' trousers as being cornflower blue with a silver stripe, the waist sash of yellow silk.

The *Light Battalion Bremen-Verden* was also clothed in dark green at first. The coatee had black pointed cuffs, collars, shoulder straps and wings; it was double-breasted and the buttons were yellow. Trousers were a very dark blue. The black shako had a yellow badge with a crown and 'GR', a black cockade, a green plume and white cords. Belts were black. NCOs had chevrons on the upper right arm. The knapsacks were yellow-brown, bread bags and canteens as for the KGL. The black cartridge box did not have a badge on it.

Officers of the *Field Battalion Bremen* had black shakos with a black cockade, green plume, black cords and a yellow hunting horn badge. The red tunic had two rows of yellow buttons, and black pointed cuffs with gold lace; the lining was white. Trousers were dark blue with a broad gold stripe. The waist sash was yellow and the sword belt white.

Formerly the Harz Sharpshooters, the *Battalion Grubenhagen* had dark green coatees with black facings. Officers had two rows of 11 yellow buttons. The coat-tails had two buttons and a hunting horn in each corner. The black stovepipe shakos had a yellow badge and crown, the badge bearing a hunting horn and two crossed hammers. Cords were black, epaulettes gold with fringes. Officers had a green cap with a yellow and white band. Later on, the battalion wore black shakos with a silver hunting horn, yellow band, black cockade and pompon; the black shako cords hung on the left.

Regt.	Field Bn.	Militia Bns.
1. Bremen	Bremen	Otterndorf, Stade, Bremervoerde
2. Verden	Verden	Verden, Bremerlehe, Harburg
3. Hoya	Hoya	Hoya, Nienburg, Diepholz
4. Osnabrueck	Osnabrueck	Osnabrueck, Quakenbrueck, Melle
5. Lueneburg	Lueneburg	Lueneburg, Celle, Gifhorn
6. Lauenburg	Lauenburg	Ratzeburg, Bentheim, Luechow
7. Calenberg	Calenberg	Hannover, Hamlem, Neustadt
8. Hildesheim	Hildesheim	Hildesheim, Uelzen, Peine
9. Grubenhagen	Grubenhagen	Alfeld, Salzgitter, Springe
10. Goettingen	Feldjaeger	Osterode, Muenden, Northeim

Staff officer, 1st Light Dragoons, KGL—dark blue coatee faced red, gold lace and 'metal': cf. Plate F1, *Wellington's Light Cavalry*, MAA 126. (Schwertfeger)

Officer, 1st Hussars, King's German Legion—dark blue dolman and overalls, dark blue pelisse, gold lace and frogging, red dolman collar and cuffs, red and gold barrel sash, brown busby with gold lines and cords and red bag. (Schwertfeger)

The dark green coatee had a black collar, pointed cuffs and one row of white buttons. Sergeants had silver epaulettes and a silver sash; their arms were a rifle and an officer's épée. Trousers were grey.

Field Battalion Langrehr had a black-covered shako. The black *Litewka* coat had two rows of yellow buttons, blue collar and Brandenburg cuffs; the unit had grey trousers, black belts and white bread bags. The later uniform consisted of a red coatee with white tail turnbacks, and light blue collar, Swedish cuffs and shoulder straps, all piped white, and small wings attached to the shoulder straps. The stovepipe shako had yellow fittings, white cords, a black rosette and white plume. Belts were black.

Field Battalion Bennigsen received white-covered shakos originally designated for use in India. It is not clear if these were stovepipes or Belgics, and later artists show both. However, they did have

white plumes and cords, yellow fittings and a black peak. The red coatees had apple green cuffs with three white buttons and white lace, green collars piped white, and similar shoulder straps with short white fringes. The coatees had a single row of eight white buttons and bars of white lace. Trousers and greatcoats were light grey, belts white. The yellow belt-plate was probably marked 'GR'.

Field Battalion Verden, which was formed from Bennigsen, had the same uniform but with black stovepipe shakos, white wings, and no belt-plate. Sergeants and officers had yellow sashes; NCOs had silver chevrons on a green background on the upper right arm.

Kielmannsegge's Field Jaeger Corps had dark green coatees with apple green collars and pointed cuffs. Officers had yellow metal epaulettes lined green, and two rows of yellow buttons. Tail turnbacks and shoulder straps were also apple green. NCOs had a

Officer, 3rd Hussars, KGL—brown fur cap with peak, red bag, gold lines; blue dolman and pelisse with silver trim and frogging, yellow dolman collar and cuffs; black fur and red lining to pelisse; red and gold barrel sash; grey overalls, gold stripe. (Schwertfeger)

green epaulette, piped white with yellow fringes on the right shoulder. Single-breasted coatees were also worn. Belts were black; brown powder horns were carried on green cords. Headgear was a dark green peaked cap piped in apple green with a yellow hunting horn badge. Trousers were light grey with an apple green stripe. Officers wore yellow sashes, and carried their sabres in a steel scabbard on a white belt. The men, being trained huntsmen, were armed with rifles and sword-bayonets. Other sources show dark green *Litewka* coats being worn. Brown hide knapsacks were carried.

In 1815, *Field Battalion Calenberg* wore a single-breasted red coatee with dark blue collar, cuffs and shoulder straps, the collar and cuffs piped white; buttons were white. As well as a pair of cross belts, a waist belt was also worn, all being white. Trousers were grey. The stovepipe shako had a yellow badge, a black cockade, white plume and white cords. The

knapsack was black, with a red greatcoat rolled on top of it.

The Light battalions were partly armed with rifles, partly with muskets; the Field battalions, with muskets and bayonets. Kielmannsegge's Jaeger had two 2 pdr. cannon served by Jaeger. Twelve members of this Corps were mounted.

The Militia wore stovepipe shakos with a black cockade and a yellow or white plume, and a white metal shako plate with the crown and 'GR'. The officers' coatees were red with a blue collar lined red, blue cuffs with three gilt buttons, and blue lining; there was a gilt button on the collar, and two rows of five on the front. The red coatee worn by the men had one row of five white buttons and bars of white lace; the collar, cuffs and shoulder straps were dark blue trimmed white; the cuffs had three buttons. The wings and tail turnbacks were white for both officers and men; the officers' tails had vertical pockets with four gilt buttons, as well as two buttons on the tail itself. Officers had a yellow sash, and a white cross belt with a yellow plate bearing 'GR'. Officers also had a yellow epaulette on the right shoulder. Belts were white, trousers were mid-grey. Militiamen were armed with a musket and bayonet and did not have a short sword.

There were variations on the above. For instance, the *Verden Militia Bn.* at Waterloo had dark blue lapels with five pairs of gilt buttons. The *Osterode Bn.* in Paris in 1815 wore a shako with green cords and plume. Their coatee had green cuffs with four gilt buttons and white lace; green collar and shoulder straps, both piped white; and green wings. The greatcoat was grey, pack straps brown, other belts white; grey gaiters were worn under the trousers. Sergeants wore the red British waist sash instead of the more common yellow. Officers wore a red peaked cap with a yellow band, and wore their greatcoats rolled over the shoulder.

In March 1813 two hussar regiments were raised in Hanover, the *Bremen-Verden* and the *Lueneburg*; and at the end of the year a third, the Duke of Cumberland's Regiment. Each regiment was initially three and later four squadrons strong; each squadron had 150 troopers divided into two companies.

The uniform of *Regt. Bremen-Verden* consisted of a green dolman with a red collar and cuffs and black trim and cords; there were three rows of 15 to 18 white buttons. The red pelisse had a black trim and cords. Trousers were light grey with a silver stripe and red piping for officers, and probably a red stripe for troopers. The waist sash was yellow and white for men, silver and gold for officers. Headgear was a brown colpack with a red bag, white plume and yellow and white cord for the 2nd and 3rd squadrons; the 1st had shakos with a red-white plume. Officers had a silver crossbelt with red piping. The black sabretache hung on three black belts. The pointed saddlecloth was green with red corners, silver piped red for officers. The greatcoat bag was also green, piped red. Horse furniture was tan.

This regiment also had a detachment of volunteers who were clothed in black. The shako had black cords, black plume, yellow fittings and a white cockade with the red cross of Bremen. Buttons, sashes, cords, belts and gauntlets were black.

The first uniform worn by the *Regt. Lueneburg* was a blue dolman and pelisse, white buttons and cords, blue trousers with a broad yellow stripe and white piping. Collar and cuffs were yellow, as was the wolf-tooth edging on the blue saddlecloth. Everything was piped white. Belts were white, sashes were red, sabretaches black on white belts. The pelisse was trimmed white. Headgear was a felt hussar cap with a white band at top and bottom, a white-over-red plume and white cords. Horse furniture was black.

Their later uniform was a blue dolman with red collar and cuffs, red pelisse, white cords for the men and silver for officers. Officers had silver piping on their collars and cuffs, men two thin lines of white. Officers' sashes were red and yellow, as were the cords on the grey colpacks. The troopers had brown colpacks with a blue bag. Officers had a white-over-red plume. Trousers were grey with red piping. Belts were white. Officers had a silver crossbelt trimmed yellow. Sabretaches were probably black. Men had yellow and white sashes, trumpeters yellow and red. Trumpeters wore reversed colours, that is red dolmans and blue pelisses.

The *Duke of Cumberland's Regt.* wore black shakos with a yellow rosette, trim, cords, cockade, clasps and chinscales, and black plume. The dolman was green with yellow frogging and three rows of yellow buttons; officers had five rows. The green pelisse

Identified as the dolman of the sergeant-major of the 3rd Hussars, KGL, 1812-16, this dark blue jacket has yellow facings and chevrons with silver lace trim and frogging. (Bomann Museum, Celle)

was lined red and also had yellow frogging; the fur was black. Collars and cuffs were either red or green. Trousers were grey with a yellow stripe, and officers also had green piping. Sashes were yellow and white. Officers had either green and yellow or red and yellow. Officers wore a yellow crossbelt piped green. The men had white belts. The saddlecloth was green with a yellow trim as was the greatcoat roll. Horse furniture was tan.

A cadre of 40 KGL gunners was sent to Hanover where it trained a battery ready for the campaign of autumn 1813; two more batteries were raised in December 1813. Uniforms were as the KGL. Battery von Wiering had four light 6 pdrs. and two $5\frac{1}{2}$ in. howitzers; von Rettberg, 9 pdrs. and howitzers; Braun, light 6 pounders.

* * *

About 25,000 Hanoverian soldiers participated in the Battle of Waterloo, the Hanoverians and KGL

41

suffering about 3,250 casualties. A new Hanoverian army was organised during 1816 from the KGL and Hanoverian formations raised after liberation from the French. The Army of Occupation of France included a contingent of 5,000 Hanoverians under Gen. von Alten, which returned home in November 1818. The post-Napoleonic reorganisation of the Hanoverian Army was completed then.

The Plates

A: Hanoverian Army, c.1790
This plate is based on a series of contemporary watercolours; the first part, known as the *Gmundener Prachtwerk*, covers the Seven Years' War period. The second part consists of 19 plates dated between 1781 and 1791, showing the army close to the turn of the century.

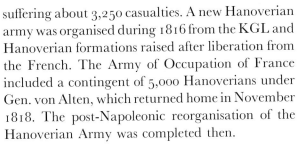

Gunners of Foot and Horse Artillery, KGL, in uniforms almost identical to their British Army contemporaries of equivalent corps: dark blue faced red, with yellow lace. (Schwertfeger)

A1: Private, 1st Infantry Regiment, c.1790
A typically British, late 18th century style of uniform. The cartridge box is carried on a broad crossbelt, the hanger on a waistbelt. The regiment's green distinguishing colour is shown here on the hat details, the lapels and the cuffs. Note eight white tape loops on the former, pairs on the latter.

A2: Gunner, Artillery, c.1790
Note the different cut of the lapels of this coat, which is a fairly bright blue with red facings. Lace and metal are gold. Note the pickers on the crossbelt, which supports a white or white-covered pouch. Waistcoats changed from buff to white in 1769.

A3: Trooper, 2nd Cavalry Regiment, c.1790
The dark blue coat is faced white, with brass buttons bearing the regimental number, and blue-

and-gold heart-shaped patches on the turnbacks. The gold lace and metal colour is seen in the hat details. The breeches are whitened leather. Note double crossbelt, the upper and narrower one with a spring-clip for the carbine, the lower one supporting a pouch with a white-covered flap. This regiment took part in the 1794 campaign in Holland.

B: Hanoverian Army, 1792
This plate is based on the contemporary series of watercolours by Ronnenberg.

B1: Trooper, Life Guards, 1792
The uniform of the Leibgarde of the Prince Elector is basically similar to that shown as A3, but in scarlet with royal blue facings. The valise, cloak-bag or simple rolled cloak behind the saddle is hard to interpret—it may be meant to show the appearance of a white-lined red cloak. Gold and red details are visible on the hat, sword-knot, etc.

B2: Trooper, 9th Dragoons, 1792
A typical light dragoon style of uniform of the period, with an ornately styled helmet or jacked cap. Its shape is hard to interpret from Ronnenberg's naif plates, but it appears to be of felt or leather with brass trim, and a silver leaping horse badge on the fancy front flap; the large red feather plume seems to be trained sideways over the skull. Note the flat, gold-on-red epaulettes; and the gold loop on a red patch at the front corner of the collar. The rectangular silver plate of the swordbelt seems to have a gold applied cypher. The carbine and pouch belts appear to follow the pattern of A3 and B1.

B3: Officer, 12th Infantry Regiment, 1792
The officer's coat had buttons, but not lace loops, on the lapels. The lemon facings of this regiment are repeated in the form of a collar patch. The silver metal and lace of this regiment show in the hat trim and epaulettes. Note the officer's swordbelt plate, a silver wreathed cypher on red backing.

C1: Private, 14th Light Infantry Regiment, 1794
The black 'Corsican' hat had a green plume and yellow loop. The pale grey coatee has a dark green collar, possibly piped white; and dark green cuffs

with yellow worsted lace loops; these also appear on the pocket flaps. The turnbacks are green. The buff leather breeches are worn with stockings and black half-gaiters. The Hanoverians, like so many other German states, appreciated the value of light troops early on, and the uniform of this unit reflects the élite status of such soldiers, while making at least a nod in the direction of low visibility in the field. (After Herbert Knoetel)

A crude drawing in the *Landwehren u. Freiwilligen* series shows this hastily-equipped volunteer of the Lueneburg Light Battalion in spring 1813—cf. Plate E2 for colours. This drawing seems to show the bayonet and pouch belts reversed from the usual arrangement.

A shako, supposedly identified to the Landwehr Battalion Osterode, 1814: black felt, leather peak, conventional British brass plate of type worn on Belgic shako, green tuft and cords. CF. Plate F1. (Stadtmuseum Hannover)

C2: Officer, 14th Light Infantry Regiment, 1794
The distinctions of an officer appear to include a feather plume and gold hat trim; the sabre; black full-length boots; and the sash. Knoetel makes no obvious distinction between the shades of epaulette worn by officer and man: gold and yellow respectively would be normal, but conceivably all ranks wore one or other. (After Herbert Knoetel)

C3: Trooper, 10th Light Dragoons, 1800
Another figure taken from Herbert Knoetel, whose rather free style of drawing leaves some questions unanswered. The shape of the lace loops is unclear, as Knoetel seems to suggest something approaching a 'bastion' rather than a straight doubled loop with a pointed end.

D: The King's German Legion, 1806–16
These figures are taken from various plates by Richard Knoetel, and from surviving items, mostly in the Bomann Museum at Celle.

D1: Grenadier, Line Infantry, c.1812
Knoetel made a number of minor errors, particularly in showing shoulder wings as blue rather than the correct red, and turnbacks as blue rather than the correct white – though his accompanying notes acknowledge that Beamish and Von Brandis show white. We have corrected these points. The uniform was of British design and manufacture, and virtually identical to that of the British infantry with whom the KGL was brigaded and alongside whom they fought with such distinction. See also MAA 119, *Wellington's Infantry (2)*, Plates G and H.

D2: Officer, 1st Hussars, c.1813
This regiment converted from the light dragoon to the hussar rôle—and uniform style—in 1805. Knoetel based his study on information from Beamish, who served in the Legion. See also MAA 126, *Wellington's Light Cavalry*, Plate F, for hussar and light dragoon uniforms in 1815.

D3: Officer, 2nd Light Dragoons, c.1814
From Knoetel, again based on Beamish. Grey overalls were worn in the field, white breeches with full dress. See MAA 130, *Wellington's Heavy Cavalry*, Plate E, for the uniform worn by this regiment before its conversion from the heavy dragoon rôle in 1813.

E1: Jaeger, Feldjaegerkorps von Kielmannsegge, 1814
Raised from foresters and huntsmen in spring 1813, this unit wore a costume reflecting that origin. The cap is 'semi-civilian', of the shape already worn by Prussian and other German state armies for undress and in volunteer and second-line units. (After Knoetel and Elberfeld)

E2: Private, Light Battalion Lueneburg, spring 1813
A mixture of national features: a British shako with green tuft and cords, a German *Litewka* coat in green with pale blue details, perhaps British trousers with an added stripe, and untreated leather equipment; the musket is British. (After a plate in the '*Landwehren und Freiwiligen*' series, and Knoetel)

E3: Bugler, Light Battalion Lueneberg, 1815
A much more conventional uniform, based on a British 1812 pattern shako dressed with red tuft and cords, a British Rifles coatee with added red-tufted wings, and black Rifles equipment—though note the interesting pair of small pouches on the belt. The horn is of local pattern. Assembled on the Lower Elbe in spring 1813, this unit was originally equipped as rapidly as possible in the expectation of immediate action. Cloth caps were worn alongside British 'stovepipe' shakos (see E2). During summer 1813 the uniform of the 1st Light Bn., KGL was gradually introduced, though with the Belgic shako. (After Herbert Knoetel)

F1: Private, Landwehr Battalion Osterode, 1814
The Landwehr battalions formed in 1814, each with a small headquarters and four companies and averaging 500 or so men, were uniformed by local Hanoverian authorities, who could draw upon British stocks. The proposed headgear was the Belgic shako with a yellow metal plate, black cockade, white (later, white-over-yellow) tuft, and white cords. A shortage of the 1812 pattern led to issue of the 1806 'stovepipe' shako in many cases. A supply of white shakos, made for British troops serving on tropical stations but infrequently issued, was also made available. Jackets were to be red, faced blue, with white lace with a blue stripe or worm (e.g. the same as worn by the KGL). In practice, however, there were numerous exceptions, which also extended to the Field Battalions.

Landwehr Battalion Osterode (illustrated here after Knoetel, Siborne, and surviving items) wore light green facings; note the shako decorations, including a plate which Knoetel shows as distinctly different from the standard British issue. (Knoetel illustrated a sergeant, with gold chevrons, a sash, sword, and musket.) The knapsack appears to be untreated hide, of a tan-yellow shade.

Other discrepancies included the Field Battalion Grubenhagen, who wore dark green faced black; Landwehr Battalions Hildesheim and Peine had pale yellow facings. A surviving jacket of a senior NCO of Field Battalion Bremen-Verden has black facings; Siborne indicates black for the 'Verden' Battalion, but light green for the 'Bremen'; other sources indicate blue facings for the 'Verden'; and Richard Knoetel shows blue for the 'Bremen-

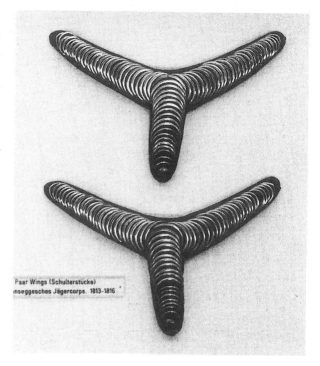

Metal-ring 'wing' worn by a member—presumably an officer—of Kielmansegge's Feldjaegerkorps, 1813–15. (Stadtmuseum Hannover)

Verden' unit. Other discrepancies which appear in Siborne's schema are black equipment and 1812 shakos for the Quakenbruck Battalion; dark blue trousers, black equipment and 1812 shakos for the Bremen Battalion.

F2: Officer, Hanoverian militia, winter walking-out dress, 1814–16
Richard Knoetel shows this strikingly 'modern' costume.

F3: Gunner, Hanoverian Artillery, 1814
An interpretation from various sources; the overall British style of the uniform is obvious. One of the more eccentric Elberfeld studies shows a supposed uniform of dark blue with what appear to be broad red lace loops, trimmed yellow, across the chest; red collar, shoulder straps and pointed cuffs trimmed with yellow; yellow-trimmed white turnbacks; and dark grey trousers with a yellow stripe. A covered Belgic shako is worn.

G: Estorff's Hussars, 1813–14
Sources give varying versions of the uniforms of the three new hussar regiments raised in 1813; see

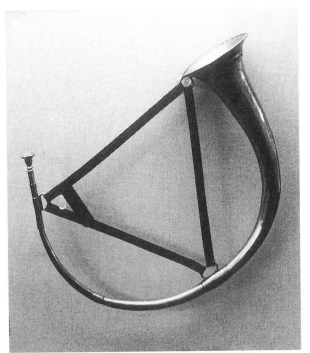

Traditional buglehorn, typical of those carried by buglers of Hanoverian light formations. (Stadtmuseum Hannover)

descriptions in the body text for some examples. The regiment raised in the Lueneburg area, also known as the Estorff Hussar Regiment after the brigade commander, had two distinct uniforms. The 2nd Regt., raised in Bremen and Verden, wore green jackets with red facings and pelisses; one source gives white lace and trim, another black. Squadrons were supposedly identified by headgear: 1st and 4th Sqns., black shakos, black and red trim respectively; 2nd and 3rd Sqns., grey colpacks with red bags. The volunteer hussar regiment 'Herzog von Cumberland' was dressed in green, the jackets having red facings, yellow braid and buttons, and the black shakos having yellow ornaments. This is the unit which behaved badly at Waterloo, marching off the field when ordered to engage.

G1: Trumpeter, Estorff's Hussars, 1814
Also known as the Lueneburg or Prince Regent Hussars. This trumpeter is reconstructed from a primitive drawing in the Elberfeld Collection; he appears to wear reversed uniform colours, as would be conventional for trumpeters.

G2: Hussar, Estorff's Hussars, 1813?
Suhr's drawing, on which this figure is based, seems

to be the only source for the original uniform with the mirleton cap.

G3: Hussar, Estorff's Hussars, 1814?
Based on the 'Landwehren und Freiwilligen' series, this shows the more conventional version of the unit's uniform.

H: Battalion von Bennigsen
The object of this plate is to show the development of uniforms within one unit. Freikorps Czernischeff was absorbed by the Battalion von Bennigsen, which later became Field Battalion Verden.

H1: Freikorps Czernischeff, spring 1813
(After George Schaefer) Note the simple 'stable jacket', the now rather outdated 'Corsican' hat, and the French equipment.

H2: Skirmisher, Field Battalion von Bennigsen, 1813–14
An interesting uniform, taken here from a rather crude early drawing, which does however make a point of showing a green, rather than the more usual white/red tuft, indicating light or skirmisher status. The white or white-covered shako, from British stocks intended for tropical use, is clearly the Belgic type, rather than the 'stovepipe' shown in Roechling's well-known painting of the Goehrde unit.

H3: Corporal, Field Battalion Verden, 1814–15
The Waterloo infantryman, completely British in appearance, uniformed from British stocks as an official unit of the Royal Hanoverian Army. Schaefer shows green facings, other sources blue or black—see under F1.

Sources
Uniform plates
Abbildungen der Chur-Hannoverschen Armee-Uniformen, Ronnenberg, Hanover & Leipzig, 1791.
Darstellung der vom 9 November 1813 bis zum 14 April 1819 durch Elberfeld passierten Truppen, Anonym. (Often known as the *Elberfeld Manuscript*.)
Landwehren und Freiwilligen 1813–1815, Anonym. (Possibly contemporary, more likely a later copy of contemporary material. In the Lipperheide collection, Berlin.)
Abbildung der Uniformen aller in Hamburg seit den Jahren

1806 bis 1815 einquartirt gewesener Truppen, Christ. & Corn. Suhr, Hamburg 1815–1820.

Uniformenkunde and other plates by Richard and Herbert Knoetel.

Printed Sources

Die Chur-braunschweig-lueneburgische Armee im Sieben-jaehrigen Kriege, Niemeyer/Ortenburg, Beckum 1976.

Die Hannoversche Armee 1780–1803, Niemeyer/Ortenburg, Beckum 1981.

Nec aspera terrent! Eine Heereskunde der hannoverschen Armee von 1631 bis 1803, Fr. Schirmer, Hanover 1929.

Militaergewehre und Pistolen der deutschen Staaten 1800–1870, Hans-Dieter Goetz, Stuttgart 1978.

Die Armee des Koenigreichs Hannover, Udo Vollmer, Schwaebisch Hall 1978.

Orden norddeutscher Staaten des 19.Jahrhunderts, Hans Georg von Gusovius, Celle 1984.

Des Koenigs Deutsche Legion 1803 bis 1816, B. von Poten, Berlin 1905.

Geschichte der Koeniglich Deutschen Legion 1803–1816, Bernard Schwertfeger, 2 vols, Hanover & Leipzig, 1907.

Mittheilung zur Geschichte der militaerischen Tracht, Richard & Herbert Knoetel, 1892–1921.

Zeitschrift fuer Heereskunde. Various issues.

Farbtafeln

A1 Die gesamte Tafel wurde der Gmundener Prachtwerk-Serie zeitgenössischer Aquarelle entnommen. Der Unterschied in den Details zu den Ronnenberg Abbildungen ist auffallend, und von dem unsere Uniformdarstellungen stammen. Diese typisch britische Uniform aus dem späten 18. Jahrhundert zeigt die Regimentsunterschiede im roten und grünen Rock und Hut. **A2** Der Rock der Artillerie wies, ausser den verschiedenen Farben, kleine Unterschiede im Schnitt auf. Bemerkenswert sind die Details am Kreuzbandelier. **A3** Zu bemerken ist das doppelte Kreuzbandelier. Das engere, obere Bandelier hat eine Klammer, um den Karabiner umzuhängen und am breiten unteren Bandelier ist eine Patronentasche mit einer weissen Klappe befestigt.

B1 Diese Illustrationen entstanden durch Ronnenberg. Sie entsprechen im Schnitt grundsätzlich denen von A3, sind aber in den königlichen Farben gehalten. Von den Originalzeichnungen ist es schwer festzustellen, ob es sich um einen aufgerollten Umhang oder eine Reisetasche hinter dem Sattel handelt. Es sieht jedoch eher wie ein aufgerollter Umhang mit weissem Futterstoff aus. **B2** Die Mütze ist nur schwer im Detail auf dem naiven Originalgemälde zu erkennen; sie ist etweder aus Filz oder Leder gefertigt und mit Messing verziert. Auffallend sind die flachen Epauletten und das gefärbte Stück Stoff am Kragen mit goldener Litze. **B3** Der Offiziersrock hat Knöpfe auf den Aufschlägen, aber keine Litzen. Die zitronengelbe Farbe des Regimentsaufschlags ist am Stück Stoff des Kragens zu sehen. Ausserdem ist das Offiziersmuster auf dem Koppelschloss des Schwertes zu erkennen.

C1 Diese Illustrationen sind von Herbert Knoetel. Das typische Uniformsmuster der deutschen leichten Infanterie aus dieser Zeit. Die matten Farben wirken wie eine 'Tarnung'. **C2** Die Unterschiede in der Offiziersuniform umfassen eine Hutfeder, Kleiderbesatz, Säbel, Stiefel und Schärpe. Knoetel stellt nicht deutlich dar, ob Offiziere goldene und die Männer gelbe Epauletten trugen, obgleich dies der Fall gewesen sein mag. **C3** Der freie Stil von Knoetel lässt Einzelheiten wie die Form der Litzen klar erkennen.

D1 Diese Illustrationen stammen von Richard Knoetel und wurden in einigen Fällen an hand von noch existierenden Uniformen im Bomann Museum von Celle verglichen und korrigiert. Diese Uniform wird hier mit der richtigen roten 'Schwalbennestern' und dem weissen Futter des Rockschosses gezeigt, welches buchstäblich demjenigen der britischen Infanterie gleicht. **D2** Aus dieser Einheit der leichten Dragoner wurden Husare, dementsprechend auch die Uniform aus dem Jahre 1805. Knoetel erhielt Informationen von Beamish, der in der Legion diente. **D3** Nochmals von Beamish. Weisse Breeches wurden mit der gesamten Uniform und grauem Umhang im Feld getragen.

E1 Nach Knoetel und der Elberfeld MS: Die Uniform spiegelt den Ursprung der Einheit wider, deren Männer Förster oder Jäger waren. **E2** Eine typische Mischung als nationalen Stilrichtungen der Uniformen ist in der eilig zusammengestellten Einheit im Jahre 1813 zu erkennen. Knoetel malt in seiner Serie Landwehren und Freiwillige nachvollzogen. Britischer Tschako mit grünen Verzierungen, deutscher Litewka-Rock, möglicherweise britische Umhänge mit einem Streifen, naturfarbenes Lederzeug und britische Muskete. **E3** Im Sommer des Jahres 1813 wurde diese Einheit mit Tailen der Uniform des 1. Leichten Bataillons der Königlichen Deutschen Legion versehen; Knoetel veranschaulicht diese zusätzlichen Kleidungsstücke am Hornisten.

F1 Zahlreiche widersprüchliche Quellen haben das Wissen über Uniformen, welche diese Bataillone trugen undeutlich werden lassen, die auf verschiedenen britischen und anderen Informationsquellen beruhen. Knoetel, Siborne und anderes existierendes Material lassen auf diese Merkmale der Bekleidung für das Osterode Batail on schliessen. **F2** Eine auffallend 'moderne' Uniform, die von Richard Knoetel entworfen wurde. **F3** Eine Rekonstruktion aus verschiedenen Quellen; die Ähnlichkeit mit der Uniform der britischen Artillerie kommt deutlich zu Tage.

G1 Die Lüneburger oder Estorffer Husare hatten zwei unterschiedliche Uniformen; diese wurde nach einer naiven Zeichnung von der Elberfeld MS entworfen und scheint das umgekehrte Farbschema der anderen Stils aufzuweisen, der in der Regel von den Trompetern getragen wurde. **G2** Eine Zeichnung von Suhr zeigt die einzig bekannte Nachbildung der frühen Uniform mit 'Mirleton'-Kappe. **G3** Die zweite Uniform wurde der Serie Landwehren und Freiwillige entnommen.

H1 Auf dieser Bildtafel sind die Veränderungen der Uniform innerhalb der Einheit zu sehen: Freikorps Czernischeff ging im Bataillon von Bennigsen auf, aus dem wiederum das Feld-Bataillon Verden wurde. Georg Schaefer illustriert diese schlichte frühe Uniform bestehend aus einer kurzen Jacke, korsischem Hut und französischer Ausrüstung. **H2** Eine frühe, naive Zeichnung zeigt den weissen Tschako, der aus den Beständen des britischen Tropeneinheiten stammte. Der grüne Büschel lässt auf die Einheit der Scharfschützen schliessen. **H3** Fast vollkommen britisch in der Erscheinung. Schäfer zeigt die grünen Aufschlagfarben, andere Quellen zeigen blau oder sogar schwarz.

Notes sur les planches en couleur

A1 Toute cette planche provient du Gmundener Prachtwerk, une série d'aquarelles contemporaines; notez que celles-ci diffèrent par certains détails des illustrations du Ronnenberg d'après lesquelles nous avons établi notre diagramme pour les pièces d'uniforme. Cet uniforme de la fin du 18è siècle de style typiquement britannique présente en vert. **A2** Ce manteau de l'artillerie a une coupe légèrement différente, sans évoquer les couleurs distinctives. Notez les détails spéciaux de la bandoulière. **A3** Notez la bandoulière double dont la partie supérieure plus étroite porte l'attache pour suspendre la carabine, tandis que la partie inférieure est plus large pour la giberne dont le rabat est blanc.

B1 Ces figures sont reconstituées d'après Rennenberg. D'une coupe similaire à A3, mais dans les couleurs royales. L'interprétation exacte, d'après l'oeuvre originale, du manteau roulé ou du sac de voyage derrière la selle est difficile, mai il semble que le manteau soit rouge avec doublure blanche. **B2** Le chapeau est difficilement interprétable en détail d'après la peinture naïve originale; il se peu qu'il soit en feutre ou en cuir avec ornement en laiton. Notez les épaulettes plates et l'écusson de couleur sur le col, avec boutonnière à galon brodé doré. **B3** Les manteaux des officiers avaient des boutons sur les revers mais pas de boutonnière à galon brodé. L'écusson du col révèle la couleur du parement régimentaire jaune-citron; notez également le motif de la bouclerie à plaque plate du ceinturon des officiers.

C1 Ces figures sont reconstituées d'après Herbert Knoetel. Modèle caractéristique des uniformes de l'infanterie légère allemande de cette période, la couleur terne sacrifiant au 'camouflage'. **C2** Les distinctions d'officiers comprennent le plumet du couvre-chef et les ornements en dentelles, le sabre, les bottes et l ceinture d'étoffe. Knoetel ne montre pas clairement si les officiers portaient de épaulettes dorées et les hommes des jaunes, bien que cela soit probable. **C3** L style libre de Knoetel laisse subsister des doutes quant aux détails tels que la form des galons des boutonnières.

D1 Ces figures sont reconstituées d'après Richard Knoetel, dans certains cas ave des révisions après comparaison avec des uniformes préservés au musée Bomann Celle. L'uniforme qui est présenté ici avec la doublure correcte blanche de l queue et les nids d'hirondelle rouges, est pratiquement identique à l'uniform réglementaire de l'infanterie britannique. **D2** Cette unité est passée de dragoi légers au rang de hussards, style de son uniforme, en 1805. Knoetel s'est inspiré d informations de Beamish qui fit son service dans la Légion. **D3** D'après Beamish également. Les culottes blanches se portaient avec l'habit de grande tenue, d surtouts gris en campagne.

E1 D'après Knoetel et Elberfeld MS: le costume reflète l'origine de cette unité elle était recrutée parmi les gardes-forestiers et les chasseurs. **E2** Mélang caractéristique d'articles nationaux dans la tenue d'une unité levée précipitamment en 1813, une reconstitution d'après Knoetel et les séries de Landwehren un Freiwilligen. Shako britannique avec décorations vertes, manteau Litewk allemand, il est possible avec des surtouts britanniques dont la rayure est ajouté équipement de cuir non coloré, mousquet britannique. **E3** Pendant l'été 1813 d éléments de l'uniforme de la Légion allemande royale, le 1er Bataillon léger, on été distribués à cette unité; herbert Knoetel présente ces distinctions ajoutées pou les clairons.

F1 De nombreuses sources divergentes ont semé la confusion sur not compréhension des uniformes portés par ces bataillons, prélevés sur différen matériaux britanniques et autres sources. Knoetel, Siborne, et des éléments d ont subsisté ici pour le bataillon d'Osterode. **F2** U costume dont la 'modernité' surprend, une illustration d'après Richard Knoet **F3** Une reconstitution d'après des sources variées; la similarité avec l'uniform de l'artillerie britannique.

G1 Les hussards de Luneburg ou d'Estorff avaient deux uniformes distinct celui-ci, une illustration d'après un dessin naïf dans Elberfeld MS, semble êtr version en couleur inverse du second modèle, ce qui serait normal pour d trompettes. **G2** Un dessin par Suhr présente la seule reconstitution connue l'uniforme précédent avec chapeau de mirliton. **G3** Le deuxième uniform d'après les séries d'illustrations de Landwehren et Freiwilligen.

H1 Cette gravure montre les transformations de l'uniforme dans cette unité; Freikorps Czernischeff furent intégrés au Bataillon von Bennigsen, qui devin son tour le Feld-Bataillon Verden. Georg Schaefer décrit le simple uniform antérieur avec veste courte, chapeau corse et équipement français. **H2** Un dess naïf datant des premiers jours présente le shako blanc ou couvert en blan provenant des stocks du service sous les tropiques de l'armée britannique, avec houppe verte qui suggère qu'il s'agit du rang de tireur d'élite. **H3** D'apparer entièrement britannique. Schaefer présente les parements en vert, d'aut sources en bleu ou même en noir.

Men-at-Arms Series Titles in Print

ANCIENT & MEDIEVAL PERIODS:

- (109) Ancient Middle East
- (137) The Scythians 700–300 B.C.
- (69) Greek & Persian Wars 500–323 B.C.
- (148) Army of Alexander the Great
- (121) Carthaginian Wars
- (46) Roman Army:
  - (1) Caesar–Trajan
- (93) (2) Hadrian–Constantine
- (129) Rome's Enemies:
  - (1): Germanics & Dacians
- (158) (2): Gallic & British Celts
- (175) (3): Parthians & Sassanids
- (180) (4): Spain 218–19 B.C.
- (154) Arthur & Anglo-Saxon Wars
- (125) Armies of Islam, 7th–11th C
- (150) The Age of Charlemagne
- (89) Byzantine Armies 886–1118
- (85) Saxon, Viking & Norman
- (75) Armies of the Crusades
- (171) Saladin & the Saracens
- (155) Knights of Christ
- (200) El Cid & Reconquista 1050–1492
- (105) The Mongols
- (50) Medieval European Armies
- (151) Scots & Welsh Wars 1250–1400
- (94) The Swiss 1300–1500
- (136) Italian Armies 1300–1500
- (166) German Armies 1300–1500
- (195) Hungary & E. Europe 1000–1568
- (140) Ottoman Turks 1300–1774
- (111) Crécy and Poitiers
- (144) Medieval Burgundy 1364–1477
- (113) Armies of Agincourt
- (145) Wars of the Roses
- (99) Medieval Heraldry

16TH AND 17TH CENTURIES

- (191) Henry VIII's Army
- (58) The Landsknechts
- (101) The Conquistadores
- (14) English Civil War Armies
- (110) New Model Army 1645–60
- (203) Louis XIV's Army
- (97) Marlborough's Army
- (86) Samurai Armies 1550–1615
- (184) Polish Armies 1569–1696 (1)
- (188) Polish Armies 1569–1696 (2)

18TH CENTURY

- (118) Jacobite Rebellions

NAPOLEONIC PERIOD

- (87) Napoleon's Marshals
- (64) Nap's Cuirassiers & Carabiniers
- (55) Nap's Dragoons & Lancers
- (68) Nap's Line Chasseurs
- (76) Nap's Hussars
- (83) Nap's Guard Cavalry
- (141) Nap's Line Infantry
- (146) Nap's Light Infantry
- (153) Nap's Guard Infantry (1)
- (160) Nap's Guard Infantry (2)
- (90) Nap's German Allies (3)
- (106) Nap's German Allies (4)
- (122) Nap's German Allies (5)
- (199) Nap's Specialist Troops
- (88) Italian & Neapolitan Troops
- (176) Austrian Army: (1) Infantry
- (181) Austrian Army (2): Cavalry
- (152) Prussian Line Infantry
- (149) Prussian Light Infantry
- (192) Prussian Reserve & Irregulars
- (162) Prussian Cavalry 1792 1807
- (172) Prussian Cavalry 1807–15
- (185) Russian Army (1): Infantry
- (189) Russian Army (2): Cavalry
- (114) Wellington's Infantry (1)
- (119) Wellington's Infantry (2)
- (126) Wellington's Light Cavalry
- (130) Wellington's Heavy Cavalry
- (204) Wellington's Specialist Troops
- (167) Brunswick Troops 1809–15
- (206) Hanoverian Army 1792–1816
- (96) Artillery Equipments

19TH CENTURY AND COLONIAL

- (173) Alamo & Texan War 1835–6
- (170) American Civil War Armies:
  - (1): Confederate
- (177) (2): Union
- (179) (3): Staff, Specialist, Maritime
- (190) (4): State Troops
- (207) (5): Volunteer Militia
- (37) Army of Northern Virginia
- (38) Army of the Potomac
- (163) American Plains Indians
- (186) The Apaches
- (168) US Cavalry 1850–90
- (193) British Army on Campaign:
  - (1): 1816–1853
- (196) (2): The Crimea, 1854–56
- (198) (3): 1854–81
- (201) (4): 1882–1902
- (67) The Indian Mutiny
- (57) The Zulu War
- (59) Sudan Campaigns 1881–98
- (95) The Boxer Rebellion

THE WORLD WARS

- (80) The Germany Army 1914–18
- (81) The British Army 1914–18
- (208) Lawrence and the Arab Revolts
- (182) British Battle Insignia:
  - (1) 1914–18
- (187) (2) 1939–45
- (117) The Polish Army 1939–45
- (112) British Battledress 1937–61
- (70) US Army 1941–45
- (24) The Panzer Divisions
- (34) The Waffen-SS
- (139) German Airborne Troops
- (131) Germany's E. Front Allies
- (103) Germany's Spanish Volunteers
- (147) Wehrmacht Foreign Volunteers
- (142) Partisan Warfare 1941–45
- (169) Resistance Warfare 1940–45

MODERN WARFARE

- (132) Malayan Campaign 1948–60
- (174) The Korean War 1950–53
- (116) The Special Air Service
- (156) The Royal Marines 1956–84
- (133) Battle for the Falklands:
  - (1): Land Forces
- (134) (2): Naval Forces
- (135) (3): Air Forces
- (127) Israeli Army 1948–73
- (128) Arab Armies 1948–73
- (194) Arab Armies (2): 1973–88
- (165) Armies in Lebanon 1982–84
- (104) Vietnam War Armies 1962–75
- (143) Vietnam War Armies (2)
- (209) War in Cambodia 1970–75
- (183) Modern African Wars:
  - (1): Rhodesia 1965–80
- (202) (2): Angola & Mozambique
- (159) Grenada 1983
- (178) Russia's War in Afghanistan

GENERAL

- (107) British Infantry Equipts. (1)
- (108) British Infantry Equipts. (2)
- (138) British Cavalry Equipts.
- (205) US Army Combat Equipts.
- (157) Flak Jackets
- (123) Australian Army 1899–1975
- (164) Canadian Army at War
- (161) Spanish Foreign Legion
- (197) Royal Canadian Mounted Police

Please note that for space reasons abbreviated titles are given above; when ordering, please quote the title number given in brackets, e.g. 'MAA 109' for 'Ancient Armies of the Middle East', etc.

ISBN 0-85045-887-0

9 780850 458879

Avec annotations en francais sur les planches en couleur
Mit Aufzeichnungen auf deutsch uber die Farbtafeln

Wellington's Peninsular Army

Text by

JAMES LAWFORD

Colour plates by

MICHAEL ROFFE

MEN-AT-ARMS SERIES

EDITOR: PHILIP WARNER

Wellington's Peninsular Army

Text by JAMES LAWFORD

Colour plates by MICHAEL ROFFE

Research for uniforms and illustrations T. A. HEATHCOTE

OSPREY PUBLISHING LIMITED

Published in 1973 by
Osprey Publishing Ltd, P.O. Box 25,
707 Oxford Road, Reading, Berkshire
© Copyright 1973 Osprey Publishing Ltd

All the illustrations in the black-and-white section
are reproduced by kind permission of the National
Army Museum, except for the illustrations of the
howitzer and the mortar which are by kind
permission of the Commandant of the Royal
Military Academy Sandhurst. Many of the
illustrations have been taken from those made by
Major St Clair. This officer accompanied Wellington
on his campaigns and depicted episodes as they
occurred; he is the nearest equivalent to the present
day press photographer.

ISBN 0 85045 145 0

Printed in Great Britain.
Monochrome by BAS Printers Limited,
Wallop, Hampshire.
Colour by Colour Reproductions Ltd.,
Billericay.

The Staff

During Marlborough's Wars at the beginning of the eighteenth century the muskets of the infantry and the guns of the artillery were smooth-bore and muzzle-loading, cavalry relied on shock tactics and the sabre, engineers based their fortifications on the principles of Vauban. When Wellington took the field nearly a hundred years later weapons had barely altered; a few British infantry were armed with the new-fangled rifle which the French had not thought worth adopting, and a few French or Polish/French cavalry regiments used the lance as well as the sabre, guns fired projectiles that were a little heavier than before and were slightly more mobile, while the technique of fortifications and sieges remained completely unchanged. Over the century weapon technology had hardly advanced at all. But paradoxically, perhaps in part from the very fact that weapons had altered so little permitting their characteristics to be thoroughly understood, perhaps in part because large regular armies remained continuously in existence, during that century military theory, organizationally, tactically and strategically, made remarkable progress. After the forcing-house of the Napoleonic wars, European armies reached levels of technical excellence which have probably never been surpassed, perhaps never equalled. The theories of Clausewitz, which were to dominate military thought for the next century and more, were almost entirely based on the detailed analysis he and other military thinkers made of the principles underlying the great battles of the Napoleonic period.

At the beginning of this period the record of the British army left something to be desired. But during the Peninsular War, 1808–14, Wellington led and trained a British army that, fighting against the French, the masters of Europe, never knew a major defeat in the field. Wellington himself, whose terse unflattering comments on his men have long been remembered, described his army as 'able to go anywhere or do anything.'

The staff by which he controlled his magnificent army reflected his own personality and the conditions of the time. Battlefields were small and regiments fought close together; generals could assemble all their men in a single place and transmit their orders by the power of their lungs; there was no need for the elaborate staff organizations of a later day. Napoleon it is true, co-ordinating the activities of a number of armies operating

Arthur Wellesley, Duke of Wellington. He was thirty-eight years old when, in 1808, as Sir Arthur Wellesley, he first landed in the Peninsula and forced the French out of Portugal.

3

The Battle of Fuentes de Onoro, British Headquarters. A staff officer is galloping off with a message. Wellington, wearing his usual low cocked hat and plain frock-coat, is attended by a light dragoon and other staff officers. In the background Royal Horse Artillery are changing ground (After St Clair)

hundreds of miles apart, evolved the idea of a chief-of-staff who could interpret and elaborate directions from the commander and even possibly assist him in his planning. Wellington desired nothing of this; he wanted advice or assistance from no one; modern planning staffs would have filled him with horror. In his view the formulating of plans and giving out of orders were the responsibility of the commanders. Staff officers were there to transmit these orders and to smooth out minor administrative difficulties.

In consequence, in Wellington's headquarters there was no eqivalent of the general staff. He had a small personal staff under a lieutenant-colonel to handle his military correspondence, but the colonel was a secretary, nothing more. The most important branch of the staff was the department of the Quarter-Master-General. It was headed by a major-general and initially consisted of a small group of officers, perhaps twelve in number (as the army grew bigger so their numbers increased); in addition an officer from the department served in each division.

The duties of these officers extended to such matters as quartering, the moving of equipment, the layout of camps, duties differing little from those of the present day; but their duties also included some of those now discharged by the general staff such as mapping, the compiling of information about the countryside and its resources, the organizing of all forms of movement and the drafting of orders. The Quarter-Master General's department provided the executive staff of the army, so far as such may be said to have existed.

The other great department was that of the Adjutant-General, also under a major-general. Initially this comprised fourteen officers but with the passage of time this number too increased; again a staff officer from the department served with each division. The responsibilities of these officers included such matters as discipline, statistics about unit strengths, reinforcements etc., and differed little from those of the modern 'A' staff.

The distinctions between the two departments were by no means rigid and an officer from one might well find himself deputizing for an absentee from the other. But one thing Wellington made absolutely clear, the function of the staff officer was to transmit the instructions of his commander, he had no right to arrogate to himself the authority of his general.

Besides the staff proper, Wellington kept in his headquarters the field commanders of his engineers, artillery and medical services. In addition Marshal Beresford, the Commander-in-Chief of the Portuguese army, after one disastrous experience commanding an army at Albuera, generally accompanied army headquarters, as did Sir Stapleton Cotton, from 1812 onwards the commander of the cavalry in the Peninsula. Thus Wellington had with him two senior generals whom he could send off at a moment's notice to take over an independent command or disentangle some unfortunate situation; it gave him a flexibility that allowed him to dispense with the system of Army Corps originated by the French.

On the civil side there was an important department, the Commissariat, under a Commissary General with assistants serving with every division and brigade. These were responsible for the provision of rations and the procurement of all local produce. In the nature of things a thin or ill-provided commissary officer was rarely seen, and they were apt to receive more kicks than credit.

Working direct to Army Headquarters were the divisions; there was only an intermediate headquarters when two or more were grouped together for an independent task. Here staffs were kept to the minimum. Leith Hay, an A.D.C. with the 5th Division, records that at the Battle of Salamanca the divisional staff consisted of Colonel Berkeley, probably Assistant-Quarter-Master-General, and Major Gomm, probably Deputy-Assistant-Adjutant-General, and four A.D.C.s, possibly one per brigade and one to look after the domestic arrangements of the headquarters.

Marshal Beresford in hand-to-hand combat with a Polish lancer at Albuera. He was a man of immense physical strength and the lancer had short shrift

The high sounding titles for staff officers have been retained to the present day, generally abbreviated to the initials, thereby ensuring that the army staff should be confusing to the other services and incomprehensible to other nations.

At the level of the infantry brigade, there was a single staff officer, the major of brigade; he was a captain or sometimes an able young subaltern drawn from one of its regiments. During the later stages of the war, when regimental officers had recognized the wisdom of wearing the same type of headdress as their men, staff officers could be distinguished by their courageous refusal to abandon the traditional cocked hat.

The Infantry

When Wellington took the field in the Peninsula in 1808, Britain lagged behind France in the higher organization of her armies, divisions had yet to be formed, and Wellington dealt direct with individual brigade commanders. In June 1809, however, he adopted the divisional organization originated by the French, in which a number of brigades were grouped together under a single commander. Initially he formed four divisions, but by 1812 the number had risen to eight British and one Portuguese; he numbered his British divisions consecutively from one to seven, the eighth, the most famous, was known simply as the Light Division. Each was commanded by a lieutenant-general and usually comprised three brigades; two of which were British, each under a major-general, and one foreign, often under a British brigadier-general – a rank otherwise seldom encountered in the Peninsular Army.

There were some exceptions. All three brigades of the 2nd Division were British, but since it normally operated with General Hamilton's Portuguese Division, both under the command of Wellington's most trusted subordinate, General 'Daddy' Hill, the two together virtually amounted to the equivalent of a small Anglo-Portuguese Army Corps. In the 1st Division the foreign brigade was from the King's German Legion recruited by George III from the remnants of his Hanoverian Army, in the remainder (except for the Light Division which had a peculiar organization of its own) it came from the Portuguese Army

which had been reorganized under the command of Marshal Beresford and stiffened by British officers who had transferred to the Portuguese service.

The composition of the Light Division derived from an essential feature of Wellington's tactics. He had served under the Duke of York in Flanders where he had noted how the French light troops, their Tirailleurs and Voltigeurs, could harass and weaken a battle line, so that when the heavy French columns attacked it they often broke through. He resolved to counter this gambit by deploying forward of his positions such a mass of his own light troops that the Tirailleurs and Voltigeurs would be held well short of his main position. As a first step towards achieving this aim, he constituted the Light Division with the function of screening the army both at rest and on the move. It consisted of only two small brigades each containing a Caçadore battalion (Portuguese Light Infantry) four companies of riflemen from the 95th (later increased when the 2nd and 3rd battalions of that regiment joined his army) and a British light infantry battalion (the role in which the 43rd and 52nd won immortal fame).

The 7th Division also was rather unusual; perhaps at first Wellington toyed with the idea of producing another light infantry division: it had two light infantry brigades, one containing two light battalions of the King's German Legion and nine rifle companies of the Brunswick Oel Jägers and the other two newly trained British light infantry battalions, the 51st and the 68th, and a battalion originally recruited from French emigrés and deserters, the Chasseurs Britannique, a regiment famous for the speed with which its men deserted; in addition there was the normal Portuguese brigade. This division, perhaps owing to its diversity of races, never won much renown; the malicious affected to disbelieve in its very existence, and in 1813 it reverted to a more normal organization, the light infantry battalions from the King's German Legion being transferred to the 1st Division.

In the British brigades there were generally three line battalions. Occasionally a fourth might be added, and in Guards Brigades, since a battalion of Foot Guards invariably outnumbered

General Lord Hill, wearing the uniform of the post Napoleonic period

by a considerable margin those of the line, there were only two. On average a brigade numbered about 2,000 men, but sickness and casualties, or the arrival of a strong battalion, could cause wide fluctuations. The Portuguese brigades followed the continental model and embodied a Caçadore battalion and two line regiments each of two battalions; these had seven companies and an authorized strength of 750, but rarely put more than 500 in the field; even so, Portuguese brigades on average numbered 2,500 and were almost always larger than the British.

The organization of the British battalions remained remarkably constant throughout the war. Each was commanded by a lieutenant-colonel and consisted of a grenadier company, a light company, and eight line companies, all commanded by captains. The colonel had two majors serving under him, nominally to command the two wings into which the battalion was customarily split; their main function, however, was to deputize for him when he was away and to take charge of any large detachments the battalion might be called upon to make; within the battalion their duties tended to depend on the particular whims or eccentricities of their commanders.

In the companies, the captains had under them two junior officers, in theory a lieutenant and an ensign, but there was no set proportion between the two ranks. A full-strength battalion, therefore, would be commanded by a lieutenant-colonel with under him two majors, ten captains, twenty lieutenants or ensigns, the adjutant, (generally a lieutenant), and the quarter-master; an assistant surgeon was normally attached. Sir David Dundas shows the strength of a company as being three officers, two sergeants, three corporals, one drummer, and thirty privates. This must have been at the peace-time establishment of one platoon. At war establishment, another platoon

Portuguese infantry at Penmacor 18 March 1811. (St Clair) The mounted officers wearing the 'stove-pipe' shako are below field rank. The pioneers are wearing bearskin caps and leather aprons. Their axes are not visible. The drummers carry their drums slung on their backs by means of the drum cords. (The length of the drum cord was governed by this requirement)

7

was added without any increase in the number of officers. When going to the Peninsula companies might number nearly 100 including a pay sergeant, perhaps four other sergeants and six corporals. The 52nd went to the Peninsula with 54 sergeants and about 850 rank and file. But sickness and other casualties soon took their toll, and when in 1810 the 2nd battalion of the 52nd disbanded its total strength was 20 sergeants, 12 buglers, and 572 rank and file of whom 10 sergeants, 5 buglers, and 85 rank and file were unfit for duty.

A battalion with 700 men present in the field was looked on as strong, many fell well below this figure, and some had little more than 500. In a battalion of 700 men, deducting the musicians, the adjutant's batman, the clerks, the storemen and others of that ilk likely to find their way into headquarters – say forty men – there would be 660 men serving with the companies; allowing again for the various duties that inexorably sap the strength of a regiment such as baggage guards, storemen, men just gone sick, absentees and so on, the company could probably put not much more than fifty-five men into the line. Captain Sherer remarked that at the Battle of Vitoria he had eleven casualties out of a company of thirty-eight and does not comment that at this time his company strength was abnormally low. The company for administrative purposes was divided into two platoons, but organizations were far from standardized and commanding officers were often men of character who liked to run their battalions after their own fashion and did not welcome interference from the nincompoops of the staff. The private soldier in the ranks carried sixty rounds of ball ammunition, a knapsack, a haversack, rolled blanket or great coat, a full waterbottle and probably some other articles he had managed to acquire; his load might amount to nearly sixty pounds. At first the heavy camp-kettles for cooking were carried on a company mule, but when, in 1812, Wellington managed to issue tents

to his men at a scale of three twelve-men bell-tents per company, the tents were carried on the mule and a lighter type of camp-kettle was carried in turn by the men of the company.

Their clothing and in particular that of the officers might be curious and fanciful and be only remotely related to the regulation pattern; Wellington himself never worried over such matters so long as his men resembled soldiers and would not be mistaken for the French.

'BROWN BESS'

Officers were armed with the sword, and sergeants with halberds or short pikes, called spontoons, rather to assist them in dressing the ranks than as weapons of offence. Most of the soldiers were armed with the musket, affectionately known as Brown Bess, that the Duke of Marlborough when Master-General of the Ordnance was said to have introduced. Its barrel was about 42 inches long with a diameter of ·75 of an inch; its firing mechanism was reputedly the most reliable in Europe, although at this time that was not necessarily a very great feat; its heavy triangular bayonet, 17 inches long, fitted on the barrel well clear of the muzzle. Each soldier carried his 60 rounds of ball made up into cartridges, the propelling charge and the ball being sewn together in cartridge paper to make a small cylindrical parcel. When the time came to load, the soldier bit the end of the cartridge, shook a little powder on his priming pan and emptied the rest down the barrel; he then used his ramrod to ram home his ball with the cartridge paper on top to act as a wadding. When he pulled the trigger a spark from the flint ignited the powder in the pan which in turn caused the powder in the barrel to explode; the proportion of misfires, however, could be as high as one in six and, if the powder became damp, the musket would not fire at all.

A Brown Bess, otherwise known as a Tower musket, the principal firearm of the infantry during the war

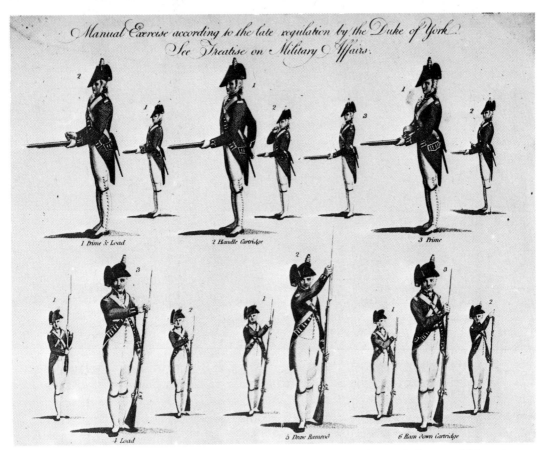

1 Prime & Load   2 Handle Cartridge   3 Prime

4 Load   5 Draw Ramrod   6 Ram down Cartridge

Loading and firing, from a manual of musketry exercises. The uniform is that of an earlier period; the hat had been replaced by the 'stove-pipe' shako in 1796, and the coat by the single-breasted short-tailed coatee. White gaiters continued to be worn only by the Foot Guards in full dress

The ball was not always a very close fit in the barrel, and the gases from the exploding charge might escape around it making it spin and swerve wildly in flight. Brown Bess had a certain feminine capriciousness; at fifty yards it could be aimed with some hope of success; up to two hundred yards it could be usefully fired at a group, the man actually aimed at being almost certain to escape harm; but over 200 yards, although the ball could carry up to 700, its behaviour was so eccentric that the noise of the discharge was more likely to excite terror than the ball. Rates of fire depended on how thoroughly the soldier performed his loading drills and the care that he took when he aimed; he could fire up to five rounds a minute if he was satisfied with producing an imposing number of bangs without worrying overmuch what happened to his ball; taking into account battle conditions a well-trained soldier should have been capable of firing nearly three effective rounds a minute.

Owing to the relative inaccuracy of the musket, the high number of misfires, and also the moral effect of a sudden blast of fire, a volley from a number of men was likely to produce a more awe-inspiring result than a comparable number of single shots, and the more concentrated the fire the more devastating it was likely to be; hence, throughout most of the eighteenth century, soldiers stood shoulder to shoulder in a line that was three ranks deep; the French experimented with four but found that the fire of the fourth was more likely to endanger their comrades than the enemy. At this time the three-deep line was still the normal practice on the continent as it gave the line a certain solidity and catered for the replacement of casualties.

TACTICS

During the War of American Independence, especially in wild country against irregular bodies

Pombal, 11 March 1811 (St Clair). Infantry on the approach march. Company officers wearing shakos have dismounted. The Colours, uncased, are in the middle of the column. An officer of the light company (wings on his shoulders) is talking to one of the staff.

of riflemen, the British army had become accustomed to a looser order. Battalions frequently fought in only two ranks and these were not properly closed up by European standards; this was beneficial in that it led Wellington to adopt a two-rank line in the Peninsula, but with the loose order regiments had come to devise tactical manoeuvres of their own and drill had become sloppy and haphazard; the results in Flanders had not always been happy. In 1792 the Duke of York, the Commander-in-Chief, decided that a common tactical doctrine must be adopted by the whole of the infantry and issued a manual entitled *Rules and Regulations for the Field Formation Exercise of Movements of His Majesty's Forces*, which he proceeded rigorously to enforce. The manual, written by Sir David Dundas, was largely based on formations current in the Prussian army and has been reviled as intolerably rigid in outlook; nevertheless it gave a sound tactical doctrine to the infantry and was the basis

of the battle-drills used in the Peninsula.

Dundas envisaged the men in a battalion standing shoulder to shoulder in a line three ranks deep. (As already mentioned, Wellington reduced this to two.) The first part of his manual was devoted to the individual drills such as turning, marching and wheeling, that the soldier had to master before he was fit to take his place in his company. In the remainder he laid down a series of drills which, while retaining the rigid, slow-moving line as the battle formation yet enabled a battalion to move swiftly and easily over the battlefield. He divided the battalion into eight equal divisions; these roughly corresponded to the eight line companies if the grenadier and light companies were both excluded; if they were present he allowed the number of divisions to be increased to ten; on the other hand if the battalion was weak the number could be reduced proportionately. In practice it was rare for the light company to form part of the battle line; its

A brigade fording the Mondego, 1810 (St Clair). An example of a brigade advancing with its battalions in column of divisions. The divisions seem well closed up, probably to hasten the crossing.

normal task was to screen the front or flanks of the battalion or brigade. The grenadier company, no longer specifically armed with grenades, was composed of the steadiest soldiers in the unit; it might be used for some particularly dangerous or difficult task, but the habit of brigading the grenadier companies to make up *ad hoc* grenadier battalions had largely disappeared. In some regiments the grenadier company was divided, half being placed on the right and half on the left of the line. Dundas does not seem to have thought that any specific provision was necessary for its deployment.

Although he described some eighteen manoeuvres in detail, in essence his drills were based on four key formations, column of route, column of divisions, line and square. Column of route was used for all movement when there was no immediate threat of contact with the enemy. Dundas laid down that this could be carried out in fours if the line formed two deep, sixes if three

deep. Since marching men required double the space occupied by the men when stationary, the length of a column of route should equal the frontage of the same unit in line, and he emphasized that this length should not be exceeded. March discipline much resembled that in force in the British Army until the 1930s when the threat from the air enforced a greater degree of dispersion. Battalions started off from their camping grounds with arms at the slope or shoulder and bands playing. After a short distance the men marched at ease and were permitted to break step. At every clock hour there was a short halt to enable the men to rest and adjust their equipment. Before the hourly halt and immediately after it, men marched to attention and in step for a few minutes, and the same drill was observed when they arrived at their destination or were called upon to execute a manoeuvre.

When contact with the enemy became a possibility, column of route was changed to column of divisions, or if the company organization had been preserved, column of companies. In this formation each division deployed in a two-deep line with the divisions ranged one behind the other, No. 1 Division leading; occasionally it might be convenient to have No. 8 in front. Here two rather confusing terms were apt to be used. If No. 1 led, the battalion was said to be 'right in front' if No. 8 'left in front', the terms referring to their respective positions when in line. In some circumstances it was desirable to adopt a compromise between column and line. For this purpose Dundas had enacted that besides being divided into eight divisions, the battalion line should also be divided into four grand divisions, and column of grand divisions, generally formed by grouping in pairs, might be substituted for column of divisions.

Intervals might be varied. In close column there might be only seven paces between the front rank of one division and the front rank of the one immediately behind it. On the move open column was more usual; in this formation the distance between divisions was equal to their front for an important reason; with these intervals the battalion could form line facing left or right very quickly indeed, as each division needed to do no more than execute a separate right or left wheel for the whole to be in line. This was the manoeuvre so brilliantly executed by Pakenham and the 3rd Division at the battle of Salamanca. Forming line to the front was a slower process. Each division came up in succession on the right or left of the division in front of it, depending on the flank ordered, until the line had been formed, while the leading division normally halted to

The Battle of Castalla. A British infantry battalion in line faces an attack by French infantry in column. On the hill the colonel rides in his correct position behind the Colours. One of the majors has been wounded and fallen off his horse; the other (cocked hat and dismounted) brings up a company on the right. Company officers (shakos, straight swords) are in their positions on the flanks of their companies. In the right foreground a light infantry officer brings up his reserve in close order to support his skirmishers. The light infantry bugler, one trusts, is sounding the advance while a French drummer is probably responding with the 'pas de charge'. (Light infantry, often working dispersed, used bugles not drums for the passage of orders)

allow the others to catch up; the rear division might therefore find it had some 200 yards to cover, and if, as sometimes happened, the whole brigade was advancing in column of companies or divisions this distance might be tripled.

Once in line, the colours took post in the centre with the Colonel, mounted, six paces behind. The senior major and the adjutant, also mounted, took post respectively behind the 3rd and 6th Divisions; the company commanders, dismounted, took up a position on the right of the front rank of their company or division with a sergeant covering them in the rear rank. The remaining officers and sergeants, the drummers, pioneers and any other hangers-on formed a third supernumerary rank with orders as Dundas phrased it to 'keep the others closed up to the front during the attack and prevent any break beginning in the rear'. The second-in-command of the left-hand division, however, covered by a sergeant, took post on the left flank of that division.

When advancing in line the men on the flanks kept their alignment by dressing on the colours in the centre. If a brigade advanced in line it was the duty of the colour parties to align themselves on the colours of the particular battalion that had been detailed to set pace and direction. In this formation the senior battalion was on the right the next senior on the left and the junior in the centre.

The last formation, that of square, Dundas shows as being formed from line. With No. 1 Division on the right and No. 8 on the left the procedure was as follows. The 4th and 5th Divisions stood fast, the 2nd and 3rd wheeled to their right rear forming a line at right angles to the right flank of No. 4 Division, while the 6th and 7th in a similar manner wheeled to their left rear forming a line at right angles to the left flank of No. 5 Division. The 1st and 8th Divisions closed the square and faced the rear; the officers and colours took post in its centre, the officers waving their swords exultantly in the air whenever a volley was fired.

There were many other drills for forming square; sometimes it was formed in two ranks, sometimes in four; on occasion two battalions might unite, as at Waterloo, to make up a single square. When two or more squares were necessary,

A British infantry square being attacked by lancers

alternate ones would be echelonned back, so that the fire from one could sweep the face of the next. It is evident that if a square were to be formed quickly and without confusion, companies had to be of equal strength, and that some system, such as that of divisions, was probably unavoidable. Nevertheless, the advantages of the fighting unit and the administrative being identical, so that officers and N.C.O.s knew the men they led in action, became more and more apparent, and the custom of using the company as the tactical unit became steadily more widespread as the war progressed.

To give still greater flexibility in manoeuvre, Dundas decreed that a division should be divided into two sub-divisions and four sections, but added that a section should never number less than five files (fifteen men if the ranks were three deep); these would operate the same formations within a division as a division within a battalion. As the division was the smallest sub-unit under an officer it may be surmised that these smaller formations were rarely used, unless a company was operating independently on its own.

As regards frontages, Dundas stated that a man should occupy twenty-two inches. Two feet, however, would seem a more realistic figure, besides being easier to use for purposes of calculation. A battalion 700 strong, subtracting the light company, the musicians, and those in the supernumerary third rank, would probably muster about 560 men actually in the battle line; assuming a front rank of 280, the frontage for such a battalion would be in the region of 200 yards. Since a brigade normally fought with all three battalions in line its front would extend about

The Regimental Colour. The colour parties of the infantry carried two flags each borne by an ensign or subaltern and known as the First or Royal Colour and the Regimental Colour. The First Colour was a Union Jack with the regimental number in its centre; the Regimental was more complicated. Its background colour matched the facings of the regiment; in its right-hand corner there was a small Union Jack and in its centre a red shield containing the regimental number or emblem, normally surrounded by a wreath of the union flowers, the rose, thistle and shamrock. Other honours might be painted on it. In the illustration the officer has removed the staff from its socket and is carrying the colour partially furled; its oilskin case can be seen over his right shoulder. A sergeant in the party stands close to defend the nearly helpless officer with his spontoon

600 yards. Infantry divisions on the other hand seldom had all three brigades in line. At the Battle of Salamanca the 4th Division did so with disastrous results; Wellington had, however, with customary prescience placed the 6th Division behind it to give the attack depth, and Cole commanding the 4th may well have taken this into account when determining his formation.

When the manoeuvring had ended and the fighting had begun it was important that at no time should a battalion be discovered with all its muskets unloaded; if this should happen it would be helpless before cavalry, and enemy infantry would be able to close and blast it off the battlefield with impunity. Dundas frowned on file firing whereby each front rank and rear rank man fired immediately after the man on his right, and favoured the firing of volleys. He stated: 'Line will fire by platoons, each battalion independent, and

firing beginning from the centre of each.' In his regulations Dundas uses the terms platoon and company as though they were the same, and presumably meant here that firing would be by company or division; since there was only one officer in the front rank of each division, except for the left flank one, it seems logical to suppose that these were the units of fire; on the other hand it is likely that battalions developed procedures of their own. After the first volley men almost certainly fired independently as fast as possible, the initial method of opening fire ensuring that firing remained continuous. At close range this fire could be murderous; after two or three minutes one side would almost certainly begin to fall into disorder, and seeing this the other would probably clinch matters with the bayonet. Captain Sherer describing his action at the Battle of Albuera gives some idea of what the reality must have been like:

Just as our line had entirely cleared the Spaniards, the smoky shroud of battle was, by the slackening of fire, for one minute blown aside, and gave to our view the French grenadier caps, their arms, and the whole aspect of their frowning masses. It was a momentary, but a grand sight; a heavy atmosphere of smoke again enveloped us, and few objects could be discerned at all, none distinctly. The murderous contest of musketry lasted long. We were the whole time advancing on and shaking the enemy. At the distance of about twenty yards from them we received orders to charge. We ceased firing, cheered and had our bayonets in the charging position . . . The French infantry broke and fled, abandoning some guns and howitzers about sixty yards from us . . . To describe my feelings throughout this wild scene with fidelity would be impossible: at intervals a shriek or a groan told that men were falling about me; but it was not always that the tumult of the contest suffered me to catch these sounds. A constant feeling [i.e. closing] to the centre of our line and the gradual diminution of our front more truly bespoke the havoc of death.

For a battalion the sequence of action might be an approach march in column of route, then a

The 57th Foot (West Middlesex Regiment), 'the die-hards', at the Battle of Albuera. Grenadier caps were commonly worn by the drummers and the colours of their coatees were the reverse of those of their regiments; in this case the coatee was yellow with red facings

halt at an assembly area where the battalion might close up in column of grand divisions, and stand poised ready to swing into action. Here colours would be uncased and primings checked. Then would come the advance in open column, deployment into line and finally trial by fire.

During the later stages of the advance the light infantry might well have been deployed in front; while capable of taking their place in the battle line, they generally had other more important functions to perform. They were equipped with a lighter version of the Brown Bess that had a barrel only thirty-nine inches long. They always acted in pairs – from the time he joined his unit each man had to choose a comrade from whom he was separated neither in camp nor on the battlefield. When a light infantry company operated on its own a few men would be kept in close order as a reserve immediately under the hand of the commander, the rest would be spread in pairs across the front, one member of each a little in front of his comrade so that they could cover each other either advancing or retiring; the intervals between pairs would vary from two to twelve paces depending on the extent of the front they had to cover. These skirmishers, as they were called, preserved only the roughest of lines, selecting individual firing positions where the best cover could be obtained. Being widely

separated, they worked to bugle calls like the cavalry, not the drums of the line. In an advance they would close with the enemy's line and while themselves presenting an insignificant target, gall it unmercifully with their fire. In defence they had to present an impenetrable front to the light troops of the enemy; but, once attacked in force, their task was done and they were permitted to withdraw to a flank, taking the utmost care not to mask the fire of their own line as they went. Light companies might work independently, but more often those in a brigade were grouped together under a single commander to form a small light infantry unit, and in the Portuguese brigade all the light companies were already concentrated in the Caçadore battalion.

In front of the light infantry the riflemen, the élite of the skirmishers, might be seen weaving their way forward. Initially Wellington had three rifle battalions, the 95th, the 5th/60th Rifles and the Brunswick Oel Jägers. Later these were increased by the arrival of two more battalions of the 95th, and in addition a number of rifles were made available to the Light Battalions of the King's German Legion. (Oman has stated that the Caçadore battalions were armed with rifles and a number of authorities agree with him. However, taking into account the total production of the Baker rifle in the United Kingdom, the

15

Riflemen of the 95th covering the right flank of the line. The short brass-hilted sword they carried in lieu of a bayonet, and the powder horn under the right arm, show up clearly

contention is open to doubt. Possibly some Caçadore battalions were so armed.) All were armed with the Baker rifle, a muzzle-loader with a barrel 30 inches long and ·615 inches diameter; to load it the ball had to be forced home against the resistance of the rifling grooves, a serious handicap which limited the rate of fire to approximately one round a minute. However, the rifle was sufficiently accurate for aimed fire to be possible at ranges of up to 200 yards, four times the range of a musket, and effective fire at 300 yards was by no means uncommon.

Wellington always allotted at least one company of riflemen to each infantry division; they operated ahead of everyone, slinking from cover to cover like hunters or poachers, rather than the brightly-hued soldiers of the day, and they were the first troops to wear an elementary form of camouflage clothing. The 60th having been raised as the Royal American Regiment wore green to match the forests where they had origi-

nated and the 95th did the same; the Brunswick Oel Jägers wore black, but this was partially to mourn for the rape of Brunswick by Napoleon, while the Caçadores, when not clothed by the British in rifle green, wore brown, perhaps the earliest use of a version of khaki.

Wellington looked to his infantry for his victories and indeed initially with few guns and less cavalry he was given little choice. Perhaps in consequence, although in two of his greatest battles, those of Vitoria and Salamanca, he was the attacker, he won his greatest renown as the master of defence. When selecting his position for a defensive battle he selected a ridge, wherever possible, deploying his troops below its crest and out of sight of the enemy. French commanders encountering such a position rarely saw more than a few scattered guns with small groups of light infantry dotting the forward slopes, who discouraged close reconnaissance by accurate fire at remarkably long ranges. When the French came to launch their attack, their massed artillery, unable to see a true target, would be largely ineffective, while their skirmishers would fail to dislodge Wellington's light infantry; then, when their heavy columns, groping their way uncertainly up the ridge through a swarm of skirmishers, finally reached the crest they would suddenly find in front of them a long steady scarlet wall of infantry and their leading files would be blown away before they had recovered from their surprise. Even as late as the closing stages of the Battle of Waterloo, Napoleon's Imperial Guard thought they had broken through the British line only for the Foot Guards to emerge out of a cornfield, and drastically enlighten them. It is probable that infantry have never been handled with greater skill than under Wellington and equally that no general was better served by his infantry soldiers.

6th Inniskilling Dragoon officer, 1814, in review order. The epaulette on the right shoulder is hidden but the crimson waist sash, a distinction of commissioned rank, is clearly visible. On active service overalls replaced boots and breeches, and the ornate sabretache (the purse-like object hanging down behind his left leg) was replaced by one of black leather

The Cavalry

Paradoxically enough, the basic organization of a cavalry regiment bore a marked similarity to that of an infantry battalion. It was commanded by a lieutenant-colonel with two majors, ten captains and twenty lieutenants or cornets under him; it consisted of ten troops, each under a captain, and had a war establishment of about eighty privates (the term trooper was not then used) and eighty horses. From time to time there were minor variations in the numbers, but substantially these figures held good for the whole period of the war.

The number of men actually present with the regiment, especially after a long period in the field, was considerably less. In *Rules and Regulations for the Cavalry, 1796* for instance, it was directed that 'Each troop should be divided into two squads when under forty, into three or more when above, according to the number, with an equal number of non-commissioned officers in each . . . The squads must be as separate and distinct as

possible . . . The squad is entirely in charge of its own sergeant.' This seems to have relieved the junior officers of all administrative responsibilities. However, they were ordered to 'look in on the men at dinner hours', regrettably not so much to check the quality of the rations as to see that their men 'do not dispose of their meat for liquor'. In an optimistic vein the Regulations continued, 'nor is any dragoon to give way to that blackguard practice of swearing'. Officers too, had to preserve a certain decorum and the Regulations emphasized, 'on no account is an officer to wear his hat on the back of his head'.

In some minor ways the cavalry organization took into account the differences of that arm from the infantry. The senior non-commissioned-officer in a troop was the troop quartermaster and in regimental headquarters there was a riding master with rough riders under him to train horses and men. As in the infantry there was an adjutant and a sergeant-major; the latter's duties included

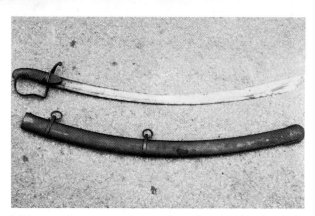

Light cavalry pattern trooper's sabre carried by light dragoons and hussars throughout the war; heavy dragoons carried a straight sword

drilling the young officers and these had to pay him a guinea and a half for the privilege of listening to his words of counsel couched, no doubt, in traditional terms.

Cavalry regiments fell into two main categories, heavy and light. The distinction at this time had little significance so far as their duties in the field were concerned. Heavy cavalry might find themselves on outpost duty, as did Le Marchant's Heavy Cavalry Brigade during the siege of Ciudad Rodrigo, while the Light might execute a fierce charge as they did at the cavalry combat at Villa-Garcia. The heavy cavalry tended to be larger men on larger horses and to carry heavier weapons, but unlike the French cuirassiers wore no body armour; in theory they were better suited for shock action on the field of battle, while the nimbler and more agile light horsemen might be expected to excel at outpost duty, patrolling and the pursuit. Wellington himself paid little attention to such niceties, using regiments as convenient without much regard for their official classification.

The heavy cavalryman went into action with a cut-down version of the Brown Bess musket, labelled a carbine, which has a barrel twenty-six inches long; his main weapon was a long, heavy, badly balanced sword, according to some critics the worst weapon ever issued to the British Army. The light cavalryman was also armed with a carbine, the Paget, which had an exceptionally short barrel, only sixteen inches, but again his main weapon was his sabre about thirty-three inches long and reputedly a light and handy weapon.

Officers carried a similar pattern sword to that of their men, and all ranks carried pistols. It was in their uniforms that the two types of cavalrymen differed most distinctly. Historically, the regular cavalry had developed from regiments of dragoons and in origin the dragoon had been little more than an infantryman on horseback. Marlborough, however, believed in shock action and the sword, limiting his cavalrymen to no more than three or four rounds for their carbines in battle, and this view had become generally accepted. The heavy cavalry regiments, still called dragoons or, more grandiosely, dragoon guards, however, retained in their uniform their old infantry connection, and at the beginning of the war were attired in red coats and white breeches. The light cavalry, light dragoons or more rarely, hussars, by now had totally renounced their origin. The colour of their jackets was basically blue, but became so adorned with wonderful and exotic additions that the modern Paris fashions would have had little to offer the well-dressed light dragoon.

But here the differences largely ended; neither in drills nor in composition does there appear to have been any great distinction; however, a marked difference soon developed between cavalry and infantry. Cavalry regiments had no battalions or depots, and were responsible for recruiting and training their own men; in addition, with their imposing chargers and cutting swords that could wound but seldom kill, they were far better at controlling riotous mobs than the infantry with their deadlier firearms and vicious bayonets that could be used only for the far more lethal thrust. Since the free-born Briton of the day was accustomed to voicing his views with no little force, the government made a habit of keeping a number of cavalry regiments in the country to help enforce its less popular decrees. For these reasons, cavalry regiments serving in the Peninsula normally left behind two troops to form a depot, going overseas with only eight, and later some regiments left behind four.

When the 10th Royal Hussars left England to join Wellington for his campaign of 1813, four troops under a major were sent to York to form a depot and keep an eye on the local populace, while according to its official history the regiment embarked six troops strong, with the following:

Hussars charging French cavalry. The metal chin-straps shown here are unusual. The pelisses are slung over the left shoulder to free the sword arm, but even so it was a common criticism that the coats were cut too tight in the arm. Plumes are not worn in the headdress; these were generally preserved for the less exacting conditions of ceremonial parades

lieutenant-colonels – 1; majors – 1; staff officers – 4 (presumably these were officers in regimental headquarters and included the adjutant, the quartermaster, and perhaps a doctor and veterinary surgeon); captains – 6; subalterns – 12; assistant adjutant – 1; regimental sergeant-major – 1; troop quartermasters – 2; troop sergeant-majors – 4; sergeants – 29; corporals – 24; trumpeters – 6; privates – 513; troop horses – 523. It is interesting to note that troop sergeant-majors appear to have begun to take over from troop quartermasters.

Although the regiment had only six troops, with about 580 rank and file, it was considerably stronger than many of the eight-troop regiments serving in the Peninsula at this time. Here the strength of most regiments fluctuated between 400 and 500; a number were considerably less. Yet in 1809 some of the cavalry regiments serving under Sir John Moore had mustered as many as 750 men. Even allowing for the wastage to be expected on service, it seems clear that the smaller regiments had proved more effective in the field.

On operations, no doubt for what must have appeared at that time good reason, the troop organization was almost entirely abandoned; troops worked in pairs to form squadrons under the senior troop commanders, and, curiously, the half-squadron, not the troop, was the basic sub-unit for manoeuvre. Captain Neville, in his treatise on light cavalry which was largely embodied in the cavalry manual of 1803, put forward the view that thirty-six or forty-eight files (i.e. seventy-two or ninety-six men and horses) composed a manageable squadron. This suggests that an eight troop regiment organized in four squadrons was at its best with under 400 men present in the ranks.

To adopt the operational organization troops first paraded and sized; then each pair of troops came together to form a squadron in a two-rank

Sabugal on the River Coa. (St Clair). A light cavalry outpost. The hussars are wearing their fur pelisses buttoned up. A dragoon in his helmet with a flowing mane sits on a log with two comrades wearing some strange headgear of their own. The men butchering the sheep are probably Portuguese light cavalry

line with the largest men from both in the centre; when in line the men on the flanks tended to lean inwards setting up a considerable pressure on the centre, and for this reason the heaviest men were placed there to prevent them being forced out of the ranks like corks from bottles of champagne. It seems unlikely that during operations this clumsy procedure was always followed, and in an emergency squadrons must surely have fallen in as such.

The intervals to be observed within the squadron were carefully defined. Between the front and rear ranks there was to be a horse's length; men in close order rode with their boot tops touching; in loose files boot tops were to be six inches apart, and in open files there was an interval of a horse's length between every man. When the squadron had been formed and the men had checked their dressing on the centre file, they were numbered and detailed into half-squadrons, quarter-squadrons and threes; (as in the infantry

the nomenclature was somewhat haphazard and such phrases as divisions and sub-divisions were occasionally used).

The numbering in threes was important. The space taken by a horse in the ranks was reckoned at three feet, or a third of a horse's length. Hence if every three men in a rank wheeled their horses independently to the right, the rank would face in that direction in column of threes with a horse's length between each three. It would then be in a very manageable formation, and when it had reached its new position, on the command 'front' the men could wheel to the left and, since there was a horse's length between each three, could resume line without falling into disorder. In a squadron both ranks would perform this manoeuvre simultaneously, the rear rank wheeling up beside their opposite numbers in the front rank and the whole squadron facing to the right or left in a column of sixes. (The drill was in practice a little more complex than that outlined here, as it involved men reining back.) Movement by threes was normally used for all changes of formation. In true British style, when the order 'threes about' was given, in fact the squadron moved on a front of six men.

For movement over any distance, it was recommended that regiments should move in column of half-squadrons, or if this was impossible, by threes (i.e. sixes) or as a last resort in file or single file. The principle was that wherever feasible the length of the regimental column should not exceed that of the regiment in line.

As in the infantry, the main battle formations were columns of half-squadrons or squadrons, and line. In line, owing to the peril of pressure developing on the centre, an interval was preserved between squadrons, and in an advance the men in each aligned themselves on the centre file of their own particular squadron; the squadron leader himself rode a horse's length in front of his centre man and therefore could control the pace and direction of the whole squadron; to ensure that the regiment preserved its line the squadron leaders of the flank squadrons aligned themselves on those in the centre, while these in turn took their positions from the commanding officer who gallantly rode in the centre of his regiment a horse's length in front of the rank of squadron leaders, a rather more hazardous position than that occupied by the infantry colonel happily ensconced six paces behind his colours. Of the remaining officers and sergeants in the squadron, an officer, covered by a sergeant took post on each of its flanks, three sergeants occupied positions on the right of quarter-squadrons, and the rest made up a serre-file, or supernumerary rank, a horse's length behind the rear rank. The trumpeter or trumpeters, rode in the serre-file, but directly behind the squadron leader. Commands were initially given by word of mouth, generally repeated by the appropriate call on the trumpet; the most important calls such as 'charge' or 'rally' were taken up by all the trumpeters. Bugles were sometimes used instead of trumpets, but the manual of 1803 clearly thought this was a deplorable surrender to utility. It stated of the bugle horn: 'Soundings are exactly the same as those for the trumpet in place of which the bugle horn may occasionally be substituted. The trumpet is always to be considered as the principal musical instrument for the sounding; it particularly belongs to the line and the bugle horn to detached parties.'

The main cavalry method of attack was the charge. On this subject the manual of 1803 stated, 'When cavalry attack cavalry, the squadrons must be firm and compact; when they attack infantry the files may be opened; when they attack a battery, they must not ride up in front of it, but they must in two divisions attack on each flank, the files opened.'

'When cavalry attack infantry they should in general do it in column; the squadrons of the column should have at least three times as much distance between them as the extent of their front. The leading squadron, after breaking the enemy's line should move forward and form, the two succeeding ones should wheel outwards by half squadrons and charge along the line.' The action after a charge was important, the manual continues, 'In a charge of either infantry or cavalry the instant the enemy gives way the line must again be formed and the pursuit continued by light troops.' This was easy enough to lay down, but it was a ruling all too often forgotten in practice. Time and again the British cavalry failed to rally after a successful charge, galloping off in a wild pursuit of their beaten enemy, only to be confronted when horses were blown by fresh French cavalry and their triumph to be turned into disaster.

In a charge against infantry, the gallop began about 300 yards away to cut to a minimum the time under fire; against cavalry, on the other hand, the most important consideration was to arrive with reasonably fresh horses for the mêlée, and only the last 150 yards were covered at a gallop. It is difficult to believe that two squadrons ever galloped at each other in a compact mass. If they did so they would have resembled two motorists driving along the crown of the road and colliding with a closing speed of thirty miles an hour, and the drivers would have been in a much happier position than the cavalryman on his horse. Colonel Tomkinson, who served throughout the Peninsular War in the 16th Light Dragoons, made some illuminating comments when describing a skirmish:

Captain Belli's squadron with one of the Hussars, was in advance; and the enemy having sent forward two or three squadrons, Major Myers attempted to oppose them in front of a defile. He waited so long and was so indecisive, and the enemy coming up so close, that he ordered the squadron of the 16th to charge. The enemy's squadron was about twice their strength and waited their charge.

This is the first instance I ever met with two bodies of cavalry coming into opposition, and both standing, as invariably as I have observed it, one or the other runs away.

Our men rode up and began sabring, but were so outnumbered that they could do nothing and were obliged to retire across the defile in confusion, the enemy having brought up more troops to that point.

The ability to outflank an enemy was clearly one of the keys to a successful cavalry action and the length of front was of critical importance. The manual specified, 'Two or three squadrons in attack may divide into small bodies with 14 or

Lieutenant-General Sir Stapleton Cotton. He is wearing the shako of a light dragoon and the epaulettes of a field officer. He must be wearing the uniform of the colonel of a regiment

16 files in each and intervals between them equal to their front, the second or reserve covering the intervals 150 yards to the rear; if only two squadrons, the first line should be four small troops, the second of two again sub-divided, three covering the intervals and one outflanking.' The use of the word 'troop' here illustrates the remarkably casual attitude to terminology typical of the period.

In the rugged country of the Portuguese border and of much of Spain, the cavalry had few opportunities to exert a decisive influence in battle. Their most valuable functions were to act as the eyes and ears of the army and to screen it in movement and at rest. Single well-mounted sentries called vedettes could observe and hang around an enemy and gallop away if threatened. The tactics of the cavalry when patrolling or on outpost were strikingly similar to those of the light infantry. They worked in pairs in open order, covering each other and using their carbines to fire from the saddle – apart from the difficulty of persuading their horses to stand still

Firing from the saddle. The uniform is that of a former period. The horse seems to be rearing, perhaps to register a protest at the odd happenings over his head

The Battle of Salamanca, 1812. Le Marchant's heavy brigade making the charge that broke the French infantry. Both the infantry and cavalry uniforms shown are those of ceremonial parades and not service where overalls had replaced breeches. In particular the cocked hat of the cavalrymen had proved useless on service, and until it was replaced by a helmet the troopers generally wore forage caps

while aiming and firing, reloading must have presented nearly insuperable problems and one suspects that the effect of such fire was moral rather than physical.

The standard cavalry formation was the brigade composed of two, three or, less usually, four regiments. During the early stages of the war Wellington formed two cavalry divisions; although these on occasion consisted of two brigades, one heavy, one light, their organization was far more fluid than that of the infantry and tended to reflect the needs of a particular situation. He was plagued by incompetent divisional commanders, and from 1812 onwards discarded the divisional organization, leaving the cavalry brigades largely independent under the general direction of a single cavalry commander, General Sir Stapleton Cotton, who normally exercised control from army headquarters.

For most of the war Wellington was heavily outnumbered in cavalry by the French; during the first three years he had only eight regiments, but towards the end of 1811 matters improved; during the Salamanca campaign of 1812 he had sixteen, and used his new-found strength to decisive advantage at the Battle of Salamanca; here Le Marchant, with a Heavy Cavalry Brigade, in brilliant charge shattered a tottering French line to turn a French reverse into utter defeat.

The following year at Vitoria and during the battles in the Pyrenees the country inhibited the use of large bodies of horsemen. However, during Wellington's great advance through Spain to the borders of France the cavalry faithfully imposed an impenetrable screen in front of his armies and enabled him utterly to deceive the French commanders.

Artillery

The organization of the Royal Artillery reflected the somewhat casual fashion in which that arm had evolved; it had a logic all its own. Gunners were men who fired guns; guns were tubes down which various types of projectiles could be stuffed to be subsequently blown to a remote destination. The process clearly required certain specialized skills not to be found in the infantry, but since one tube, give or take a few feet in length and a few inches in diameter, much resembled another, a man who could deal with one manifestly could deal with another. It would be a false and expensive move, therefore, to train gunners to deal with only one particular type of equipment; what was needed was a number of all-purpose gunners capable of firing any type of cannon that might be appropriate to the task of the moment.

At the beginning of the eighteenth century, when it had become clear that artillery was likely to be a permanent feature of the battlefield, the British Army raised a Regiment of Artillery consisting of a single battalion. The old Roman organization of tens and centuries which seemed to work well enough for the infantry was obviously equally suitable for gunners. When over the years more battalions were raised they were composed of ten companies each about a hundred strong. These companies were expected to man any type of cannon, so there seemed little point in issuing them with a standard number of guns, or indeed any guns at all. When the need arose a battery of guns could be drawn from the gun-park, the number and type being those deemed suitable for the particular task. Since it might

Royal Horse Artillery changing position at speed. The gun detachments normally rode separately as outriders. Presumably in this incident it has not proved possible to bring forward their horses. A field officer of the Royal Foot Artillery seems to be enquiring about the move

1 General, review order, 1814
2 Staff Officer, service dress, 1814
3 Ensign, 9th or East Norfolk
   Regiment of Foot, service dress, 1814

MICHAEL ROFFE

A

1 Field Officer, 7th Foot (Royal
   Fusiliers), full dress, 1813
2 Infantry Officer, Line Regiment,
   cold weather uniform, 1812
3 Private, 3rd or East Kent Regiment
   of Foot (Buffs), marching order, 1814

B

1 Rifleman, 95th Foot (The Rifle
   Brigade), service dress, 1811
2 Portuguese Rifleman, 5th Cacadores,
   campaign dress, 1811
3 Corporal, Portuguese 8th Infantry,
   full dress, 1810

1

2

3

MICHAEL ROFFE

C

1 **Corporal, Grenadier Company, 42nd of Foot (Royal Highland Regiment or Black Watch), service dress, 1810**

2 **Officer, 52nd Light Infantry, service dress, 1814**

3 **Colour Sergeant, 11th Foot, full dress, August 1813**

D

**Private, 10th (Prince of Wales's Own Royal)
Regiment of Light Dragoons (Hussars), campaign dress, 1814**

MICHAEL ROFFE

E

1 **Officer, 9th Light Dragoons,**
   parade dress, 1812
2 **Private, 3rd Dragoon Guards,**
   service dress, 1814
3 **Gunner, Royal Horse Artillery,**
   service dress, 1810

F

1 Officer, Marching Battalion,
Royal Artillery, service dress, 1814
2 Gunner, Royal Artillery,
service dress, 1810
3 Sapper, Royal Sappers
and Miners, service dress, 1814

MICHAEL ROFFE

G

1 **Field Officer, Royal Engineers,**
  service dress, 1811
2 **Pioneer, Line Regiment,**
  29th Foot, service dress, 1811
3 **Drum Major, 57th Foot,**
  ceremonial dress, 1812

H

MICHAEL ROFFE

prove unnecessary to move the guns it would be folly to provide any form of transport. The infantry humped their muskets, there seemed no reason why the gunners should not pull their guns; if transport should be necessary, the sensible answer was to hire contractors for the occasion and discharge them when the occasion was over.

It was a delightfully simple approach and one likely to appeal strongly to those in financial authority. The possibility that, while it might provide the cheapest form of artillery, the system was hardly likely to produce the most efficient, was only slowly and reluctantly accepted. The first reform came when some astute member of the Board of Ordnance, which controlled such matters, realized that invalid companies were quite fit enough to man the guns on permanent fortifications, and thus the first tentative attempt at specialization was introduced. This reform, being an economy, was relatively painless. But the next, the decision to discontinue the hiring of civilian contractors to transport guns, was another matter. Yet civilian transport had indisputable disadvantages. Civilians, for some inscrutable reason of their own, were very apt to depart from the battle-field at the most critical moments, leaving the guns stranded or without ammunition. As these civilians were not subject to military law, the only punishment was to discharge them, a service that they had frequently already performed for themselves. By the time of the Peninsular War, however, a Corps of Royal Artillery Drivers had been raised, but this corps was completely separate from the Royal Regiment of Artillery and was commanded by officers from the Commissary. It was organized in troops from which drivers and horses were allotted to the artillery companies as might be necessary. This was the organization in force in the Peninsula. When a company of artillery had been allotted a battery of guns and the wherewithal to move them, it was known as a 'Brigade of Artillery'. This term, which had a completely different significance for most of the first half of this century, may be confusing; since these brigades corresponded to what in modern parlance would be called a field battery, it will, perhaps, be less confusing to use this title.

In the early days of the Peninsular War the finding of the gunners from one source and transport and guns from others had the unfortunate results to be expected; in particular the gunners tended to suffer from a critical shortage of transport. However with the passage of time the artillery companies operated for long periods with a particular type of gun and a roughly standardized amount of transport, but even then a company might find itself suddenly drafted to man siege guns, and the provision of horses and drivers to make the guns mobile still had its problems. In 1813 Captain Cairns commanding an artillery company wrote, as quoted in the Dickson papers:

We, that is our brigade [i.e. battery] and the Household Cavalry, arrived here on the 27th. Although marching with them we are not in their brigade; however, as we are of the Reserve, I am quite well pleased with them, as with no superior officers of our corps being now left to myself to forage and arrange as I please.

I am getting my naked drivers clothed here as well as I can. These lads were only three days in Lisbon, when they were pushed up to the Army and unluckily fell to my lot.

They leave England paid in advance, sell half their necessaries when lying at Portsmouth and the other half either at Lisbon or on the road, the driver officers never inspecting their kit. Thus they join a brigade perfectly naked. In my establishment of 100 drivers, I have men from three different Troops. I am resolved to

Royal Artillery Drivers. They wore blue jackets with red facings and the same pattern helmet as the Royal Horse Artillery. The non-commissioned-officer is in full dress with yellow braid and velvet trimmings. The man on the wagon is in undress uniform and wearing a forage cap and stable jacket. Artillery drivers carried no personal weapons

see that my officer of drivers, Lieutenant Dalton, does his duty in supplying them with necessaries, soap and salt. That is all I allow him to interfere with. My own officers look to the stable duties, and inspect the drivers' kits of their division every Saturday. The poor drivers are sadly to be pitied – considering the labour of taking care of two horses and harness they are worse paid than any other troops, and when left to the management of their own officers they are luckless indeed. By being with a brigade there is some hope of instilling into them the idea that they are soldiers.

The first part of this letter indicates another curious aspect of the artillery organization. At any one time an artillery battalion might have its companies spread as far apart as the West Indies, Spain and Sicily. All attempts to concentrate battalions in particular regions invariably failed and the commanding officers, accepting with philosophy the impossibility of visiting their companies, generally stayed in Woolwich, contenting themselves with organizing drafts and looking after the administration of their companies overseas. In consequence there tended to be no real gunner hierarchy with the armies in the field. In operations near England, such as that at Walcheren, a reasonable number of senior officers might take part, but farther afield there was often only one senior artillery officer, perhaps a major, who acted as the Commander Royal Artillery, and his duties rarely extended to more than solving the many administrative problems which the peculiar gunner organization was likely to produce. The artillery company commanders were virtually independent, and as Cairns's letter shows, they were probably far from dissatisfied with their fate.

In the Peninsula the artillery initially was officially in charge of a Major-General, Royal Artillery. He seldom accompanied the army in the field, partly because his most important duties were administrative, partly because Wellington seems to have taken a dislike to the two generals who successively occupied the post. During most of the war he took as his artillery adviser Major Alexander Dickson (later Major-General Sir Alexander Dickson) a captain in the Royal

Artillery who had transferred to the Portuguese service to obtain a step in rank. It was a fortunate choice, and quite possibly Wellington was happy to have as his artillery adviser an officer too junior to press on him gratuitous advice, something he detested. During the course of the war, Dickson was promoted Lieutenant-Colonel and in 1813 was appointed to command all the artillery in the field. By the time of the Battle of Vitoria he had accumulated the nucleus of a staff and majors were to be found on occasion co-ordinating the activities of two or more batteries.

This lack of a gunner hierarchy, particularly during the early period, may have influenced Wellington against using his artillery massed. He allotted one battery semi-permanently to each division and that battery rarely strayed far from its parent formation. The reserve artillery was generally minimal in strength and artillery tactics seldom rose above the level of the battery. At this level the standard became remarkably high.

But although the company of Royal Foot Artillery in the Peninsula remained a maid-of-all-work,

Sir Alexander Dickson wearing a post-Napoleonic uniform. He has the Army gold cross with a number of Peninsular clasps

the first step in producing a battery trained and equipped for the field had already been taken. On 1 January 1793 orders were issued for the formation of A and B Troops Royal Horse Artillery. These Troops were designed to act with the cavalry, and, therefore, had to be highly mobile, fast into action and quick and accurate in their shooting. They were trained almost exclusively in their own particular role, and their drivers, although initially drawn from the Corps of Royal Artillery Drivers, were carried on the Troop strength and to all intents and purposes formed an integral part of the unit. Only officers of proven ability and the pick of the recruits were posted in. As a result these troops soon established a very high reputation. Since they supported the cavalry, they adopted a light cavalry style of uniform quite different from that of their comrades with the infantry. Troops R.H.A. supported the two cavalry divisions in the Peninsula and that most famous of divisions, the Light Division.

In an embarkation return dated 8 June 1809 quoted in Captain Duncan's *History of the Royal Artillery*, Captain Ross's Troop R.H.A. is shown as being composed as follows:

Captains	2
Subalterns	3
Assistant Surgeons	1
N.C.O.s	13
Trumpeters	1
Artificers	7
Gunners	81
Drivers	54
Total	162
Horses	162
6-pounder guns	5
$5\frac{1}{2}$ in. Howitzers	1
Ammunition wagons	6
Baggage wagons	3

This shows a troop R.H.A. at full strength. Whether horse or field, batteries were commanded by captains with 'second captains' to understudy them. The light six-pounders and the howitzer were generally drawn by teams of six horses, but for the wagons mules might be substituted. Gunners carried sabres but the drivers were unarmed. During the campaigns the R.H.A. fully justified their position as the right of the line, and at the Battle of Fuentes de Onoro under Captain Ramsay, their second captain, Bull's Troop R.H.A. performed a famous feat. The Troop was cut off by French cavalry and was given up for lost by the remainder of the army. Ramsay however, limbered up his guns and charged the French cavalry at the gallop. The gunners broke through the astonished French horsemen and rejoined the Army with their guns intact.

The work of the Companies Royal Foot Artillery, although less glamorous, was no less vital to the success of British arms. Since their guns were heavier than those of the horse artillery, these companies had rather more gunners on establishment. In the Dickson papers a company was shown with an authorized establishment of 2 captains, 3 subalterns, 4 sergeants, 4 corporals, 9 bombardiers, 120 gunners and 3 drummers, giving a total of 145 all ranks. In the field, its strength probably fluctuated between 110 and 130. The battery was armed with five field guns, 9-pounders or heavy 6-pounders, and one $5\frac{1}{2}$ inch howitzer. In addition it might have allotted to it about 100 drivers and horses and mules totalling altogether nearly 200. Teams of eight horses harnessed in pairs were normally used to drag the guns, but for the ammunition and baggage (a standard field battery might have eight ammunition and three baggage wagons plus a travelling forge) mules were often employed. However, the companies were far from standardized and would reflect in their organization the prejudices of their company commanders, or the needs of a particular task. The drivers would have a commissary officer theoretically in charge of them, and being mounted and therefore unable to understand drum calls, had their own trumpeter.

The characteristics of the guns in both field batteries and the Horse Artillery troops differed little, those in the horse artillery being merely lighter for greater speed of movement. There were three main types of projectile, roundshot, grape and shell. Round shot was a solid iron ball that had an extreme effective range of about 1,200 yards. It depended for its effect on the velocity with which it struck its target, hence field guns

The passage of the River Douro by Murray's Division, 1809 (St Clair). In the foreground foot artillerymen have taken the barrel of a field gun, probably a heavy six-pounder, off its carriage preparatory to embarkation – the triangular ornaments on the back of the gunners' coatees show up clearly. Behind them a light dragoon who has left his carbine on his horse is having trouble coaxing it into the boat, while on the left an infantry sergeant, clutching his spontoon, superintends the embarkation of his men

needed long, heavy barrels to stand up to large charges and impart a high muzzle velocity. On the other hand, since these barrels had to be mounted on robust yet light carriages that could travel across country unharmed and at a reasonable speed, the weight of the barrel had to be severely limited; British field pieces initially only took a six lb. ball, not a very daunting missile, and later a model was introduced capable of firing one of nine lb.

Roundshot, unless striking a column of troops, was comparatively harmless, but it was the only missile that could be used against a moving target at ranges of over 300 yards. Under this distance grape was far more effective. This name was applied indiscriminately to grapeshot itself, canister and case. Grapeshot consisted of about nine iron balls sewn together in a canvas bag that dissolved after the rounds left the gun, and

received its title from its resemblance to an over-size bunch of grapes; it was issued only to the eighteen-pounder and twenty-four-pounder guns of the siege train. Case and canister, as the names imply, were metal containers filled with a hundred small bullets or forty large ones. The container disintegrated as the round left the muzzle and the shot fanned out to produce a deadly pattern of destruction for a distance of nearly 300 yards.

Between 300 and 1,000 yards shells could be very effective, but only if the target was reasonably stationary. The common shell, as it was called, consisted of a hollow iron ball containing a fuze and a bursting charge. The fuze was ignited by the explosion of the charge that propelled the shell, and if all went well, it would cause the bursting charge to explode after the shell had landed; fragments of the exploding shell case would, it was hoped, strike anyone rash enough to be standing near by. To achieve this desirable result it was necessary that the shell should have thin walls and carry a large bursting charge, so that the casing broke up into numerous fragments moving with a lethal velocity; in consequence the shell was too large and too fragile to be fired from a field gun. However the shell did not need to be given the high muzzle velocity of roundshot and a shorter, lighter piece could be used. The $5\frac{1}{2}$ inch howitzer, the standard field piece for firing shells, although capable of accommodating a 24 lb. ball, owing to its light construction and short barrel (only 33 inches compared with 72 inches for the light 6-pounder, 96 inches for the heavy, and 84 inches for the 9-pounder) could keep up even with the cavalry.

Since field guns could not fire shells, every battery included a howitzer. This complicated arrangements for ammunition, and experiments were made with all-howitzer batteries, but these proved too specialized to suit the dispersed way in which Wellington generally deployed his guns.

There was an obvious need to make field guns more effective at ranges over 300 yards and Lieutenant Shrapnel developed a shell originally called spherical case, but which later attained more fame under the name of its inventor. He filled his shell with bullets; now the bursting charge had only to be strong enough to break open the shell case and let loose the bullets, it could be much reduced and the walls of the shell could be thicker. Spherical case was issued to all field guns, although technical difficulties prevented its being fully effective at that time.

In a regimental order the following proportions

A $5\frac{1}{2}$-inch howitzer

were laid down for a hundred rounds. Field guns were to carry 60 rounds roundshot, 30 of spherical case and 10 of common case; howitzers 50 rounds spherical case, 10 rounds common case and 40 rounds common shell. Ammunition was to be carried at the scale of 180 rounds per 6-pounder gun, 116 per 9-pounder and 84 per howitzer.

In action guns were aimed by lining up the barrel with the target, hence the gun-layer for either field guns or howitzers had to have a clear view of his target. Range was obtained by elevating the barrel, but even with howitzers it was rare to elevate it more than 10° with the horizontal.

To load the gun, first a charge of gunpowder was rammed down the barrel, then the missile, and finally some wadding to keep it in place. At the same time powder was trickled down a vent which led to the charge, or some combustible material was inserted. When the order to fire was given, a slow match or port-fire was applied to this powder which burnt down to the charge and caused it to explode. Immediately after firing, the gun barrel had to be sponged out to remove any burning embers that might remain and prematurely ignite the next charge; if for any reason a sponge was not available the gun was out of action. Five or six men were sufficient to load and point a gun but four or five more were needed to prepare the ammunition and help haul it back to its firing position, as the shock of each discharge would cause it to recoil a few feet. Rates of fire are not known for certain. General B.P. Hughes, perhaps the best authority on the subject, calculated that under battle conditions guns could probably fire two rounds of roundshot or three of grape in a minute. Dickson merely observed that the rate of fire for howitzers was slower than that for guns: it may be guessed at about three rounds in two minutes.

Besides the field artillery there were two more categories in the Peninsula, the siege train, which will be considered later, and rockets. Although in the Peninsula no complete battery of rockets ever operated, as Wellington viewed their uncertain behaviour with considerable distaste, it is recorded that 'Captain Lane's rocket detachment did good service during the crossing of the R. Adour before the battle of Orthes.'

Wellington's handling of his artillery has sometimes been called in question, yet his method corresponded exactly to his own particular tactical policy. Napoleon concentrated his artillery and signalled his attacks by massive bombardments. Wellington, generally fighting on the defensive, was determined to conceal his dispositions until the last possible moment; he therefore spread his artillery across his front, placing the batteries under the control of his divisional commanders, so that it was possible for the commander on the spot to use his guns to best advantage without the hampering rigidity inevitable under a system of centralized control. Concentrations of artillery might indeed pave the way for a successful attack, but in defence it could result in furnishing an easy target for the guns of the enemy and might rob an area of vitally needed artillery support.

At the same time Wellington was quite competent to deploy his individual batteries to best advantage himself. At the battle of Salamanca the French had a considerable superiority in artillery, but it was the British guns that exercised the most influence on the battle. During the initial attack on the French flank, they were positioned at right angles to the infantry line of advance and raked the front of the French columns with deadly effect. When later in the battle Clausel launched a counter-attack that achieved a considerable initial success, the French infantry found themselves advancing up a shallow valley with the British artillery, personally posted by Wellington long before, pouring in a devastating cross-fire from the high ground on either side, a fire which contributed powerfully to their eventual repulse. It was perhaps natural for the Royal Artillery to watch enviously Napoleon's technique for handling guns *en masse*, a technique perfectly suited to the tactics he used. It did not follow that Wellington's less ostentatious use of that arm was any less well suited to the tactics that at Waterloo led to the defeat of the Emperor of the French.

Badajoz. The 3rd Division takes the Castle by escalade. A bare-headed field officer, probably Major Ridge of the 5th, is stepping on to the ramparts while a grenadier waves his comrades forward

Sieges and Sappers

The organization of the Royal Artillery may have seemed peculiar, but the organization of the Royal Engineers had the distinction of being barely discernible. For most of the eighteenth century, like the inmates of a college at a university with fellows and dons but no undergraduates, Royal Engineer officers were unencumbered by the presence of soldiers. They moved in the aura of a mysterious craft no lesser mortals could comprehend, and depended on contract labour for the execution of their designs.

However, after the capture of Gibraltar it was realized that contract labour might not relish repairing fortifications while a siege was actually in progress, and a company of military artificers was raised for this purpose. Later, when revolutionary France threatened invasion, new companies under Engineer officers were formed to fortify the English coastline and the name was changed to the Corps of Royal Military Artificers.

But this corps remained distinct from the Royal Engineers and at the time of the Peninsular War Engineer officers still had virtually no troops under their command; in addition, although they were competent enough in the art of fortification, as they showed when constructing the Lines of Torres Vedras, they had no experience and little knowledge of how to conduct a siege. Since sieges were considered pre-eminently the province of the Engineer assisted by the Artilleryman, being clearly too complicated for the ordinary army officer to understand, the inexperience of the engineers, and above all the lack of trained engineer units was to cost the Peninsular Army very dear. The tragedy was the greater in that during the eighteenth century an elaborate ritual had developed by which a siege, if the attackers had sufficient men and siege guns, became largely a formal and relatively bloodless exercise in excavation and mathematics. General Jones, who as a young engineer officer was present at all Wellington's major sieges, has described the accepted procedure: the besiegers broke ground about 700 yards from the ramparts of the fortress:

This is effected by secretly approaching the place in the night with a body of men carrying entrenching tools and the remainder armed. The former dig a trench in the ground parallel to the fortifications to be attacked, whilst those with arms remain in readiness to protect those at work should the garrison sally out. During the night this trench is made of sufficient extent to cover from the missiles of the place the number of men requisite to cope with the garrison . . . This trench is afterwards progressively widened and deepened till it forms a covered road called a parallel, and along this road guns, wagons and men can securely move equally sheltered from the view and the missiles of the garrison. Batteries of guns and mortars are then constructed on the side of the road next the garrison and in a short time by superiority of fire silence all those [enemy guns] which bear on the works of the attack.

The procedure was continued at distances progressively nearer the enemy and from about 500 yards onwards heavy guns using groundshot would start to batter a gap, called a breach, in the ramparts of the fortress. While the guns demolished a selected section of the wall the mortars had an important task to perform. They resembled stocky wide-mouthed howitzers with barrels permanently set at an angle of forty-five degrees: their role was to lob large bombs into or over the fixed defences of the enemy subduing their fire and enabling the construction of the parallels and the covered road to proceed until the covered road led into the breach itself. At this juncture it was customary for the garrison to admit defeat and walk out with the 'honours of war'. If properly carried out, time and gunpowder were consumed rather than lives.

The main difficulty arose when the approaches came within 300 yards of the enemy ramparts. Jones continues:

Then the work becomes truly hazardous and can only be performed by selected brave men who have acquired a difficult and most dangerous art called sapping from which they themselves are styled sappers. An indispensable auxiliary to the sapper is the miner, the exercise of whose art requires an even greater degree of skill, courage, and conduct, than that of his principal. The duty of the miner at a siege is to accompany the sapper, to listen for and discover the enemy's miner at work underground, and prevent his blowing up the head of the road either by sinking down and meeting him, when a subterranean conflict ensues, or by running a gallery close to his opponent and forcing him to quit his work by means of suffocating compositions and a thousand arts of chicanery, the knowledge of which he has acquired from experience. Sappers would be unable of themselves, without the aid of skilful miners, to execute that part of the covered road forming the descent into the ditch, and in various other portions of the road, the assistance of the miner is indispensable to the sapper; indeed without their joint labours and steady co-operation no besieger's approaches ever reached the walls of a fortress. A siege, scientifically prosecuted, though it calls for the greatest personal bravery, the greatest exertion and extraordinary labour in all employed, is beautifully certain in its progress and result.

Unhappily this was never true of the British sieges in the Peninsula. Wellington had neither the trained sappers to accomplish the final stages of the siege, nor sufficient guns to silence those of the enemy; he always lacked time. In consequence he was forced to storm imperfectly blasted breaches from too far away. Even if he was successful the cost of life, as at Badajoz, could be appalling, while he frequently risked a bloody repulse, as at Burgos and San Sebastian.

The number of trained engineers at his sieges is revealing. At the unsuccessful attempt on Badajoz in 1811 he had seventeen engineer officers distributed at two per brigade, excluding

The siege of Ciudad Rodrigo. On 19 January 1812 the French garrison made a sally while the covering troops were being relieved, and nearly captured the breaching batteries. Here the working party are seen putting up a stout resistance with anything that came to hand

The Kurnool Mortar

the commander in charge of the siege. He had besides twenty-five men of the Royal Corps of Military Artificers who were no more than store-keepers responsible for the engineer park and the issue of engineer stores. He formed an *ad hoc* engineer unit by calling in forty-eight carpenters and forty-eight miners from his infantry battalions. At the sieges of Ciudad Rodrigo and Badajoz in 1812 his engineer resources were much the same and he supplemented them with twelve officers and 180 men culled again from the infantry, but these were no substitute for properly trained men.

After the atrocious number of casualties he suffered at the storm of Badajoz, he wrote home bitterly complaining of the lack of trained sappers, and Horse Guards responded by creating the Royal Corps of Sappers and Miners. At the siege of San Sebastian he had 105 rank and file from the newly-formed corps, but their numbers were quite inadequate and the fortress fell only after the second attempt at a storm.

Guns were the other half of the siege equation. Siege guns were heavy and difficult to move, requiring long trains of oxen if they travelled by

An artillery officer personally lays a siege gun while two others stand ready to observe the fall of shot. The artillery-man with the handspike wears two fringed epaulettes and is therefore a corporal (bombardiers, equivalent to the modern lance corporal, wore only one fringe on the right shoulder). Chevrons, although officially adopted by the Royal Artillery in 1802 to conform with the infantry, were not actually worn until 1813

33

road. The siege train sent out from England for the siege of Ciudad Rodrigo is fairly typical. Jones quotes this as being:

24-pounders iron	32
18-pounders ,,	4
10 inch mortars iron	8
$5\frac{1}{2}$ inch mortars ,,	20
$5\frac{1}{2}$ inch mortars brass	10
8 inch howitzers ,,	2

However, for various reasons only thirty-eight of these were actually used at the siege and to man them there were 171 British gunners and 371 Portuguese, giving a total of 542 non-commissioned-officers and men; of these, Jones noted, '85 men over two reliefs for laboratory and magazine duties and escorts and to replace casualties'. The actual gun detachments were only six men strong; this may seem strangely small, but the guns were aimed with a deliberation that was almost pedantic, and care had to be taken to avoid overheating the barrels; as a result rates of fire as compared with field guns were slow. At San Sebastian a breaching battery of ten guns fired 350 rounds per gun over a period of $15\frac{1}{2}$ hours, giving an overall average of a little more than one round per gun every three minutes. Jones said of this, 'such a rate of firing was probably never equalled at any siege'.

As regards supplies and the movement of stores there was a small British unit, 'the Royal Waggon Train', but for most of his transport Wellington had to depend on locally engaged Spanish bullock carts and pack mules, and for rations on the local purchases of his commissary officers. Medical arrangements were rudimentary. Every regiment had its own surgeon, but there were no ambulances or field hospitals, and the sick and wounded were cared for, so far as they were cared for at all, in improvised hospitals set up at nearby towns.

The Royal Waggon Train. The coatee was blue with red facings and the cut of the jacket resembled that of the artillery drivers

Conclusion

It can be said with justice that despite its many anomalies the Peninsular Army under Wellington was probably one of the finest that the world has known. Clausewitz suggested that as a war progressed the best men in the armies engaged became casualties resulting in a general levelling of standards. This process almost certainly happened to the Napoleonic armies, but Wellington was always careful of the lives of his men, and in the later stages of the war he and his army together merited the somewhat abused title, invincible. He himself remarked that if he had had his old Peninsular Army under him at Waterloo, instead of the astonishing miscellany of nationalities with which he was presented, the issue would never have been in doubt and the whole affair ended in three hours. Finally, a point not to be forgotten, one third of that magnificent army was Portuguese, and when he came to confront Napoleon in Belgium, he tried to have some of his veteran Portuguese regiments sent to him, but he appealed in vain.

The Plates

A1 General, review order, 1814

The 'loops' (the technical term for the long, false button-holes) on the lapels, cuffs and tails of the coatee were spaced evenly for generals, in threes for lieutenant-generals, and in pairs for major-generals. Two gold epaulettes were worn until 1811, when they were replaced by a gold aiguillette on the left shoulder. The cocked hat and feather were worn as shown in review order, but on active service a lower version was worn fore-and-aft for greater convenience.

A2 Staff Officer, service dress, 1814

This officer is wearing the uniform of an assistant adjutant-general or an assistant quarter-master-general. The embroidered loops were distinctive of all staff officers below general rank. They were in silver for the A and Q staff, and gold for aides-de-camp. Deputy assistants and brigade majors also wore silver lace, with only one epaulette, worn on the right shoulder by infantry and on the left by cavalry. Brigade majors were usually captains in rank, but those who were regimental majors did not wear the two epaulettes of a major when in staff pattern uniform, as they would then have been wearing the uniform of the senior grade posts of assistant adjutant- or quarter-master-general.

A3 Ensign, 9th or East Norfolk Regiment of Foot, service dress, 1814

The ensign was the junior commissioned rank in the infantry, corresponding to the cornet of cavalry and the second lieutenant of artillery. He wears the so-called 'Belgic' shako, officially adopted in 1812; earlier pattern 'stovepipe' shakos remained in use until stocks were exhausted, however. The double-breasted coatee came into use at the turn of the century. The tails, originally long as in a civilian tail-coat, were gradually shortened for convenience. The coatee could be worn buttoned up, but usually the top three buttons were left undone and the lapels turned back to reveal the same facing colour as on the collar and cuffs. The ground of the Regimental Colour he carries is of the same facing colour.

B1 Field Officer, 7th Foot (Royal Fusiliers), full dress, 1813

Wings were worn on the shoulders by all ranks of the grenadier and light companies of infantry battalions, and by all companies of light infantry and fusilier regiments. The Royal Fusiliers have blue facings, a distinction of all 'Royal' regiments. Their fur 'grenadier' caps, and grenade skirt ornaments, were worn to mark the original connection of the Fusiliers with the artillery; they were formed to escort the artillery, being armed with the then new flintlock fusil. Field officers at this time wore two epaulettes, but company officers had one on the right shoulder only.

Grenadier and light company officers wore two lace wings, as did all officers of fusilier and light infantry regiments. Field officers of these regiments wore small epaulettes over their wings.

B2 Infantry Officer, Line Regiment, cold weather uniform, 1812

The stovepipe shako is protected by an oilskin cover with a flap at the neck. Other types of headdress, including the helmets of the cavalry, had similar covers adapted to their shape. The greatcoat is the approved dismounted version (although some officers had shorter, fur-trimmed coats, while others had very long patterns reaching almost to the ground). The crimson waist sash was the distinction of an officer, tied on the left by cavalry and all field officers, and on the right by dismounted and all company officers. The gorget was worn by officers of the battalion companies when on duty, attached to the collar of the

coatee by a ribbon of the facing colour. Light infantry officers wore curved swords, as did most field officers; the remainder carried a narrow, straight sword.

B3 Private, 3rd or East Kent Regiment of Foot (Buffs), marching order, 1814

The 3rd of Foot took their ancient nickname from the buff facings of their coats. The 'Belgic' shako shown here was made of felt, and the plume was carried on the left-hand side to avoid confusion with the French when viewed from a distance. Grenadier companies had a white plume, light companies a green one, and the battalion companies the national colours of white and red. Grey trousers and spat gaiters were officially sanctioned for active service in 1811, replacing the white breeches and black gaiters previously worn. The shade of grey depended on the quality of material and the effects of weathering.

The Battle of Fuentes de Onoro, 5 May 1811 (St Clair). The regimental surgeons, wearing the cocked hat of battalion staff officers, have set up a regimental dressing station to which stretcher-bearers are carrying a wounded man on an improvised stretcher. The musicians in a regiment were normally trained to perform this duty

C1 Rifleman, 95th Foot (The Rifle Brigade), service dress, 1811

The dark green uniform worn by the 95th, and by the rifle companies and 6th Battalion of the 60th Foot. This was in imitation of the corps of sharp-shooters recruited from the huntsmen or jägers of the German forests, who wore on military service the same traditional and practical green clothing that they wore in their peacetime occupation. (Another German-imported custom was the moustache, worn at this time only by riflemen and Hussars, whose style of uniform was also copied from the Continent.) Officers of Rifles wore a uniform based on that of the Hussars, with a braided jacket, fur-trimmed pelisse, curved sword, barrelled waist sash, and tasselled Hessian boots. Rifle regiments, like Fusiliers, eventually saw the rest of the army equipped with their own special weapon; but, at this time, they alone were armed with the muzzle-loading Baker rifle. Tactically, they operated in the same way as the light infantry. The black collar, cuffs and shoulder-straps outlined in white braid were peculiar to the 95th, the 60th wearing red facings. Note the special black rifleman's equipment, with its distinctive silver 'snake' belt-buckle; the cord fastened to the cross-belt of the cartridge pouch supported a flask of fine-grain powder, used for loading and priming the rifle when there was leisure to do so. At other times the normal paper-wrapped cartridge is thought to have been used. Note also the brass-hilted Baker rifle sword-bayonet.

C2 Portuguese Rifleman, 5th Caçadores, campaign dress, 1811

The Portuguese army was completely re-organized and trained from 1808 by British officers and N.C.O.s, under the supreme command of William Beresford. They soon became extremely reliable troops, capable of operating as a matter of course in mixed divisions with British Line formations. The Caçadores were the light troops, equivalent to British Riflemen, French Chasseurs à Pied and German Jägers. Some were armed with the Baker rifle, others with muskets. The basic brown uniform had different coloured facings and decorations according to unit, and exact cut seems to have varied, according to surviving illustrations of

the period. This figure is based on a reconstruction in the Lisbon Military Museum.

C3 Corporal, Portuguese 8th Infantry, full dress, 1810

Although the Portuguese conformed in general terms with British patterns of uniform and were, in fact, supplied with them largely from the looms and mills of northern England, they kept their own particular distinctions – notably the blue coatees of the infantry, and the distinctively shaped shoulder-straps. Grey trousers, in the British style, were often worn on active service, although the uniform illustrated officially included blue breeches and high black gaiters (see C2). The rank distinction of the Cabo or corporal is the double gold stripe around the cuff, and the sabre with yellow or gold sword-knot. The colours of collar, cuffs, and piping varied according to regiment; they were dark blue, yellow, and red respectively for this unit, the 8th (Castello de Vide) Line Infantry. Light companies wore the same uniform with a brass *cor-de-chasse* replacing the national arms on the shako, and a green fringe on the outer edge of the shoulder-straps.

D1 Corporal, Grenadier Company, 42nd of Foot (Royal Highland Regiment or Black Watch), service dress, 1810

The Highlanders wore many distinctions of uniform based on their national dress, but otherwise conformed to the rest of the army. Thus the corporal illustrated has two chevrons, and wears the white hackle and wings of the grenadier company. The 42nd had the privilege of wearing red plumes, so their grenadiers had white with red tips. The dark blue facings identify a 'Royal' regiment. The diamond-ended or 'bastion' loops were worn by several units, including the Royal Artillery and Royal Sappers and Miners. The feather bonnet could be fitted with a detachable peak, like that of a shako, for active service. Officers of Highland regiments carried a Scottish broadsword, and mounted officers wore tartan trews and a plaid. Officers and sergeants of Highland regiments wore their sashes over the left shoulder. (For further details, see the Men-At-Arms title *The Black Watch*.)

D2 Officer, 52nd Light Infantry, service dress, 1814
Light infantry regiments were dressed and equipped in much the same way as the light infantry companies of Line battalions. Thus they wore shoulder wings, and the green plume, and the officers carried curved swords and did not wear the gorget. The stovepipe shako continued in service with the light and rifle regiments when the rest of the infantry adopted the Belgic style, and remained the headgear of these élite corps until 1816. The sergeants carried light muskets instead of spontoons, and both sergeants and officers used whistles to signal orders in the field. These were carried attached to the crossbelt by a metal chain.

D3 Colour Sergeant, 11th Foot, full dress, August 1813
The rank of colour sergeant was introduced in July 1813. There was only one to each company, and the appointment, intended to improve the career structure of the non-commissioned ranks (always a pet reform of the Duke of Wellington) corresponded to that of the modern company sergeant-major. The badge of rank was worn on the upper right arm: a crown above a Union Flag, below which were two crossed swords, and below this again a single chevron. The three chevrons of a sergeant were worn on the left arm. N.C.O.s wore chevrons on both arms, with a gap of about half an inch between them; corporals wore two, sergeants three, and sergeant-majors (corresponding to the modern regimental sergeant-major) four. Sergeants wore scarlet coats like those of officers, instead of the madder-red of corporals and privates. Their distinctive weapon was the spontoon or short pike; in general usage this continued to be referred to as a halberd, although the true halberd – a pike with an axe-head – had been replaced by the spontoon in the 1790s. Additionally, sergeants were armed with a sword of the same type as that carried by their officers; and, like them, wore a crimson waist sash, although sergeants' sashes had a central stripe of the regimental facing colour.

E Private, 10th (Prince of Wales's Own Royal) Regiment of Light Dragoons (Hussars), campaign dress, 1814
Originally hussars were a branch of light cavalry raised from the half-wild mounted herdsmen of the Hungarian plains; and a number of distinctive items of dress, evolved in accordance with local fashion and working conditions, were later taken up by military tailors and adapted into more formal styles. The braided waistcoat became the laced hussar jacket; the wolf-skin worn around the shoulders as protection against the weather became the fur-trimmed pelisse; the fur cap with a long 'night-cap' bag became the fur busby with a flat bag hanging down one side; and the cords worn around the waist became a corded gold sash clasped together with crimson 'barrels' or hoops. The gradual adoption of these items by some regiments of British Light Dragoons was recognized in 1805, when the 7th, 10th and 15th regiments were permitted to add the suffix 'Hussar' to their title. The 18th were converted in 1807. Despite their flamboyant uniforms and continental moustaches, their tactical employment remained identical to that of conventional Light Dragoons. Note that this trooper is wearing his pelisse over his laced jacket for warmth. Leather trouser cuffs were not uncommon among both cavalry and dismounted troops in the field, and leather inserts on the inside of the leg were normal for the mounted branches.

F1 Officer, 9th Light Dragoons, parade dress, 1812
Most of the British Army's light cavalry work – reconnaissance and patrolling – was done by the Light Dragoons. The uniform illustrated was introduced in 1811 and was in fact less functional than that worn previously: the bell-topped shako so closely resembled that already in use by the French light cavalry that the possibility of mistakes under campaign conditions was considerable. The coatee had short tails reaching to the saddle, and the lapels were usually worn buttoned back to give the effect of a plastron or cloth breast-plate. When worn in this way they were buttoned back all the way down to the waist, and the coatee was fastened in the centre with hooks and eyes. The cap lines were to prevent the shako being lost while galloping, and terminated in tassels and 'flounders' or knots of cord, plaited in the shape of the flat fish whose name they borrowed.

F2 Private, 3rd Dragoon Guards, service dress, 1814
Until 1811 British heavy cavalry (the Life Guards, the Royal Horse Guards, Dragoon Guards and Dragoons) wore the large cocked hat, long-tailed coatees with looped button-holes on the chest, cuffs and collar, white breeches and high boots. However, regiments on active service had generally worn various types of forage caps as head-dress; and overalls, buttoned over boots and breeches, were common for some years before this point, when they were officially sanctioned for all mounted personnel on active service. For parades and reviews boots and white breeches remained the rule for all mounted officers and cavalrymen. The 1811 reforms included a new heavy cavalry coatee without loops, and fastened down the middle with hooks and eyes. Dragoons had pointed cuffs, Dragoon Guards square ones. Heavy gauntlets were worn. The metal helmet, resembling the Romanesque patterns used by French cavalry formations, had a bearskin crest curling forward for the Household Cavalry, and a flowing horsehair tail in the Line Cavalry. The brass chin-scales were not entirely decorative, as they gave a degree of protection from horizontal cuts to the throat and face.

F3 Gunner, Royal Horse Artillery, service dress, 1810
The Horse Artillery continued to wear this uni-form – based on that of the Light Dragoons before 1811 – until after the Napoleonic Wars. The shell jacket was in the artillery colours of blue with red facing and gold lace, and the black helmet with the fur crest also bore the artilleryman's white plume. The numerous rows of loops were a Light Dragoon characteristic before the adoption of the coatee. Officers of the R.H.A. wore a hussar-type pelisse trimmed with brown fur, and all ranks wore the sabretache, or wallet, when this was introduced into the cavalry in 1811.

G1 Officer, Marching Battalion, Royal Artillery, service dress, 1814
The Royal Artillery at this time conformed to infantry patterns of dress in most respects; the major difference was that they traditionally wore blue coats, as servants of the Board of Ordnance, rather than red, as soldiers of the monarch. They wore the white plume of grenadiers.

G2 Gunner, Royal Artillery, service dress, 1810
The gunner wore the infantryman's stovepipe shako until 1812, when both arms adopted the Belgic pattern. The diamond-ended or 'bastion' loops were worn by all Ordnance Corps, as well as by a few infantry regiments. The pouch belt carried a small hammer and prickers, and the red cord carried a powder flask for priming. The sword bayonet was the most common personal weapon carried by the gunners of field batteries; one or two light muskets were carried on the limber for use in emergencies or by sentries. Gunners of garrison batteries carried muskets and infantry equipment, to defend their guns if the enemy came too close for the fixed armament to bear on them.

G3 Sapper, Royal Sappers and Miners, service dress, 1814
This sapper wears ordinary infantry pattern uni-form, with the white plume and bastion loops of an Ordnance Corps. The red coatee with blue facings came into use in 1813; prior to this, the army's few sapper units had worn a blue coatee similar to the artillery pattern, with black facings. The change to red was ordered to make the sappers less conspicuous when serving with infantry working parties.

H1 Field Officer, Royal Engineers, service dress, 1811
The Royal Engineers were at this time an all-officer corps, selected from those cadets who came highest in the final order of merit at the Royal Military Academy, Woolwich. Engineer and artillery commissions could not be purchased, but depended on completing the R.M.A. course. They were therefore a type of specialist staff officer, and wore the cocked hat rather than the shako.

H2 Pioneer, Line Regiment, 29th Foot, service dress, 1811
The pioneers of the infantry provided local engineer support, obstacle clearance, and so forth. The grenadier cap could be worn with or without a peak, and with several minor variations of shape and size. The other distinctions of appearance were the felling axe, the leather apron, and the beard – in an otherwise clean-shaven army.

H3 Drum Major, 57th Foot, ceremonial dress, 1812
The drum-major illustrates the widespread – and international – convention by which trumpeters, drummers and bandsmen wore the colours of their regiment reversed; i.e., if the regiment had red coats faced with yellow, the musicians wore yellow coats faced with red. Drummers and bands of marching battalions wore shoulder wings (as they still do) and heavily laced coatees. The trumpeters of cavalry units wore especially ornate uniforms, carrying on the traditions of the heralds of chivalry. Musicians usually wore the normal headdress of the company or regiment to which they belonged with various embellishments, except for the drum-major, who was distinguished by a feathered cocked hat. He wears the infantry sergeant's sword and sash, and a baldric, richly laced, bearing two miniature drum-sticks. The brilliant uniforms of trumpeters and drummers not only looked impressive on parade but fulfilled a useful tactical purpose; it was important for an officer to be able to pick them out quickly to sound field calls in battle.

Men-at-Arms Series

TITLES ALREADY PUBLISHED

THE STONEWALL BRIGADE *John Selby*

THE BLACK WATCH *Charles Grant*

FRENCH FOREIGN LEGION *Martin Windrow*

FOOT GRENADIERS OF THE IMPERIAL GUARD *Charles Grant*

THE IRON BRIGADE *John Selby*

CHASSEURS OF THE GUARD *Peter Young*

WAFFEN-SS *Martin Windrow*

THE COLDSTREAM GUARDS *Charles Grant*

U.S. CAVALRY *John Selby*

THE ARAB LEGION *Peter Young*

ROYAL SCOTS GREYS *Charles Grant*

ARGYLL AND SUTHERLAND HIGHLANDERS *William McElwee*

THE CONNAUGHT RANGERS *Alan Shepperd*

30th PUNJABIS *James Lawford*

GEORGE WASHINGTON'S ARMY *Peter Young*

THE BUFFS *Gregory Blaxland*

LUFTWAFFE AIRBORNE AND FIELD UNITS *Martin Windrow*

THE SOVIET ARMY *Albert Seaton*

UNITED STATES MARINE CORPS *John Selby*

THE COSSACKS *Albert Seaton*

BLUCHER'S ARMY *Peter Young*

THE PANZER DIVISIONS *Martin Windrow*

ROYAL ARTILLERY *W. Y. Carman*

JAPANESE ARMY OF WORLD WAR II *Philip Warner*

MONTCALM'S ARMY *Martin Windrow*

THE KING'S REGIMENT *Alan Shepperd*

THE RUSSIAN ARMY OF THE NAPOLEONIC WARS *Albert Seaton*

THE ENGLISH CIVIL WAR ARMIES *Peter Young*

THE RUSSIAN ARMY OF THE CRIMEA *Albert Seaton*

THE BLACK BRUNSWICKERS *Otto von Pivka*

AUSTRO-HUNGARIAN ARMY OF THE NAPOLEONIC WARS *Albert Seaton*

THE AMERICAN PROVINCIAL CORPS *Philip Katcher*

FREDERICK THE GREAT'S ARMY *Albert Seaton*

THE AUSTRO-HUNGARIAN ARMY OF THE SEVEN YEARS WAR *Albert Seaton*

THE ARMY OF THE GERMAN EMPIRE 1870–1888 *Albert Seaton*

FUTURE TITLES INCLUDE

WOLFE'S ARMY *Gerald Embleton*

THE ROMAN IMPERIAL ARMY *Michael Simkins*

THE BRITISH ARMY OF THE CRIMEA *J. B. R. Nicholson*

NAPOLEON'S POLISH TROOPS *Otto von Pivka*

ARMIES OF THE AMERICAN WAR 1812–1814 *Philip Katcher*

THE KING'S GERMAN LEGION *Otto von Pivka*

BRITISH TROOPS IN AMERICA 1775–1783 *Gerald Embleton*

THE GURKHA RIFLES *J. B. R. Nicholson*

LIEUTENANT-COLONEL J. P. LAWFORD was commissioned into the Indian Army in 1937 and the following year joined the 1st Battalion, the 16th Punjab Regiment. He served with this regiment until the disbandment of the old Indian Army in 1947, and then transferred to the Royal Artillery until his retirement in 1961. He is now a Senior Lecturer at the Royal Military Academy Sandhurst. Among his published works, Colonel Lawford has edited a history of the 16th Punjab Regiment, co-edited *History of the British* ͟͟nd wrote *The 30th Punjabis* for the Men-at-Arms Series.

---

nly)

ISBN 0 85045 145 0

OSPREY
MILITARY

MEN-AT-ARMS SERIES

NAPOLEON'S
LINE INFANTRY

PHILIP HAYTHORNTHWAITE   BRYAN FOSTEN

EDITOR: MARTIN WINDROW

OSPREY MILITARY

MEN-AT-ARMS SERIES 141

NAPOLEON'S LINE INFANTRY

Text by
PHILIP HAYTHORNTHWAITE
Colour plates by
BRYAN FOSTEN

First published in Great Britain in 1983 by
Osprey, an imprint of Reed Consumer Books Limited
Michelin House, 81 Fulham Road, London SW3 6RB
© Copyright 1983 Reed International Books Limited
Reprinted 1983, 1984, 1985 (twice), 1987 (twice),
1988, 1989, 1990, 1991, 1992, 1994

British Library Cataloguing in Publication Data
Haythornthwaite, Philip
 Napoleons line infantry.—(Men-at-Arms series; 141)
 1. France *Armee Infanterie*   2. France—
 History   1789–1815
 I. Title   II. Series
 356'.11'0944   VA705

ISBN 0 85045 512 X

Filmset in Great Britain
Printed through Bookbuilders Ltd, Hong Kong

Dedication
To my mother

Organisation

Napoleon's line infantry was founded upon that of the *Ancien Régime*, comprising (in 1789) 79 French and 23 foreign regiments, each of two battalions (the 28th had four), with the artillery ranking as the 64th line, and 22 provincial regiments and 78 garrison battalions as the 97th.

A total re-organisation began on 1 January 1791 with the abolition of the old regimental titles, and over the next two years an increasing number of conscript and volunteer battalions were formed, culminating with the *levée en masse* of 1793. Their quality varied from the proficiency of the early National Guard regiments to the untrained and ill-equipped rabble of the *levée*, whose main tactic was a headlong rush, even basic manoeuvre being quite beyond them. To combine the discipline and steadiness of the regular army with the rev-olutionary fervour of the new army, the *Amalgame* was decreed on 21 February 1793 and enacted on 8 January 1794; by this measure each regular battalion became the nucleus of a Demi-Brigade, a new term to replace 'regiment', which was es-chewed for political reasons.

To every regular battalion (now the 2nd or centre battalion of a Demi-Brigade) was added a 1st and 3rd battalion from a newly-raised corps; for example, on 8 December 1794 the 2nd Demi-Brigade was created from the 1st Bn. of the old 1st Regt. (Régt. Picardie), with the 5th Paris and 4th Somme volunteer battalions. The tactical impli-cation was obvious: the centre (regular) battalion could manoeuvre in line and concentrate its firepower, while the conscripts on either flank could make rapid advances in column. Born of necessity, this system developed into the classic Napoleonic tactic of *l'ordre mixte*, operating at all levels from battalion to division, by which alternate

units provided fire-cover while others charged; the system was potentially invincible until the French encountered opponents equally innovative.

Demi-Brigade battalions (termed 'de Bataille' for line infantry and 'Légère' for light) each comprised eight fusilier companies and one of grenadiers, the latter (no longer armed with grenades) being in theory the battalion élite, the most steadfast and often largest men; there was in addition a regimental artillery company equipped with six 4-pdr. fieldpieces, reduced to three in 1795. The original 198 Demi-Brigades de Bataille increased to 211, but on 8 January 1796 a further re-

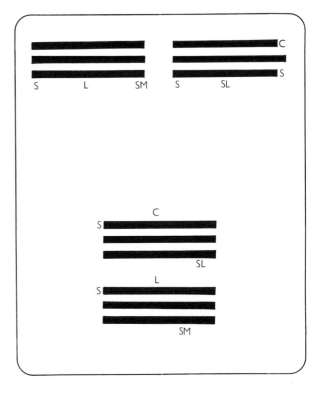

Above, **a company in line: first section (right), second (left), each three ranks deep. Positions marked: C = captain; L = lieutenant; SL = sous-lieutenant; SM = sergeant-major; S = sergeant.** *Below,* **a company in column, each section three ranks deep, key as above.**

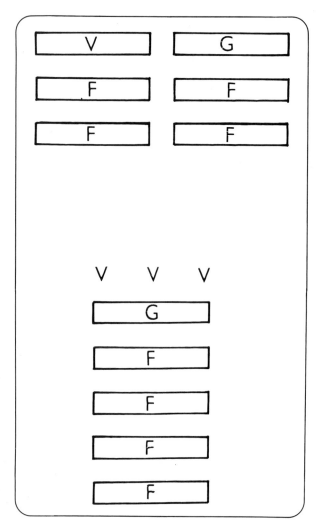

Above, **battalion column, six-company establishment, led by élite companies. Each company three ranks deep; frontage 75 yards, depth 15 yards. Key: V** = *voltigeurs*; **G** = **grenadiers; F** = **fusiliers.** *Below*, **alternative battalion column, six-company establishment. Five companies in column, each three ranks deep, preceded by screen of** *voltigeurs* **as skirmishers. Grenadiers could lead the column or bring up the rear if other companies were likely to waver.**

organisation reduced the number to 100, with the weaker corps broken up and amalgamated; for example, on 18 February 1796 the 3rd, 91st and 127th Demi-Brigades de Bataille were together formed into a new 3rd Demi-Brigade de Ligne, the term 'de Bataille' being discontinued. On 30 March 1796 the number of Demi-Brigades de Ligne was increased to 110.

In a Demi-Brigade, each fusilier company officially comprised a captain, a lieutenant, a *sous-lieutenant* (2nd lieutenant), a sergeant-major, five sergeants, a *caporal-fourrier* (quartermaster-corporal), eight corporals, two drummers and 104 fusiliers, and each grenadier company likewise except that there were four sergeants and 64 grenadiers. Throughout the entire period, however, actual strengths often bore little relation to the official establishment; for example, instead of the regulation 96 officers and 3,300 men, in February 1795 the 109th Demi-Brigade numbered only 92 officers and 1,239 men.

The term 'regiment' was re-instated on 24 September 1803, 'demi-brigade' being applied henceforth only to provisional units; the regimental artillery was disbanded at this time, being resurrected in 1809 but generally dispersed again in 1812. Ninety infantry regiments existed in 1803, 19 with four battalions and the remainder with three. Although some regiments had possessed 'light companies' as early as 1800, on 20 September 1804 a company of *voltigeurs* (literally 'vaulters') was added to each battalion by the conversion of a fusilier company; theoretically these were the smallest and most nimble members of the battalion, most adept at scouting and skirmishing.

A decree of 18 February 1808 confirmed a change in establishment which seems to have been in motion already, by which each regiment was to comprise four *bataillons de guerre* and one dépôt battalion, the latter of four companies commanded by the senior captain, with a major in command of the dépôt itself. Each *bataillon de guerre* was commanded by a *chef de bataillon* and comprised four fusilier companies and one each of grenadiers and *voltigeurs*, each company composed of a captain, a lieutenant, a *sous-lieutenant*, a sergeant-major, four sergeants, a *caporal-fourrier*, eight corporals, two drummers and 121 privates. The regimental staff consisted of a colonel, a major, four *chefs de bataillon*, five adjutants and five assistants, ten sergeant-majors, an 'Eagle'-bearer and two escorts, a drum-major and drum-corporal (*caporal-tambour*), a band-master, seven musicians, four craftsmen, a quarter-master, paymaster, surgeon-major and four assistants, the regimental establishment being 108 officers and 3,862 other ranks. In each *bataillon de guerre* were four *sapeurs* (pioneers) as part of the grenadier company, with one *sapeur* corporal per regiment. The grenadiers occupied the right of the line, the *voltigeurs* the left.

In the later campaigns the Line infantry was

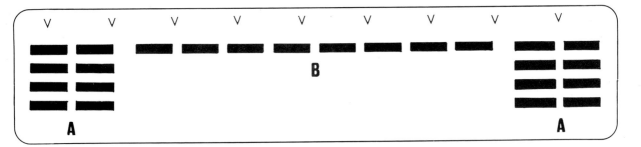

increased by the creation of 5th, 6th and even 7th battalions of existing regiments, and by the formation of new corps, including some from foreign personnel. As progressively younger conscripts were called, culminating with the teenaged 'Marie-Louises' of 1813–14, the standard of recruits declined markedly.

Formations for manoeuvre were flexible, and the accompanying diagrams show typical examples from company to brigade strength; the terms 'division', 'platoon' and 'section' referred not to sub-units but to formations, a 'division' being a tactical unit of two companies. The decree of February 1808 noted that when the élite companies (grenadiers and *voltigeurs*) were present, a battalion would act by divisions, and when they were detached, by 'platoon', each company constituting a 'platoon' and each half-company a 'section'. Such detachment of élites might be caused by the deployment as skirmishers of the *voltigeurs*, or by the consolidation of the élites of several regiments into composite battalions of selected personnel, as employed by Oudinot. (The screen of skirmishers which covered many manoeuvres was not necessarily composed exclusively of *voltigeurs*, as whole regiments could be employed thus; light infantry tactics will be covered in depth in the companion title, *Napoleon's Light Infantry*.)

Têtes de Colonne

The *Têtes de Colonne* (literally 'heads of column') comprised the musicians, *sapeurs* and colour-escort. The varied flags of the Demi-Brigades (usually in the national colours of red, white and blue and bearing republican symbols such as lictors' fasces and the Phrygian cap or 'bonnet of liberty') were replaced in 1804 by 'Eagles': gilt-bronze sculpted Imperial eagles atop a standard-pole, serving not only as the conventional rallying-point, but symbolising the unit's honour and fidelity. As this subject has been covered by a previous Men-at-Arms title (MAA 77, *Flags and Standards of the Napoleonic Wars (1)*), the briefest note will suffice here. Though the sculpted eagle was each battalion's symbol, a flag was usually attached (though often removed on campaign). The 1804 pattern consisted of a white diamond with alternate corner triangles of red and blue bearing the regimental number within a laurel wreath, the diamond inscribed in gold lettering, on one side 'L'Empéreur/des Français/au—^{me} Régiment/d'Infanterie de Ligne', and on the other 'Valeur/et Discipline' and the battalion number. In 1808, due partly to the number lost in action, it was decreed that an 'Eagle' was to be carried by only one battalion per regiment, other battalions having simple marker-flags. In 1811 the design of flag for the 'Eagle' was changed to one based upon the 'tricolour', one side bearing the presentation-inscription as before but the other emblazoned with battle-honours, reverting to the practice used by the Demi-Brigades. A third tricolour pattern, issued hastily in 1815, lacked almost all the magnificent embroidery of the previous types.

In 1808 the 'Eagle'-escort was ordered to consist of a lieutenant or *sous-lieutenant* as *premier porte-aigle*, with two veterans whose illiteracy had prevented their promotion as *deuxième* and *troisième porte-aigles*, paid as sergeant-majors and ranking as sergeants. They were usually armed with pistols and a halberd bearing a coloured pennon (often red for the 2nd and white for the 3rd, with 'Napoleon' on one side and the regimental number on the other). Many were dressed as grenadiers, but from 1812 some adopted versions of the carabinier helmet, a practice probably never widespread.

Uniforms

In the following sections it should be noted that official dress regulations were frequently not obeyed. In the 1790s matériel was so deficient that French forces resembled a ragbag; and under the Empire regimental variations were legion, even between battalions of the same regiment and within each battalion, due to the practice of reinforcing

units with drafts of men sent from their dépôts. Together with uniforms made by local manufacturers and modifications made of necessity on campaign, this rendered the appearance of Napoleon's infantry very divergent from the regulations. Examples of regimental variations are recorded below, these often being only discernible from contemporary descriptions and illustrations unsupported by other evidence; it is not unusual for sources to conflict, non-regulation examples conceivably representing a single uniform worn out of necessity or executed on the whim of an individual, as some officers and NCOs enjoyed considerable freedom in their dress. Others may represent transient variations instigated by the regimental or battalion commander.

Les Blancs et les Bleus: **French infantry wearing both the new blue uniform and the white coat of the ex-Royal army. Detail after Hippolyte Lecomte's** *Entrée de l'Armée Française à Mons.*

Table A (1791)

Regts.

(a)	(b)	(c)	(d)	(e)	(f)	(g)	Lapels	Collar, cuff flaps	Cuffs	Buttons
1, 7	13, 19	25, 31	37, 43	49, 56	67, 74	82, 102	x	x	x	yellow
2, 8	14, 20	26, 32	38, 44	50, 57	68, 75	83	x		x	yellow
3, 9	15, 21	27, 33	39, 45	51, 58	70, 78	84	x	x		yellow
4, 10	16, 22	28, 34	40, 46	52, 59	71, 79	90	x	x	x	white
5, 11	17, 23	29, 35	41, 47	54, 60	72, 80	91	x		x	white
6, 12	18, 24	30, 36	42, 48	55, 61	73, 81	93	x	x		white

Colours: (a) black, (b) violet, (c) pink, (d) sky blue, (e) crimson, (f) scarlet, (g) dark blue. First of each pair of regiments had horizontal pockets, second vertical.

The 1791 Uniform

The white uniform which gave the regulars their nickname (*les blancs*, contrasting with *les bleus* of the volunteer and conscript battalions) was designed in 1779 and confirmed on 1 October 1786, with facing colours borne on the lapels, collar, cuffs and turnbacks of the long-tailed coat. Considerable laxity of style included high or low collars, and cuffs with three- or four-button flaps or with a piped opening instead of a flap; headdress was the bicorn hat, with the white Royal cockade replaced on 27 May 1790 by one of the national red, white and blue 'tricolour' in concentric rings of varying arrangements of colours. The fur grenadier cap was re-introduced in 1789.

In 1791 some regiments were renumbered and a new sequence of facing colours introduced, with a three-button cuff flap (though the other types still persisted); fusiliers had white shoulder straps piped in the facing colour, grenadiers wearing the red epaulettes which remained their distinction throughout the period. (For facings, see Table A.)

The 1791 headdress was a peaked leather helmet resembling the British 'Tarleton', with an imitation fur turban and a fur crest; this was often of shoddy manufacture, with the crest being sometimes only a straw-filled fabric 'sausage'. The skull had metal reinforcing-bands, a tricolour cockade and a white plume with facing-coloured tip, feathers for full dress and a woollen pompon on other occasions. The 'Tarleton' was apparently never received by some regiments (which retained the bicorn) and

was unpopular. The 9th Demi-Brigade kept their helmets at least until 1798; but the 46th, receiving them in 1793, found them so noisome by 1796 that in a mass demonstration the entire regiment pitched their helmets into the river at Strasbourg, replacing them with bicorns at five francs per man! Grenadier caps had a red rear patch bearing a white lace cross, a brass plate bearing a grenade or regimental insignia, a red plume and white cords, and in some cases a peak.

The 1792 Uniform

New regiments were formed in 1792 and on 15 January new facing colours were specified for regiments numbered higher than 48 (see Table B); the short life of the 1791 facings for these regiments must cast doubts upon their use.

Other innovations in 1792 included sky-blue greatcoats with facing-coloured collars for officers, and the general replacement on campaign of grenadier caps and officers' helmets in favour of the bicorn, which had a white lace cockade-loop (silver for sergeants and sergeant-majors).

The 1793 Uniform

To eradicate the difference between *les blancs* and *les bleus*, an egalitarian blue uniform was introduced universally in 1793, based upon that of the National Guard, created in 1789. But due partly to shortage of cloth and partly to reverence for the traditional colour, it was some years before the white uniform disappeared, it being not uncommon for regular officers and NCOs to retain their white uniform

Table B (1792)

Regts. (a)	(b)	(c)	(d)	(e)	Lapels	Collar, cuff flaps	Cuffs	Buttons
49, 55	61, 72	79, 87	93, 102	108	x	x	x	yellow
50, 56	62, 73	80, 88	94, 103	109	x		x	yellow
51, 57	67, 74	81, 89	96, 104	110	x	x		yellow
52, 58	68, 75	82, 90	98, 105	111	x	x	x	white
53, 59	70, 77	83, 91	99, 106		x		x	white
54, 60	71, 78	84, 92	101, 107		x	x		white

Colours: (a) crimson, (b) scarlet, (c) dark blue, (d) dark green, (e) light green. First of each pair of regiments had horizontal pockets, second vertical.

even though their men were dressed in blue, a practice causing criticism from republicans.

Early National Guard uniform was varied; while blue coats with white lapels, cuffs and turnbacks and red collar was the eventual dress of the Paris National Guard (their original red lapels and cuffs seemingly never, or only briefly, adopted), provincial corps wore such varied styles as the scarlet with black facings of the Brest unit, the red faced with blue of Avignon and the white faced with red of Pont-St.-Esprit.

The National Guard uniform standardised in 1791 and copied as the dress of the Demi-Brigades in 1793 consisted of a long-tailed dark blue *habit* (coat) with scarlet collar and cuffs piped white; white lapels, turnbacks and cuff flaps piped red; red pocket-piping, and brass buttons (though old regulars often transferred their old buttons onto the new uniform). Blue shoulder straps piped red were specified, but red epaulettes were often worn indiscriminately, no longer restricted to grenadiers; and numerous cuff designs existed, including those with red or blue flaps, or the 1786 flapless version with piping on the opening. The bicorn bore the tricolour cockade, often with a yellow loop, and red or red-and-white pompon; but a drooping plume of red horsehair was popular, not just for grenadiers, and was used as late as 1800, when it was banned by Gen. Belliard when commandant of Cairo. Officers continued to wear gorgets and metallic lace epaulettes, as described later. Appalling shortages of everything throughout the 1790s led to almost

total disregard of uniform regulations; a soldier might consider himself lucky to receive a hat and coat, irrespective of style, and legwear and waistcoats were almost unknown as 'issue' items, the individual having to scavenge for civilian garments to supplement his wardrobe. In place of the regulation breeches and gaiters, loose trousers as worn by the *sans-culottes* of the Revolution were usual, white with red and/or blue stripes being

Typical colour of late 18th-century style: National Guard of the District de Saint-Magloire, Paris (9th Bn., 4th Division), 1790. White colour with gold scrolls and cypher, green leaves, red ribbon, silver sword with gold hilt, brown musket with silver metalwork.

LA LIBERTÉ FAIT MA GLOIRE

DISTRICT Sᵗ MAGLOIRE

popular. Footwear was so scarce that lucky men might aspire to wooden clogs stuffed with straw, while the majority of some French armies went barefoot. Uniformity of insignia was equally neglected; grenadiers might wear the regulation red grenade badges on the turnbacks, but other devices, including hearts, numbers or mottoes, were legion. Plumes occurred in all varieties of 'tricolour', both upright and drooping. Even such major variations as coats with red lapels or without turnbacks were not uncommon, the whole ensemble often in a state of total dilapidation.

The 'Egyptian' Uniform

Ordinary uniform was worn at the outset of the Egyptian expedition, at least four Demi-Brigades (18th, 25th, 32nd and 75th) wearing red-and-white striped trousers. As the campaign is covered by MAA 79, *Napoleon's Egyptian Campaigns*, brief details will suffice here. In autumn 1798 Bonaparte introduced a short-tailed, single-breasted jacket dyed with local indigo, with scarlet collar and cuffs and white turnbacks, and blue shoulder straps (red epaulettes for grenadiers); the wooden buttons were covered in cloth, brass buttons being reserved for élite units, and so scarce as to serve as currency! A peaked leather cap, the *petit casquette* or *casquette à pouf*, was worn with a tricolour cockade on the left, a flap to be lowered as a neck-shade, and a *pouf* or

woollen pompon on top; grenadiers had brass grenade badges on each side of the cap and sometimes all-red *poufs* (e.g. the 25th Demi-Brigade). Legwear usually consisted of cotton trousers and short gaiters, or one-piece 'gaiter-trousers'.

Shortage of cloth in autumn 1799 occasioned the so-called 'Kléber Ordinance' by which infantry received uniforms of the 1798 pattern but in any colour of cloth available; numerous variations are recorded (descriptions of the same colour perhaps varying as the uniforms faded), and it is possible that lapels and madder-red trousers may have been contemplated, but there is no evidence that they ever existed. Among recorded variations are the pointed cuffs (instead of round) and white bastion-shaped collar-loop of the 88th Demi-Brigade, and the green breeches (or red trousers with green stripe) of the 9th's officers. Table C lists examples of the 'Egyptian' uniform.

The pre-1806 Uniform

Confirmed by several regulations around 1800–01, the uniform evolved gradually from the 1793 pattern. The dark blue coat (*habit à la française*) was given shorter tails with false turnbacks, but which did not extend to the bottom edge of the tails until about 1810, and the lapels received an accentuated curve. The regulations specified red collar and cuffs

---

Table C ('Egyptian')

Regt.	Coat	Collar/Piping	Cuffs	Turnbacks	Piping	Pouf
9th	scarlet	blue/red	white	white	blue	red
13th	crimson	dark blue/white	puce	puce	white	blue
18th	scarlet	brown	yellow	yellow	blue	black
25th	crimson	sky-blue/white	sky-blue	sky-blue	white	white/red
32nd	brown	scarlet/blue	orange	orange	white	white/blue
61st	crimson	dark blue/yellow	dark blue	dark blue	yellow	white/black
69th	brown	scarlet/blue	white	white	white	white/yellow
75th	scarlet	sky-blue/white	sky-blue	sky-blue	white	red/blue
85th	brown	scarlet/blue	yellow	yellow	white	red/yellow
88th	violet	blue/white	green	green	white	blue/yellow

Recorded alternatives: 9th, green facings piped white; 18th, yellow facings piped white, or blue facings and scarlet collar on brown jacket; 32nd, crimson faced blue; 61st, light green cuffs and turnbacks piped white, brown faced yellow, or brown with yellow collar and light green cuffs and turnbacks piped blue; 69th, scarlet facings piped white; 88th, crimson jackets; 13th, green piping; 18th, scarlet collar and cuffs, white turnbacks and piping; blue piping for 69th, 75th, 85th; violet jackets for 32nd and 61st.

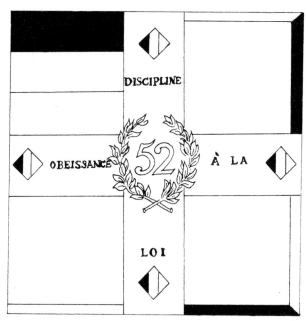

Colour of the 52nd Regt., 1793. White throughout with tricolour border and canton; green wreath; gold numerals and lettering. Tricolour lozenges cover the original fleurs-de-lys in accordance with an instruction of 28 November 1792 which obliterated previous Royal insignia.

An order of 26 October 1801 confirmed the use of the bicorn, but grenadiers were allowed to wear fur caps, usually for parade or combat, the bicorn with red plume serving at other times. Made of bearskin (hence its name *ourson*) or goatskin, the cap's cloth rear patch (nicknamed *cul de singe* or 'monkey's backside'!) was officially quartered in red and blue, but seems to have been almost invariably red with a white lace cross. The bonnet had a brass plate usually embossed with a grenade and sometimes a number (for example, the 45th had the number below a grenade, or 'No.' and '45' at either side); and officially a red plume and partially braided cords, though white cords were not uncommon (e.g. the 3rd, 18th, 21st and 57th), while the 8th wore peaks similar to the 1791-pattern cap. Red epaulettes and turnback grenades remained grenadier distinctions. The undress cap or *bonnet de police* was a pattern used since the 1780s, the *bonnet à la dragonne*, having a tasselled stocking-end folded up and tucked behind the right-hand side of a stiffened headband. The blue cap had red lace edging, piping and tassel and a company-badge for élites (red grenade, or yellow hunting-horn for *voltigeurs*), and when not in use was rolled and strapped under the cartridge box.

Officers' uniforms were of finer material, with gold lace headdress ornaments, and rank indicated by gold lace epaulettes in a scheme specified in 1786 and continuing through the Empire:

Colonel—epaulettes with bullion fringes on both shoulders; major (a rank created in 1803)—as colonel with silver straps; *chef de bataillon*—as colonel but fringe on left only; captain—gold lace fringe on left only; *capitaine adjutant-major*—lace fringe on right only; lieutenant—as captain but red stripe on straps; *sous-lieutenant*—two red stripes; *adjutant-sous-officier*—red straps with two gold stripes and mixed red-and-gold lace fringe on left. (A popular fashion was to have the red stripes on the straps in the form of interlocking diamonds).

The gorget was worn principally on 'dress' occasions, in gilt with silver devices incorporating the eagle (after 1804) and/or élite badges and regimental number. Officers' undress uniform, often worn on active service, included a single-breasted blue *surtout* without lapels, often with a red collar or (as worn by the 8th) a red cuff piping. NCOs' rank-distinctions were generally in the form

piped white, white turnbacks and lapels, and blue cuff flaps, fusiliers' shoulder straps and horizontal pockets piped red; but variations included red flaps or white flaps piped red, and the retention of the flapless cuff (perhaps as late as 1812 by elements of the 8th Line). An order of 13 July 1805 noted that: 'Many colonels have abolished the red piping on the lapels, others have made vertical pockets instead of the horizontal ones.' Turnback badges included stars, diamonds and hearts, eagles (after 1804), and regimental devices such as the 8th's red diamond bearing a white '8' and inner diamond, or the 48th's blue '4' on one turnback and '8' on the other.

The bicorn hat, worn across the head (*en bataille*) or fore-and-aft (*en colonne*) bore a tricolour cockade; 'ties' (laces to hold the sides erect) were usually black, sometimes coloured, and orange for the 4th Line, a distinction awarded for gallantry at Arcola. Short plumes or pompons began to appear to distinguish companies or battalions; on 21 June 1805 Gen. Vandamme ordered '. . . only round pompons and forbid the use of those as worn by the 57th, which place an undue strain on the hats and give generally a bad effect'—that regiment wearing carrot-shaped battalion plumes of sky-blue, orange or a violet shade known as *lie-de-vin* (literally, 'wine dregs').

of diagonal lace bars on the lower sleeve: two orange bars for corporals, a gold bar on red for sergeants, and two for sergeant-majors, and often with gold intermixed in the epaulette fringes, shako cords and sword knots and gold lace epaulette-edging for sergeants and above. Service chevrons were worn point uppermost on the upper arm, usually of red lace (gold for senior NCOs).

Hairstyles originally ranged from the dressed and powdered queues of the Royal army to the unkempt styles of the *sans-culottes*, the queue declining in use around 1803. Variations were permitted, largely according to individual taste, though as late as February 1804 cutting the hair short was an imprisonment offence in the 64th Line! Side-whiskers became popular from the early 1800s (though prohibited by the eccentric 64th), and moustaches were obligatory for élite company personnel.

Waistcoats and legwear remained basically un-changed, with loose trousers restricted to active service. White breeches with black gaiters were universal, non-regulation white gaiters being worn by many regiments in summer and on parade; off-white or grey linen were often used for everyday wear. The sleeved, single-breasted waistcoat had red collar and cuffs for some regiments (yellow for *voltigeurs*), and doubled as a drill-jacket. Walking-out dress included white stockings and gloves and buckled shoes, gloves being prohibited for rank-and-file under arms. A black stock was worn for parade and service dress and a white one for ordinary dress, often replaced unofficially by a cravat which protruded above the collar. Smocks might be used for fatigues, but not until 1805 were greatcoats issued, and even then only to troops on active service and purchased by regimental funds; before this, civilian overcoats, cloaks or capes had been provided by the individual. In April 1806 the issue was formalised, all members of *bataillons de guerre* receiving a coat. There seems to have been little standardisation, coats being either single- or double-breasted, coloured from beige through grey to brownish-maroon, with epaulettes transferred from the *habit* by élite company men.

The creation of *voltigeurs* in 1804 introduced new distinctions, initially a *chamois* or yellow collar (often piped red), virtually universal until 1815, and soon afterwards green or green-and-yellow epaulettes,

Colour of the 2nd Bn., 109th Demi-Brigade, 1795. White ground with tricolour border; tricolour bonnet over brown fasces with silver axe-heads; green oak-leaves; tricolour canton (signify-ing 2nd Bn.); white labels, gilt letters and numerals. Successive patterns of colour will be illustrated in the companion MAA **146**, *Napoleon's Light Infantry*.

plumes, sword knots and shako cords, with green or yellow bugle-horn turnback badges and similar devices on the shako plate. Originally *voltigeurs* wore the bicorn with yellow or green pompons, but in February 1806 the first Line infantry shako was authorised, replacing the bicorn generally by 1807. (The formation of light companies of 100 *carabiniers* per battalion around August 1800 in the 12th, 35th, 45th and 64th Demi-Brigades caused the issue of light infantry style shakos in that November to the 5th, 6th, 35th and 64th.)

The 1806 shako had a felt or board body, widening slightly towards the top; a waterproofed crown, leather peak and bands around the top and bottom; and usually a leather chevron stitched as strengthening to each side. On the front was borne a tricolour cockade above a lozenge-shaped brass plate bearing an embossed, crowned eagle above the regimental number, though many regimental patterns were also used. Brass chinscales were often worn even before their official sanction, with circular bosses bearing a five-pointed star or élite badges. Many regiments adopted coloured pom-pons, with plumes for élites, and braided cords for full dress in white (fusiliers), red (grenadiers) and yellow/green (*voltigeurs*). Officers' shakos had gold lace and cords and gilded fittings.

The 1806 Uniform

On 25 April 1806 it was decreed that uniforms would be styled as before but reverting to the white colour of the previous century, with coloured facings piped white and cuff flaps, turnbacks, pockets and shoulder straps piped in the facing colour, with company distinctions as before, though not all voltigeurs appear to have had *chamois* collars. Regimental differences were officially as in Table D.

It is believed that only the following received the white uniform: 3rd, 13th, 14th, 15th, 16th, 17th, 18th, 21st, 32nd, 33rd, 46th and 53rd (not

necessarily the whole regiment), of which the 13th, 15th, 46th and 53rd were not officially designated to receive the white. The 4th, 8th, 12th, 19th, 22nd, 24th, 25th, 27th, 28th, 34th and 36th were scheduled to receive it, but may not have done so; the 4th had theirs manufactured but perhaps never issued them. Among recorded variations, such as cuffs without flaps and coloured turnbacks, are the following:

3rd Line: Green or white cuffs with green flaps, apparently without buttons for *voltigeurs*, whose *chamois* collars were piped white; white buttons; red turnback badges of '3' on one side and five-pointed star on the other.

4th Line: White uniform perhaps never issued to rank-and-file, but officer shown with green cuff flaps and turnbacks.

13th Line: Suhr shows a *voltigeur* without cuff flaps,

'The raising of the siege of Thionville', 16 October 1792; after Hippolyte Lecomte. Illustrates the use of different uniforms within the same regiment; grenadiers in the foreground wear bicorn hats, the remainder the 'Tarleton' helmet.

Table D (1806)

Regts. (a)	(b)	(c)	(d)	(e)	(f)	(g)	(h)	(i)	(j)	(k)	(l)	(m)	(n)	1	2	3
1	9	17	25	33	41	49	57	65	73	81	89	97	105	X	X	X
2	10	18	26	34	42	50	58	66	74	82	90	98	106	X	X	
3	11	19	27	35	43	51	59	67	75	83	91	99	107	X		X
4	12	20	28	36	44	52	60	68	76	84	92	100	108		X	X

(above with yellow buttons, horizontal pockets)

Regts. (a)	(b)	(c)	(d)	(e)	(f)	(g)	(h)	(i)	(j)	(k)	(l)	(m)	(n)	1	2	3
5	13	21	29	37	45	53	61	69	77	85	93	101	109	X	X	X
6	14	22	30	38	46	54	62	70	78	86	94	102	110	X	X	
7	15	23	31	39	47	55	63	71	79	87	95	103	111	X		X
8	16	24	32	40	48	56	64	72	80	88	96	104	112		X	X

(above with white buttons, vertical pockets)

Colours: (a) dark green, (b) black, (c) scarlet, (d) capucine, (e) violet, (f) sky-blue, (g) pink, (h) *aurore* (orange-pink), (i) dark blue, (j) jonquille yellow, (k) grass-green, (l) *garance*, (m) crimson, (n) iron-grey. (1) lapels, (2) cuffs, (3) collar.

and with yellow-tufted white shako pompon with black centre, white cords, green epaulettes.

14th Line: Sapeur's bearskin with black-tipped red plume, buff apron with red crossed axes over grenade in each bottom corner.

17th Line: Red cuff flaps and turnbacks; *voltigeurs*, yellow collar piped white, green epaulettes with yellow crescents, yellow-over-green plume, green cords.

18th Line: Red turnbacks; *voltigeur*, red collar piped green, yellow tufted shako pompon, yellow epaulettes with green crescents.

19th Line: Red turnbacks.

21st Line: Red turnbacks.

22nd Line: Brass buttons; grenadier officer shown without cuff flaps, with gold-laced shako including side chevrons, red plume with white base.

30th Line: Presumed extant uniform (attribution perhaps doubtful) has red collar and turnbacks and narrower, longer shoulder straps than usual.

33rd Line: Violet cuff flaps and turnbacks; *voltigeurs*, yellow plume, cords, epaulettes and upper shako band, grenadier red ditto; band wore gold-laced uniforms and shakos, drummers with red (or yellow) lace including bars on sleeves.

66th Line: Apparently wore white at least until 1808, as tropical dress in Guadeloupe.

It soon became apparent that the white uniform was unserviceable. Napoleon expressed his disapproval (traditionally after seeing horrifically blood-stained uniforms on the field of Eylau), and blue was restored in October 1807, the white being allowed to wear out before being replaced; not until November 1809 did Suchet report that 'the medley is over—there are no more hats, no more white coats'.

The pre-1812 Uniform

The most significant alteration during the 1806–12 period was the introduction of a slightly taller and more robust shako on 9 November 1810, without side chevrons but with chinscales, as already adopted by many. Cords and plumes were abolished (but still continued to be worn). The plate was redesigned to show only the regimental number on a brass lozenge, though many non-regulation varieties existed, including an eagle-on-crescent plate (the 'crescent' representing the traditional 'Amazon shield' motif) adumbrating the 1812 pattern and worn by the 3rd, 5th, 11th, 14th, 21st, 26th, 40th, 42nd, 63rd, 75th, 81st, 94th and 121st, among others. On 21 February 1811 it was decreed that only senior officers were to wear plumes (white *aigrette* for colonel, red-over-white for major, red for *chef de bataillon*) with white pompons for other officers and staff NCOs, red for grenadiers, yellow for *voltigeurs*, and for the 1st to 4th fusilier companies of each battalion, dark green, sky-blue, *aurore* (orange/pink), and violet respectively. Officially there was no battalion identification, but among observed variations were pompons or padded cloth discs with a white centre bearing the battalion number, or with a tuft above resembling the flames of a bursting grenade. Officers' shako lace varied in width according to rank. Regimental variations included:

1st Line: 1806 shako plate had a letter 'N' upon the eagle's breast; *voltigeurs'* plate consisted of an eagle atop a lightning-bolt.

2nd Line: 1806 shako plate believed retained until c. 1813.

3rd Line: Recorded shako plates included eagle-on-plinth design; shield bearing eagle over '3'; czapka-style 'sunburst' plate; brass grenade

Gen. Duhesme rallies a company of grenadiers at Charleroi; note the use of fur caps and bicorns within the same unit. After Bellangé.

Reconstruction by Job of a sergent porte-fanion of 5th Co., 2nd Bn., 105th Demi-Brigade in 1796. He wears basically regulation 1793 uniform, but note curious cuff patch details, with facing and piping extending to second button only.

badge for grenadiers; eagle-on-crescent. Initially red cords and carrot-shaped plumes for grenadiers, green for *voltigeurs*; fusiliers wore tufted 'company' pompons (e.g. red over sky-blue, with sword knots in same colours), and in full dress blue plume with red tip over yellow ball. Sergeants and above had gold upper shako bands; officers' *surtout* had red collar and flapless cuffs piped white, white turnbacks piped red with gold star on one side and '3' on the other.

4th Line: Grenadiers had red shako bands and white cords c. 1809.

5th Line: Fusilier shown c. 1809 with red-tipped blue plume, red collar without piping, red lozenge turnback badge.

8th Line: Shako plate of eagle upon plinth inscribed '8' or '8me Regt.', but c. 1810 *voltigeurs'* plate had '8' without a horn upon a lozenge; officers' shakos had gold lace interlocking rings instead of an upper band. Suhr shows a *voltigeur* with blue cuff flaps piped red, *chamois* collar, green epaulettes and plume, green-and-yellow cords with green *raquettes* and yellow sliders, yellow sword knot with green strap and fringe.

10th Line: 1806 shako plate shaped as elongated lozenge, *voltigeurs'* plate an eagle upon a lightning-bolt.

18th Line: Bicorn had red lace 'ties', yellow for *voltigeurs*, whose plumes were green with

yellow tip; red-over-white-over-sky-blue plumes for senior officers and drummers. Lozenge shako plates c. 1807, but eagle-on-crescent c. 1809; red cuff flaps.

21st Line: Voltigeurs c. 1807, green epaulettes with yellow retaining strap, crescents piped red (outside) and yellow (inside), green cords, yellow-tipped green plume.

22nd Line: Grenadiers' epaulettes had white crescents.

27th Line: Élites had brass-scaled epaulettes with red crescent and fringe (grenadiers), yellow crescent and green fringe (*voltigeurs*); *voltigeur* shown with green upper shako band and cords, white lower band, green-over-yellow plume, later version (?) shows yellow shako bands and chevrons, yellow plume over green ball, yellow collar piped white.

29th Line: 1806 shako plate bore an eagle over a ball pierced with '29', upon a shield.

30th Line: In c. 1809, brass czapka-style shako plates of rays around an eagle over '30'. *Voltigeur* distinctions varied with battalion, plumes yellow-over-red, over green or yellow-over-red

'Rampon and the 32nd Demi-Brigade at Montelegino', 10 April 1796; after Berthon. Note the large colour bearing the motto *Vaincre ou mourir* **('Victory or Death'), and the uniform of various members of the regiment, including a** *sapeur***, right foreground.**

ball, with yellow upper shako band, cords and epaulettes: or green cords, green epaulettes with yellow strap, and white or orange cockade loop; c. 1810, green upper band and cords, green-over-yellow plume, green epaulettes with yellow crescents, eagle-on-crescent shako plate; officer shown with busby, silver-laced yellow bag, silver cords, yellow-over-red plume over yellow ball. Grenadier caps without plates, red cords and plume; grenadier shakos with red upper band, cords and plume.

34th Line: Officers' shakos with tricolour rosette instead of plate; *chef de bataillon*, red-over-white-over-blue plume. Grenadiers' great-coats with red collar and red cuff piping.

42nd Line: Fusiliers, tufted pompons, e.g. red over sky-blue; grenadier caps without plates, red plume, white cords.

54th Line: Eagle-on-crescent shako plate bearing

15

Infantryman of c. 1796, after Bellangé. Although he wears grenadier distinctions (red epaulettes, drooping red horsehair plume on the bicorn, in this case turned to the rear) such distinctions were not always confined to élite companies in the early revolutionary wars.

bust of Napoleon and '54'.

56th Line: 1806 shako plate pentagonal bearing eagle over number; grenadiers' plate, 1810, bore grenade over '56' on lozenge.

57th Line: Fusiliers, tufted pompons, e.g. red over yellow.

62nd Line: 1806 shako plate oval, bearing eagle over disc pierced '62'.

63rd Line: 'Capucine' facings c. 1806–08, grenadiers with brass grenade-shaped shako plate, red plume with white base; c. 1808 red plume and upper shako band, white cords. NCO in Spain shown with blue cuffs with red piping and flaps, gold upper shako band, red tufted pompon and cockade loop, large brass (?) numbers '63' instead of shako plate. Portrait of *voltigeur* officer shows dark blue overcoat with yellow collar and red piping.

64th Line: Voltigeur c. 1806 shown with bicorn, red ties and tassels, green pompon with red tuft, red collar piped white, green epaulettes with red crescents, '64' on turnbacks.

65th Line: Officers with tricolour rosette instead of shako plate, 1810–12; blue cuffs with red flaps and piping; grenadiers as Plate F in this book.

67th Line: Shako cords worn diagonally; red cuffs and flaps piped white.

71st Line: Grenadiers' shako plate of grenade shape with '71' on ball.

88th Line: Grenadier caps with brass grenade badge, red plume and cords.

93rd Line: Grenadier cap plates bore grenade with '93' on ball.

95th Line: Voltigeurs' bicorn with yellow-tufted green pompon, 1806.

96th Line: Voltigeurs had *chamois* cuff flaps piped red; Suhr shows green epaulettes with yellow crescents, yellow shako bands and chevrons, green cords and carrot-shaped pompon.

100th Line: shako plate of eagle upon a plinth bearing '100'.

102nd Line: 1806 shako plate bore 'N' on eagle's breast.

108th Line: Grenadier caps with triangular plate, upper point occupied by bursting grenade, '108' cut out below.

117th Line: Grenadiers c. 1806–08 had grenade-shaped shako plates with number on ball.

125th Line: Formed from 4th and 7th Dutch Regts.; wore white Dutch uniform with pink and yellow facings respectively for at least a year (see Plate G); by June 1812 only élites of 1st–3rd Bns. had received blue uniforms. Initially 1st Bn. had yellow facings (élites pink), 2nd Bn. pink (grenadiers yellow), 3rd Bn. pink (*voltigeurs* and two fusilier companies yellow), 4th Bn. pink (two companies yellow).

Examples of regimental *voltigeur* distinctions are noted below:

Regt.	Plume	Shako cords	Epaulettes
3rd c. 1807	green-over-yellow	green	green, yellow crescents
4th c. 1809	green, red tip (yellow shako band and chevrons)	white	green, red crescents
18th c. 1809	red with yellow tip or vice versa, over yellow ball	green	green, or with yellow crescents
26th	yellow-over-green, over green ball	green	green, yellow crescents
42nd	yellow tipped green, over green ball	green	yellow, green fringe
57th	green tipped yellow, over yellow ball	green	green, yellow crescents
63rd c. 1807	green-over-yellow (green upper shako band)	green	yellow, green fringe

Members of the Army of Italy of the late 1790s in typically wretched clothing exhibiting a wide variety of styles, with headgear including the fur-crested 'Tarleton' helmet, bicorns, a grenadier cap, mirliton caps and *bonnets de police.*

French infantry, c. 1800, wearing a wide variety of non-regulation uniform, including cavalry overalls (left); the grenadier (centre) has a large plume of 'stand-and-fall' shape. Print by Bartsch after Kobell.

Regt.	Plume	Shako cords	Epaulettes
65th 1810– 1812	red-over- green ball (green sword knot, red tassel)	green, red tassels	green, red crescents
67th	green-over- yellow	green	green, yellow crescents
94th	green tipped yellow, over yellow ball (green sword knots)	yellow	green, yellow crescents

Musicians

Governed by the whim of the colonel, musicians' uniforms fell into two categories: those of the band, and those of drummers, fifers and *voltigeur* buglers (*cornets*). Bandsmen usually wore uniforms with laced facings and almost always matching trefoil epaulettes, white shako cords and plume, laced hussar boots or officers' boots with turned-over tops, and were armed with light-bladed *épees*, which details should be presumed in the following regimental details unless stated otherwise. Drummers, fifers and *cornets* usually wore ordinary uniform with lace on facings, pockets and turnbacks and often on the sleeves; with large 'swallows'-nest' wings; and with ordinary company distinctions, shako ornaments, turnback badges, epaulettes, etc., the latter worn over the wings. Tricolour lace of various red, white and blue designs was popular. Drum majors usually wore laced coats, a laced bicorn with plume and/or feather *panache*, usually in red, white and blue; Austrian knot decorations on the thighs, gauntlets, laced hussar boots, a laced baldric to support a sabre, and a corded mace; *caporals-tambour* often wore a less elaborate version of the same uniform, with busby and smaller mace. Drums were brass, often with blue hoops, but sometimes tricolour diagonal stripes were used, e.g. the 67th and 88th. Examples of recorded uniforms are noted below:

3rd Line: Musicians (1807), sky-blue coat faced red, laced gold, white-plumed bicorn; drummers etc., same, but shakos, red wings, orange or tricolour lace.

4th Line: Musicians (1809), blue coat, red collar, green lapels, cuffs and turnbacks laced gold; drummers same with gold-laced green wings.

5th Line: Drum major (1809), sky-blue single-breasted coat laced silver, seven tassel-ended silver loops on breast, silver-laced white (or sky-blue) breeches, white plume.

9th Line: Musicians (1809) as Plate E, drum major with bicorn bearing red-over-white-over-blue plume over tricolour *panache*; drummers had blue coats with green facings and wings, *caporal-tambour's* busby with green bag, red piping and plume.

18th Line: Musicians (1805), blue coat, red collar, sky-blue facings, gold trefoils, sky-blue wings or élite epaulettes for drummers. 1809, blue faced crimson, gold lace; drummers with crimson wings, tricolour or yellow/green lace including seven inverted chevrons on sleeve; *caporal-tambour*, busby with red bag and plume, white cords.

26th Line: Musicians (1809), red coat faced blue, gold lace, blue breeches, blue-over-white plume; drummers, blue coat faced red, red wings, tricolour lace, shako with company distinctions (e.g. fusilier, green-tipped plume over green ball).

27th Line: Musicians, blue coat, pale orange lapels, other facings red, white piping, gold lace; drummers etc., same but seven inverted chevrons on sleeve; drum major's bicorn with orange-over-white plume; *caporal-tambour* with busby, red bag and plume, white cords. One source shows orange cuffs and turnbacks.

30th Line: Musicians (c. 1809), red coat faced blue, brass czapka-style shako plate; drummers etc., same but some with blue wings, tricolour lace; drum major with red epaulettes over blue wings, busby bearing brass grenade badge, red bag and plume, white piping and cords; *voltigeur cornet* same, yellow epaulettes, busby with yellow bag, white cords and piping, yellow-over-red plume over similarly coloured ball. c. 1810, yellow/gold lace, red cuff flaps, eagle-on-crescent shako plate shown, with white grenadier epaulettes.

42nd Line: Musicians, sky-blue coat faced yellow, laced gold; drummers similar with gold-laced yellow wings, tufted company shako pompons.

48th Line: Extant drummer's coat (1812) is dark blue, faced red, dark blue shoulder straps piped red, flapless cuffs, white lace with interwoven red diamond pattern on facings, including button loops on lapels and six inverted chevrons on sleeve; blue star on turnbacks.

57th Line: Musicians (c. 1803–05), blue coat faced yellow, white lace and trefoils, yellow-laced bicorn, red-over-white-over-sky-blue plume; drummers etc., same with white-laced yellow wings; c. 1809, band wore blue faced sky-blue, laced gold, drummers with sky-blue wings, orange lace.

63rd Line: Musicians (c. 1808), blue coat faced *aurore*, gold lace, *aurore* trefoils edged gold; drummers blue faced red (including wings), white lace, red upper shako band, cords and plume (including fusiliers). Musicians c. 1811–12 as before but blue turnbacks piped white, blue cuff flaps and trousers, blue waistcoat with red hussar braid, shako with *aurore* cords, plume and 'wing' wrapped around, black upper band and no plate.

65th Line: Musicians (c. 1810–12), blue coat faced red, blue cuffs, white turnbacks, yellow lace, yellow shako with black leather bands, white plume and cords; drum major, gold epaulettes with gold or red fringe, busby with red bag, white plume, gold cords with red tassels.

67th Line: Musicians as Plate E, but white plume and cords, gold lace; drummers etc., blue wings.

Line grenadiers, c. 1800; contemporary watercolour. Note the long coat-tails, with handkerchief protruding from the pocket; the trousers with slits for draw-strings around the bottom; and the civilian waistcoat of yellow-and-white stripes worn by the standing figure.

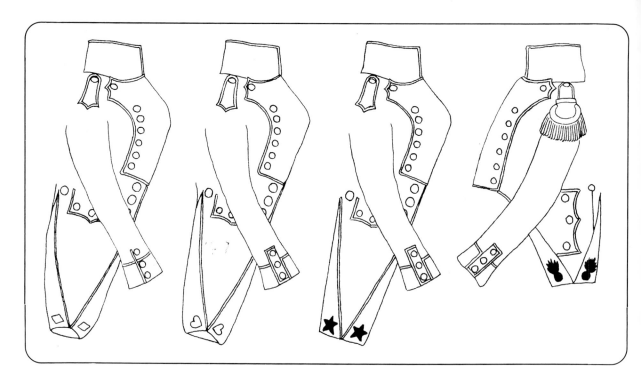

Successive patterns of infantry coat; from left to right: (a) *habit* **with flapless cuff, c. 1804 (b)** *habit* **with flapped cuff, c. 1804–10 (c)** *habit* **with reshaped turnbacks, c. 1810–13 (d) 1812** *habit-veste,* **bearing company distinctions of a grenadier.**

88th Line: Musicians (c. 1805), blue coat faced orange, gold lace, bicorn with white-over-orange plume; drummers same but red collar, gold-laced orange wings. Drummers attached to band had black gauntlets and aprons.

Sapeurs

Sapeurs normally wore grenadier uniform, with crossed axes and/or grenade badges on the sleeves, usually white or red; plateless fur caps, leather gauntlets and apron, and an axe-case over the shoulder; beards were mandatory. Recorded variations include:

3rd Line: In c. 1809–10, sky-blue faced red, red epaulettes with yellow crescents, red plume and badges, white cap cords; c. 1812, ordinary uniform with red epaulettes, white cords, red-over-sky-blue plume.

9th Line: Green facings c. 1809, red piping and plume, white cords.

18th Line: Sky-blue coat faced crimson, white epaulettes, badges and cords, red plume, adopted c. 1809; reverted to ordinary uniform

c. 1810, red epaulettes, cap with grenade-embossed brass plate.

26th Line: In c. 1809, red lapels, white sleeve badges, red epaulettes with white crescents, busby with red bag and plume, white piping.

27th Line: In c. 1808–12, pale orange lapels, red badges and epaulettes with brass-scaled straps, brass cap plate bearing grenade, red plume, white cords.

30th Line: In c. 1809, red coat, blue facings and badges, white epaulettes and cords, red plume; c. 1810, blue coat with red facings, lapels, badges and epaulettes.

42nd Line: In c. 1809, red-tipped green plume, white cords, red badges, red epaulettes with gold crescents, green fringe.

45th Line: In c. 1806–08, sky-blue facings piped dark blue, red cuff flaps, turnbacks, epaulettes, plume and cords, blue breeches with black gaiters cut to resemble hussar boots with red edging and tassel; sleeve badge of blue-shafted axes with yellow ferrule, white blade, outlined red.

46th Line: In c. 1806–08, sky-blue facings, red cuff flaps, badges, epaulettes, piping; white turn-backs and cords, red plume with dark blue tip.

57th Line: In c. 1809, sky-blue facings, with or without orange lace, red badges and plume, white cords.

63rd Line: In c. 1806–08, capucine facings, red badges and epaulettes, white turnbacks piped red, blue breeches with capucine scalloped-edged stripe, short gaiters as for 45th above, black fur shako with peak, red plume, white cords; c. 1808–09 same, but white piping, ordinary cap with same decorations.

65th Line: In c. 1810–12, red badges, cords and plume, white epaulettes with red crescents.

67th Line: In c. 1808, red plume and badges, white cords, red epaulettes with white straps edged red.

The 1812 Uniform

The regulations of 19 January 1812, named after the Major Bardin responsible for their issue, introduced a double-breasted, short-tailed blue jacket or *habit-veste*, with red collar piped blue (or white; *chamois* piped blue for *voltigeurs*), white 'plastron'-style lapels piped red, red cuffs piped white, blue flaps and vertical pockets piped red, and brass buttons. The white turnbacks bore a blue crowned 'N' for fusiliers, red grenade for grenadiers, and yellow or *chamois* horn for *voltigeurs*; fusiliers had blue shoulder straps piped red, with red or *chamois* epaulettes edged blue for élites. Rank badges were unchanged, but officers' coats had longer tails. The white single-breasted waistcoat had a slightly lower collar, round cuffs and shoulder straps of dark blue (red for élites and sometimes *chamois* for *voltigeurs*). The black gaiters no longer extended over the knee. A new pattern of forage cap was introduced, the 'pokalem', a pie-shaped blue cap with a folding neck-flap which could fasten under the chin; piped red, it bore the regimental number or élite company badge on the front.

The 1812-pattern shako had a new plate comprising a crowned eagle atop a semi-circular plate into which the regimental number was cut, with lion-head finials sometimes replaced by grenades or horns for élites, some *voltigeurs* having the number surrounded by a horn in addition. A tricolour cockade was partly covered by the eagle's head, and brass chinscales were used as before, but shako cords were discontinued (not always in practice). Grenadiers' shakos were slightly taller, with red upper and lower bands and side chevrons; these decorations were yellow for *voltigeurs*. Red and yellow plumes were re-introduced for *élites*, though tufted pompons seem to have been more popular. Grenadier caps were officially discontinued.

On 30 December 1811 an attempt was made to standardise musicians' uniform by introducing a single 'Imperial Livery', a green coat with 'Imperial' lace of alternate yellow and green segments, the yellow with an interwoven crowned green 'N', the next yellow with a green eagle; drum majors and bandmasters were to have double silver lace on the collar and musicians a single lace. Drummers received new 'Imperial Livery' by the 'Bardin regulations': a single-breasted green jacket with red collar piped green, green cuff flaps and shoulder straps piped red, and red cuffs piped white, with 'Imperial' lace on breast, back and sleeves. Company distinctions were retained, and regimental patterns continued in use.

Issue of the 1812 uniform was often delayed until 1813 or even 1814, and recorded variations include:

1st Line: Voltigeur cornet c. 1814 shown in blue jacket, yellow collar edged white, blue cuffs with yellow flaps and piping, blue lapels piped yellow and laced with mixed white-and-sky-blue, of which seven inverted chevrons on sleeve; yellow epaulettes with green crescents; blue trousers with yellow stripe; red shako with yellow bands and chevrons, yellow plume,

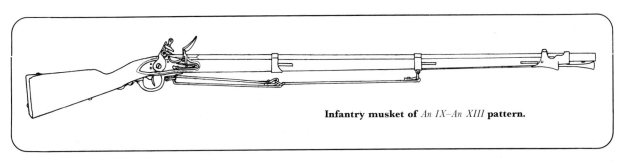

Infantry musket of *An IX–An XIII* **pattern.**

Shako plate, 16th Line, 1806 pattern.

NCO with a colour of 1804 pattern; print by Martinet.

white metal shako plate and chinscales and brass-edged peak.

3rd Line: Grenadiers as Plate H; *voltigeurs* same, except yellow instead of red, yellow collar piped red, green epaulettes with yellow crescents. Musicians wore ordinary jackets, red-over-sky-blue plume; fusilier drummers same, élites with company distinctions; drum major wore single-breasted blue coat faced sky-blue, laced gold (including seven bars on breast), busby with sky-blue bag laced gold, red plume over white and blue *panache*. *Voltigeur* (1814) shown with green tufted pompon, green epaulettes with red crescent, baggy brown Spanish trousers with yellow zigzag-edged stripe.

5th Line: Drummers wore ordinary jacket, seven inverted red-and-white chevrons on sleeve, fringeless red epaulettes for fusiliers.

8th Line: Apparent retention of old lozenge plates bearing eagle over '8'. Élites' shakos without side chevrons; red tufted pompon or plume, red cords for grenadiers; blue-tufted yellow pompon, yellow-over-red or sky-blue-tipped yellow plume for *voltigeurs*; tufted pompons for fusiliers, e.g. red with blue or green tuft, blue with white tuft. Drummers wore single-breasted blue jacket faced red, tricolour lace; musicians sky-blue *habit-veste* and breeches, yellow facings, gold lace, yellow plume tipped sky-blue, drum major's busby with gold-laced yellow bag.

18th Line: Lozenge plates bearing '18' used as well as 1812 pattern. *Voltigeurs*, green pompon, yellow-tipped green plume over yellow ball, or red-tufted yellow pompon, green epaulettes with yellow crescents. Musicians, blue *surtout* faced crimson, gold lace, white plume; drummers etc., single-breasted blue jacket faced red, laced with mixed red-and-gold or white with interwoven red diamonds.

45th Line: 1810-pattern shako plate perhaps still in use.

130th Line: Czapka-style 'rayed' shako plates.

The Restoration

Some changes were occasioned by the Bourbon restoration in 1814, some regiments being re-numbered, some being assigned 'Royal' titles, and each being restricted to three battalions. The white Bourbon cockade was restored on 13 April 1814, which often meant simply covering the red and blue centre of the tricolour with a white disc, with as easy a reversion upon the return of Napoleon. Fusiliers' 'N' turnback badges were removed, and on 8 February a cartridge box badge of a crowned and interlaced double 'L' cypher was introduced, with a shako plate bearing Bourbon symbols; but it is unlikely that many alterations could have taken effect before the Hundred Days, except for a modification of the 1812-pattern shako plate by removing the eagle, leaving only the section with pierced number—e.g. Dighton shows its use by the 45th.

Campaign Uniforms

Uniforms were modified on campaign for reasons of utility or due to the rigours of active service; uniforms might be made locally, from whatever cloth was available and often not conforming to regulations. Loose trousers or overalls were usual, grey, white or ochre in colour, with blue and (in Spain) brown not uncommon. Shako covers of black, waterprooofed fabric, or of white or buff cotton, concealed most ornaments but sometimes left the pompon, or even plume, visible; such covers were often painted with a regimental device or number, as in Plate F. So were the white fabric cartridge box covers which recorded the identity of the owner, '—Régiment d'Infanterie/—Bataillon,—Compagnie', and sometimes painted élite company badges. The trousers might be turned up at the bottom or tied around the ankle with string; the greatcoat was often worn directly over the waistcoat, with the *habit* in the knapsack; and the *bonnet de police* was often worn for comfort instead of the shako. For action, however, a regiment would often endeavour to look its best, on the premise that (as one officer stated) 'One can never be too well dressed when the cannon roars'! Exigencies of campaign life resulted in all manner of non-regulation garments, from the Arab appearance of the troops in Egypt to the fur-swathed masses on the retreat from Moscow; while the 'Marie-Louises' or conscripts of 1813–14 were often so wretchedly equipped that they received nothing save a cap and greatcoat, to be worn over civilian clothes.

Sergeant-major with the 'Eagle' of the 12th Line, c. 1809; print after P. and H. Lecomte. The scarlet colour-belt bears gold-embroidered foliate designs, and the staff is painted sky-blue and studded with gilt nails.

Equipment

Regulated by successive orders, basic infantry equipment remained reasonably standard throughout the period. The knapsack (*havresac*) was based upon the 1786 and 1791 specifications, slightly reduced in size by regulations of the Year X (*An X*) of the Republican calendar (1801–02). Made of calfskin tanned with the hair on, it was

23

Shako plate, 23rd Line, 1810 pattern.

carried on the back by means of buff leather shoulder straps attached by wooden toggles, with a flap fastened by three (or two) buff leather straps and buckles. In 1806 it was provided with three extra straps, one to pass vertically all round the middle, and two to secure the rolled greatcoat on top, this having been attached earlier by privately-acquired straps or string. When filled with two packs of cartridges, spare shoes, four days' biscuit, two spare shirts, spare trousers and gaiters, night cap, polishing brushes, pipeclay and personal impedimenta, it might weigh between 15 and 20kg, not including items fastened to the outside such as messtin, cooking pot, and spare headdress in linen cover.

The black leather cartridge box was initially constructed around a wooden block with holes drilled to accommodate cartridges; later types had box interiors. Sizes varied slightly, the 1786-pattern measuring 32.1 × 12.2 × 6.8cm (interior), with a flap 28.5 × 16.3cm; the *An X* pattern was similar, the 1812 type including an interior flap and removable container; later patterns had two straps underneath to accommodate the rolled forage cap.

The cartridge box was suspended at the rear of the right hip by a whitened buff leather belt over the left shoulder, with a strap at the left of the box fastened onto the sword belt or one of the skirt-buttons of the coat, to prevent the box from slipping; the flap carried grenade or hunting-horn badges for élites, and occasionally the regimental number.

The bayonet scabbard was carried at the front of the cartridge box belt by fusiliers, but a belt over the right shoulder was used by all those armed with sabres, when it was usual to carry sabre and bayonet in a combined frog. This practice led to uneven drill, grenadiers reaching to their left and fusiliers their right when preparing to fix bayonets. The combined frog was prohibited in 1791, all bayonets to be carried at the right thereafter; but it seems doubtful whether this system was ever adopted universally, and the combined frog was restored by the decree of *4 Brumaire An X* (27 October 1801) which regulated equipment patterns.

Non-regulation items carried on campaign included canvas satchels slung over the shoulder, fabric 'sausages' to contain flour, and the ubiquitous canteen, which was always provided by the individual; there was no official issue, and canteens ranged from wooden barrels to bottles in wickerwork cases and metal flasks, usually slung over the shoulder by a coloured cord. Officers on campaign sometimes carried knapsacks, but often had their equipment rolled in a greatcoat slung over one shoulder, across the body, a rudimentary protection from sword cuts also adopted by other ranks.

Weapons

The basic arm was the 1777-pattern musket, modified (in barrel bands and sling swivels) in Years IX and XIII. The *An IX/XIII* pattern was a smoothbore flintlock 151.5cm long, of 17.5mm calibre and 4.375kg weight; all fittings were iron. Other firearms in use included *fusils depareilles* made from spare parts of 1763, 1774 and 1777-patterns to remedy the shortage of matériel in the early Revolutionary Wars; and the *An IX/XIII* dragoon musket, 141.7cm long and 4.275kg in weight, usually carried by *voltigeurs*, selected numbers of whom carried rifled muskets until these were withdrawn in 1807. *Sapeurs* carried light musketoons of *An IX* pattern, 111cm long and with brass barrel bands.

1: Fusilier, 43e de Ligne, 1792
2: Infantryman in campaign dress, 1795
3: Grenadier, Garde Nationale de Paris, 1792

A

1: Fusilier, 61ᵉʳ Demi-Brigade; Egypt, 1799
2: Fusilier, 1800
3: Officer, 15ᵉ Demi-Brigade, 1800
4: Grenadier, 1800

B

1: Sergent-major with 'Aigle', 4e de Ligne, 1805
2: '2e Porte-Aigle' 8e de Ligne, 1811
3: Sapeur, 46e de Ligne, 1808

C

1: Grenadier, 15^e de Ligne, 1807
2: Voltigeur cornet, 18^e de Ligne, 1809
3: Voltigeur, 3^e de Ligne, 1809

1: Caporal-tambour, 67ᵉ de Ligne, 1808
2: Musician, 9ᵉ de Ligne, 1809
3: Grenadier-tambour, 57ᵉ de Ligne, 1809

E

1: Voltigeur, 88ᵉ de Ligne; Spain, 1811
2: Fusilier officer, 34ᵉ de Ligne; Spain, 1810
3: Grenadier, 65ᵉ de Ligne; Spain, 1810

1: Major, 100^e de Ligne, 1809
2: Sergent de fusiliers, 30^e Ligne, 1811
3: Officer, 125^e de Ligne, 1811
4: Voltigeur, 14^e de Ligne, 1811

G

1: Fusilier, 70ᵉ de Ligne, 1813
2: Grenadier, 3ᵉ de Ligne, 1813
3: 'Marie-Louise', 82ᵉ de Ligne, 1814
4: Tambour, 96ᵉ de Ligne, 1814

H

The 1769-pattern sabre with angular brass guard and short, slightly curved blade remained in use with minor modifications until the issue of the *An IX* and *An XI* patterns of *sabre-briquet*, the former having a cast-brass hilt of 28 ribs and a curved guard ending in a pyramidal quillon, and the latter a 21-ribbed grip and a rounded quillon. Both had a slightly more curved blade and a black leather scabbard, the *An XI* with a larger chape. The 1786 practice whereby the sabre was carried by grenadiers, musicians and all NCOs remained largely constant throughout; *voltigeurs* were initially equipped with sabres, an instruction ordering their discontinuance from 7 October 1807 clearly having limited effect, as it had to be repeated as late as 16 January 1815. The sword knot, partly decorative but originally for securing the sabre to the wrist, was coloured red for grenadiers, green and/or yellow for *voltigeurs* and white for fusiliers, but regimental variations existed. Drum majors and *sapeurs* usually carried elaborately decorated sabres, those of *sapeurs* often shaped as an antique 'glaive' with an eagle-head pommel. The bayonet was 45.6cm long, triangular in section, and secured by a locking-ring, though in the 1790s it was common to tie the bayonet to the musket with string to prevent its being wrenched off the muzzle. The scabbard was usually of brown leather.

Officers carried a straight-bladed *épée* with single-bar guard and helmet-shaped pommel, suspended from a shoulder belt, or a waist belt passing beneath the coat and front flap of the breeches, of whitened buff leather—though unofficial black or coloured leather waist belts, some with gold lace decoration and/or rectangular gilt plates instead of the usual S-clasp, were popular. Officers of élite companies carried various types of curved sabre with single-bar guard, as (unofficially) did some fusilier officers. All metal fittings were gilded, and sword knots were of gold lace.

The variety of regimental weaponry is exemplified by a return of the 14th Line in 1808–09:

134 officers: 96 *épées*, 38 sabres (élites), 9 carbines (*voltigeurs*)

27 sergeant-majors: 24 muskets, 27 sabres, 3 carbines (*voltigeurs*)

108 sergeants: 96 muskets, 12 carbines (*voltigeurs*), 108 *sabres-briquet*

27 *fourriers*: 24 muskets, 3 carbines (*voltigeurs*), 27

Shako plate, 121st Line, of the common but non-regulation 'eagle-over-crescent' design, c. 1809–10.

sabres-briquet

216 corporals: 192 muskets, 24 dragoon muskets (*voltigeurs*), 216 *sabres-briquet*

13 *sapeurs*: 13 musketoons, 13 sabres

167 grenadiers: 167 muskets, 167 *sabres-briquet*

241 *voltigeurs*: 241 dragoon muskets (regt. must have abolished *voltigeur* sabres)

2,307 fusiliers: 2,295 muskets, 12 musketoons (perhaps for 12 unauthorised musicians appearing on the rolls as privates?)

54 drummers, musicians and *cornets*: 54 musketoons, 54 *sabres-briquet*

The Regiments of the Line

For reasons of space, the following list cannot cover fully all the services of each regiment, especially as it was common for battalions to serve apart; thus elements of the same regiment might be engaged simultaneously as far apart as Spain and Russia.

Only major actions are listed below and abbreviated as follows:

A—	Austerlitz	J—	Jena
AA—	Arcis-sur-Aube	L—	Leipzig
Al—	Albuera	Lu—	Lützen
BA—	Bar-sur-Aube	M—	Montmirail
Bd—	Badajos	N—	Nivelle
Be—	Berezina	P—	Paris
Bo—	Borodino	Sa—	Salamanca
Br—	Barrosa	Sb—	Sabugal
Bt—	Bautzen	SD—	St. Dizier
Bu—	Busaco	Sg—	Saragossa
By—	Bayonne	Sm—	Smolensk
Ca—	Castalla	Ta—	Tarragona
Ch—	Champaubert	Tf—	Tarifa
Co—	Corunna	To—	Toulouse
D—	Dresden	Tr—	Trafalgar
Ec—	Eckmühl	Tv—	Talavera
Es—	Essling	U—	Ulm
Ey—	Eylau	Va—	Valencia
F—	Friedland	Vi—	Vittoria
FO—	Fuentes de Onoro	Vm—	Vimiero
G—	Gerona	W—	Wagram

'1812' and '1815' indicate to which Corps of the Grande Armée and Armée du Nord respectively a regiment was attached for the Russian and Waterloo campaigns; '1813' and '1814' refer to service in Germany and France respectively. 'NG' and numerals indicate from which cohorts of the National Guard a regiment was formed. Details are restricted to the corps formed in 1796 by the consolidation of the Demi-Brigades de Bataille into Demi-Brigades de Ligne. The complexity of this process may be demonstrated by the lineage of the 4th Demi-Brigade de Ligne, formed at Loano on 14 March 1796 from the former 39th, 130th, 145th and 147th Demi-Brigades de Bataille, and including among its personnel ex-members of the old regiments of Cambrésis (20th in 1786), de Médoc (73rd), de Boulonnois (82nd) and d'Angoumois (83rd), and the volunteer battalions of Hautes- and Basses-Pyrénées, Haute-Garonne and l'Aude.

'Infanterie de Ligne en Campagne: Sentinelle': print by Martinet, c. 1810, showing a grenadier wearing a single-breasted greatcoat and a shako which features a non-regulation 'eagle-over-crescent' plate and the plume within a waterproof cover.

Shako of the 54th Line, c. 1810, of 1806 pattern plus chinscales, with the non-regulation 'eagle-over-crescent' plate bearing the apparently unique device of a portrait-bust of Napoleon above the number. (Wallis & Wallis)

1st Regt.	W, Sa, Lu, Bt, D, L, M, P, 1815 II Corps.
2nd Regt.	Tr, Ec, Es, W, G, 1812 II Corps, D, L, 1815 II Corps.
3rd Regt.	U, A, J, F, Ec, Es, W, N, 1812 XI Corps, 1813, BA, AA, 1815 II Corps.
4th Regt.	U, A, J, Ey, Ec, Es, W, 1812 III Corps, Sm, Bo, D, L, 1814, 1815 II Corps.
5th Regt.	W, Va, 1815 VI Corps.

Infantry, c. 1812; print by Raffet. The shako 'pompons' are discs of padded cloth bearing the number of the battalion.

6th Regt.	Bt, L.
7th Regt.	1801–04 San Domingo; G, Va, Ta, Ca, Bt, L.
8th Regt.	A, J, F, Es, W, Tv, FO, Br, Bd 1811, Vi, N, BA, AA, 1815 I Corps.
9th Regt.	A, W, 1812 IV Corps, Bo.
10th Regt.	Capri 1808, Sicily 1810, Va, To, Lu, Bt, L, 1815 VI Corps.
11th Regt.	U, W, D, L, 1814, 1815 III Corps.
12th Regt.	A, J, Ey, Ec, W, 1812 I Corps, Sm, Bo, D, AA, SD, 1815 III Corps.
13th Regt.	A, W, Tyrol 1810, Bt.

14th Regt.	U, A, J, Ey, Sg, Ta, Ca, Lu, Bt, D, AA.
15th Regt.	F, Co, FO, Sa, N.
16th Regt.	Tr, Ec, Es, W, G, Ta, Va, Ca, Lu, Bt, D, L, 1814.
17th Regt.	A, J, Ey, Ec, W, D, 1815 I Corps.
18th Regt.	U, A, J, Ey, Ec, Es, W, 1812 III Corps, Sm, Bo, D, L, 1814.
19th Regt.	W, 1812 II Corps, D, L, 1814, 1815 I Corps.
20th Regt.	Va, 1814.
21st Regt.	A, J, Ey, Ec, W, Sg, 1812 I Corps, Sm, Bo, D, 1815 I Corps.
22nd Regt.	Sa, Lu, Bt, 1815 III Corps.
23rd Regt.	W, Bt, D, 1815 III Corps.
24th Regt.	J, Ey, F, Es, W, Tv, FO, Bd 1811, Vi, N, D, SD.
25th Regt.	A, J, Ey, Ec, W, 1812 I Corps, Sm, Bo, D, P, 1815 I Corps.
26th Regt.	Guadeloupe & Martinique, 1st & 2nd Bns., 1805–14; Bu, FO, Sa, N, Lu, D, L.
27th Regt.	U, J, Ey, F, Es, W, Bu, FO, Sa, N, To, Lu, D, 1815 VI Corps.
28th Regt.	U, A, J, Ey, Tv, Vi, N, Sg, 1814, 1815 I Corps.
29th Regt.	W, 1812 XI Corps, 1813, 1815 I Corps.
30th Regt.	A, J, Ey, Ec, W, 1812 I Corps, Sm, Bo, 1813, 1815 IV Corps.
31st Regt.	San Domingo 1801–04; 1804 disbanded and transferred to 7th and 105th Regts.
32nd Regt.	U, F, Vm, Tv, N, To.
33rd Regt.	A, J, Ey, Ec, W, 1812 I Corps, Bo, 1815 III Corps.
34th Regt.	U, A, F, Sg, Al, N, To, 1815 III Corps.
35th Regt.	U, W, 1812 IV Corps, Sm, Bo.
36th Regt.	U, A, J, Ey, Co, Bu, Sb, FO, Sa, Vi, N, To, 1812 IX Corps.
37th Regt.	Ec, Es, W, 1812 II Corps, Bo, Lu, Bt, 1814, 1815 III Corps.
38th Regt.	Number vacant.
39th Regt.	U, J, Ey, F, Es, W, Bu, FO, Sa, N, To, D.
40th Regt.	U, A, J, W, Sg, FO, Al, N, To, Lu, Bt, L, Ch, P, 1815 VI Corps.
41st Regt.	Absorbed into 17th Regt. 1803.
42nd Regt.	W, G, Ta, Bt.
43rd Regt.	U, A, J, Ey, Tf, Vi, N, To, Ch, M.

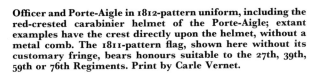

Officer and Porte-Aigle in 1812-pattern uniform, including the red-crested carabinier helmet of the Porte-Aigle; extant examples have the crest directly upon the helmet, without a metal comb. The 1811-pattern flag, shown here without its customary fringe, bears honours suitable to the 27th, 39th, 59th or 76th Regiments. Print by Carle Vernet.

Sergent-major Vaguemestre (regimental postman) and Adjutant-Sous-Officier in 1812 regulation uniform; print by Carle Vernet. The Vaguemestre has a gold piping between his rank-bars (perhaps indicating his appointment); the Adjutant-Sous-Officier wears an officers'-pattern long-tailed coat with a fringe on the right epaulette, a non-regulation feature possibly imitating those worn by commissioned adjutants.

44th Regt. J, Ey, Sg, Va, Ca, 1812 IX Corps, 1815 IV Corps.

45th Regt. A, J, F, Es, W, Tv, FO, Bd 1811, Vi, N, To, D, 1815 I Corps.

46th Regt. U, A, J, Ey, Ec, Es, W, 1812 III Corps, Sm, Bo, L, BA, 1815 I Corps.

47th Regt. Bu, Sb, FO, Co, Sa, N, To, Lu, Bt, L, 1815 VI Corps.

48th Regt. A, J, Ey, Ec, W, 1812 I Corps, Bo, 1813, 1815 IV Corps.

49th Regt. Disbanded 1803.

50th Regt. U, J, Ey, F, Bu, FO, Sa, N, To, Lu, Bt, D, Ch, M, 1815 IV Corps.

51st Regt. A, J, Ey, F, Tv, Al, Tf, Vi, N, To, 1812 IX Corps, D.

52nd Regt. W, Bt.

53rd Regt. W, 1812 IV Corps, Bo.

54th Regt. A, J, F, Es, W, Tv, FO, Bd 1811, Tf, Vi, N, 1813, 1814, 1815 I Corps.

55th Regt. U, A, J, Ey, Al, Vi, N, To, 1812 IX Corps, Bt, D, 1814, 1815 I Corps.

56th Regt. Ec, Es, W, G, 1812 II Corps, D, L, 1814, 1815 III Corps.

57th Regt. U, A, J, Ey, Ec, Es, W, 1812 I Corps, Bo, D, 1814.

58th Regt. U, A, F, Vm, Tv, Al, Bd 1812, Vi, N, To, Lu, D, P.

59th Regt. U, J, Ey, F, Es, W, Bu, FO, Sa, N, To, Lu, Bt, D, L, 1815 IV Corps.

60th Regt. Illyria and Dalmatia 1806–09; W, Va.

61st Regt. A, J, Ey, Ec, W, 1812 I Corps, Bo, 1813, 1815 II Corps.

62nd Regt. W, Sa, Lu, Bt, P.

63rd Regt. J, Ey, F, Es, W, Tv, FO, Vi, N, L, 1815 IV Corps.

64th Regt. U, A, J, Es, W, Sg, FO, Al, Bd 1812, N, By, D, 1815 III Corps.

65th Regt. Ec, W, FO, Sa, Vi, N, To, Lu, Bt, L, 1814, 1815 IV Corps.

66th Regt. Guadeloupe, Bu, FO, Sa, N, Lu, Bt, L, P.

67th Regt. Tr, Ec, Es, W, G, Lu, Bt, 1814.

Grenadier in 1812-pattern uniform; note the retention of the shako cords and the large feather plume. Print by Martinet.

68th Regt.	Disbanded and absorbed into 56th, 1803.
69th Regt.	U, J, Ey, F, Es, W, Bu, FO, Sa, N, To.
70th Regt.	Tr, Vm, Co, FO, Sb, Sa, N, Lu, Bt, L, 1814, 1815 III Corps.
71st Regt.	Disbanded 1803, 1st & 2nd Bns. joining 35th, 3rd Bn., 86th.
72nd Regt.	F, Ec, Es, W, 1812 III Corps, Bo, L, 1814, 1815 II Corps.

73rd Regt.	Disbanded and absorbed into 23rd Regt., 1803.
74th Regt.	Disbanded 1803.
75th Regt.	U, A, J, Ey, Tv, Vi, N, To, 1814, 1815 VI Corps.
76th Regt.	U, J, Ey, F, Es, W, Bu, FO, Sa, N, To, D, 1815 IV Corps.
77th Regt.	Disbanded 1803.
78th Regt.	Absorbed into 2nd Regt. 1803.
79th Regt.	Tr, W.
80th Regt.	Absorbed into 34th Regt. 1803.
81st Regt.	A, Dalmatia 1806–09, W, Va, To.
82nd Regt.	Guadeloupe & Martinique 1803–09, Vm, Bu, FO, Sa, N, Lu, Bt, L, SD, 1815 II Corps.
83rd Regt.	Absorbed into 3rd Regt. 1803.
84th Regt.	U, A, W, 1812 IV Corps, Bo, Be, 1815 I Corps.
85th Regt.	A, J, Ey, Ec, W, 1812 I Corps, Bo, D, 1814, 1815 I Corps.
86th Regt.	Vm, Co, FO, Sa, To, Lu, Bt, D, L, 1814, 1815 III Corps.
87th Regt.	Absorbed into 5th Regt., 1803.
88th Regt.	A, J, Ey, Ec, W, Sg, FO, Al, Bd 1812, Vi, N, P, 1815 III Corps.
89th Regt.	Disbanded 1803.
90th Regt.	Absorbed into 93rd Regt. 1803.
91st Regt.	Absorbed into 20th Regt. 1803.
92nd Regt.	U, W, 1812 IV Corps, Bo, 1815 II Corps.
93rd Regt.	Tr, Ec, Es, W, G, 1812 III Corps, Sm, Bo, Be, D, L, 1814, 1815 II Corps.
94th Regt.	A, J, F, Es, W, Tv, FO, Tf, Vi, N, 1813.
95th Regt.	A, J, F, Es, W, Tv, FO, Al, Vi, N, 1813, 1815 IV Corps.
96th Regt.	U, F, Es, W, Tv, FO, Bd 1811, N, To, 1813, 1814, 1815 IV Corps.
97th Regt.	Absorbed into 60th Regt. 1803.
98th Regt.	Absorbed into 92nd Regt. 1803.
99th Regt.	Absorbed into 62nd Regt. 1803.
100th Regt.	U, J, Ey, F, Es, W, Sg, FO, Al, Vi, N, 1815 II Corps.
101st Regt.	Sa, N, To, Bt, L, BA, AA.
102nd Regt.	W, Lu, L.
103rd Regt.	U, J, Es, W, Sg, FO, Al, Bd 1812, Vi, N, To, Lu, Bt, L, 1814.
104th Regt.	Absorbed into 11th Regt. 1803; reformed 1814 from bns. of 17th, 52nd and 101st Regts.

105th Regt.	J, Ey, Ec, Es, W, N, 1812 XI Corps, 1813, BA, AA, SD, 1815 I Corps.
106th Regt.	W, 1812 IV Corps, Bo.
107th Regt.	Disbanded 1803; reformed 1814 from bns. of 6th, 10th, 20th and 102nd Regts.; 1814, 1815 VI Corps.
108th Regt.	A, J, Ey, Ec, W, 1812 I Corps, Bo, Be, 1813, 1815 II Corps.
109th Regt.	Absorbed into 21st Regt. 1803.
110th Regt.	1st Bn. absorbed into 55th Regt., 2nd and 3rd into 86th, 1803.
111th Regt.	A, J, Ey, F, Ec, W, 1812 I Corps, Sm, Bo, 1813, 1815 IV Corps.
112th Regt.	W, Bt, L.
113th Regt.	Formed 1808; Ciudad Rodrigo, 1812 XI Corps, 1813, Ch, P; absorbed into 4th, 14th and 72nd Regts. 1814.
114th Regt.	Formed 1808 from 1st and 2nd Provisional Regts.; Sg, Va, Ca, Ta.
115th Regt.	Formed 1808 from 3rd and 4th Provisional Regts.; Sg, Ta, N, To, 1814.
116th Regt.	Formed 1808 from 5th Provisional Regt.; Sg, Ta, Va, Ca, To.
117th Regt.	Formed 1808 from 9th and 10th Provisional Regts.; Sg, Ta, Va, Ca, To.
118th Regt.	Formed 1808; Sa, Vi, To, AA.
119th Regt.	Formed 1808 from 13th and 14th Provisional Regts; Sa, Vi, To, 1814.
120th Regt.	Formed 1808 from 17th and 18th Provisional Regts.; Sa, Vi, N, To, 1814.
121st Regt.	Formed 1809 from 2nd *Légion de Reserve*; Sa, Ta, Va, Ca, Lu, Bt, D, L, AA, P.
122nd Regt.	Formed 1809 from 1st and 2nd Supplementary Regts., *Légion de Reserve*; Sa, Vi, N, Lu, BA, AA, SD.
123rd Regt.	Formed 1810 from Dutch troops; 1812 II Corps, Be, 1813.
124th Regt.	Formed 1810 from Dutch troops; 1812 II Corps, Be, 1813; incorporated into 25th Regt. 1814.
125th Regt.	Formed 1810 from Dutch troops; 1812 IX Corps, Be; disbanded 1813.
126th Regt.	Formed 1810 from Dutch troops; 1812 IX Corps, Be; incorporated into 123rd Regt. 1813.
127th Regt.	Formed 1811 from Hamburg Guard;

Grenadiers in undress waistcoats, a style which could be worn on active service in place of the *habit*, especially in hot climates. The blue facings are regulation, but the grenade-shaped sleeve badges are an unrecorded addition. Print by Carle Vernet.

	1812 I Corps, Bo, Be.
128th Regt.	Formed 1811 from Bremen Guard; 1812 II Corps, Be, 1813; incorporated into 40th and 53rd 1814.
129th Regt.	Formed 1811 from Westphalian troops; 1812 III Corps, Bo, Be, 1813; incorporated into 127th and 128th 1813.
130th Regt.	Formed 1811; N, M, BA, AA.
131st Regt.	Regt. de Walcheren became 131st 1812; Lu, Bt, L, 1814.
132nd Regt.	Regt. l'Ile-de-Ré became 132nd 1812; Bt, L, Ch, P, SD.
133rd Regt.	2nd Mediterranean Regt. became 133rd 1812; Bt, L.
134th Regt.	Formed 1813 from *Garde de Paris*; Lu, Bt.
135th Regt.	Formed 1813 (NG 1, 8, 9, 11); Lu, BA; disbanded May 1814.
136th Regt.	Formed 1813 (NG 12–14, 67); Lu, Bt, L, M, P; disbanded July 1814.
137th Regt.	Formed 1813 (NG 2, 84–86); L; disbanded 1814.
138th Regt.	Formed 1813 (NG 44–46, 64); Lu, L, Ch, M, P; disbanded August 1814.

Shako plate, 72nd Line, 1812 pattern. Compare with the next illustration, and note the many small but typical differences of detail.

Shako plate, 43rd Line, 1812 pattern. Regimental variation upon the 'standard' design—the number upon a raised oval surrounded by a wreath of laurel.

139th Regt.	Formed 1813 (NG 16, 17, 65, 66); Lu, Bt, L, AA, SD; disbanded June 1813.
140th Regt.	Formed 1813 (NG 40–43); Lu, Bt, L, 1814; disbanded May 1814.
141st Regt.	·Formed 1813 (NG 37, 39, 62, 63); Lu, Bt, L, P; disbanded 1814.
142nd Regt.	Formed 1813 (NG 5, 36, 38, 61); Lu, Bt, D, Ch, M; disbanded May 1814.
143rd Regt.	Formed 1813 (NG 28–31); disbanded 1814.
144th Regt.	Formed 1813 (NG 32–35); Lu, Bt, L, Ch, M, P; disbanded 1814.
145th Regt.	Formed 1813 (NG 6, 23, 24, 25); Lu, L, Ch, M; disbanded June 1814.
146th Regt.	Formed 1813 (NG 3, 76–78); 1813; disbanded 1813.
147th Regt.	Formed 1813 (NG 15, 71, 78, 87); 1813; absorbed into 154th 1813.

148th Regt.	Formed 1813 (NG 72–75); 1813; disbanded 1813.
149th Regt.	Formed 1813 (NG 47–49, 77); Bt, 1814; disbanded 1814.
150th Regt.	Formed 1813 (NG 68, 69, 80, 81); L; disbanded 1814.
151st Regt.	Formed 1813 (NG 7, 50–52); 1813, 1814; disbanded May 1814.
152nd Regt.	Formed 1813 (NG 18, 19, 53, 54); L, P; disbanded 1814.
153rd Regt.	Formed 1813 (NG 55–58); L; disbanded 1814.
154th Regt.	Formed 1813 (NG 4, 20–22); L, 1814; disbanded 1814.
155th Regt.	Formed 1813 (NG 10, 59, 60, 70); L, 1814; disbanded July 1814.
156th Regt.	Formed 1813 (NG 26, 27, 82, 83); Bt, P; disbanded 1814.

The Plates

A1: Fusilier, 43rd Line, 1792

This representative of *les blancs* wears 1791 uniform with the 'Tarleton' helmet. The 43rd Regt. in 1786 bore the name 'du Limosin', but renumbering in 1791 caused this regiment to be ranked 42nd, the number 43 passing to the old Régt. Royal Vaisseaux, hitherto the 44th.

A2: Infantryman in campaign dress, 1795

This *bleu* is based in part upon a drawing by Benjamin Zix, showing the dilapidation of uniforms on campaign, though Zix shows a coat with unflapped cuff, breeches, and neither gaiters nor shoes but bare legs below the knee.

A3: Grenadier, Paris National Guard, 1792

Uniform distinction within the Paris National Guard consisted of plume colours (blue, red, white, blue/red, red/white/blue and blue/white respectively for the city's 1st to 6th 'divisions'), insignia and even facings; for example, grenadiers of the Versailles area are believed to have worn red cuffs and a red-tipped plume. The cap plate bore both monarchist and republican symbols, the King's Arms, Phrygian cap and motto '*Vivre libre ou mourir*', the former obliterated later. Moustaches were usual but apparently not universal.

B1: Fusilier caporal, 61st Demi-Brigade, Egypt

This figure illustrates the 'coloured' uniform of the Kléber Ordinance.

The 61st Line's 1st to 4th and 6th Battalions formed part of Compans' Division of I Corps in the 1812 Russian campaign, and suffered appallingly in the assault on the Shevardino Redoubt two days before Borodino. On the following day Napoleon asked the colonel what had become of one of his battalions: 'Sire', was the reply, 'it is in the redoubt of Shevardino'; the Emperor said nothing, but passed on. Almost the entire corps of drums was annihilated by artillery fire while beating the charge; Bourgogne relates how Florencia, the regiment's young Spanish *cantinière* (sutleress), was wounded whilst searching for her father, the drum major, whom she found mortally injured, lying amid a heap of broken drums and slain drummers.

B2: Fusilier, 1800

Taken from a contemporary painting, this figure wears regulation dress.

B3: Officer, 15th Demi-Brigade, 1800

Taken from an extant costume; uniform variations include cuffs with both red and white vertical piping, and the common practice of having coat-tails without fixed turnbacks.

B4: Grenadier, 1800

Though wearing regulation dress, this grenadier follows normal practice in having a cap with a red rear patch instead of the prescribed red-and-blue quarters.

Senior officer of the 52nd Line, wearing 1812 regulation uniform including the waistbelt specified for mounted officers. Note the rank distinctions in the form of lace bands around the shako.

C1: Sergeant-Major with 'Eagle', 4th Line, 1805

This figure wears the orange hat lace peculiar to the 4th.

Though losing only 18 dead, the regiment was routed by Russian cavalry at Austerlitz and lost an 'Eagle' despite a heroice defence by Sgt.Maj. St.Cyr, 'who relinquished this trophy only after he had received a dozen wounds on his head and arms'. As Joseph Bonaparte was the regimental colonel, Napoleon felt the loss deeply and harangued the regiment with such venom that he reduced even a spectator to tears. Despite pleas by its commander and the assertion that none of the survivors of the 1st Bn. had seen the 'Eagle' fall, it was only with reluctance that Napoleon granted a new one, in return for two Austrian colours captured by the regiment.

C2: 2ᵉ Porte-Aigle, 8th Line, 1811

The 'Eagle-guard' is distinguished by his pistol belt, four sleeve chevrons (in accordance with an instruction of 18 February 1808, altered to two on 18 March 1811), and wears the regimental peaked cap.

The 8th Line lost its 'Eagle' to Sgt. Patrick Masterson of the British 87th Foot at Barrosa, after *Premier Porte-Aigle* Edmé Guillemain was killed in its defence; the *2ᵉ Porte-Aigle* at this time was Etienne Debette, who joined the 8th Demi-Brigade in 1793 and died in hospital in Spain in 1812. Incredibly, it seems that the 8th attempted to conceal the loss of their 'Eagle', replying to an official circular in April 1812 that it had been broken by a cannonball at Barrosa!

C3: Sapeur, 46th Line, 1808

This shows the usual *sapeur* uniform with grenadier distinctions and the 46th's sky-blue facings.

The 46th Line was always associated with '*le premier grenadier de France*', Théophile Malo Corret, known from 1777 as '*La Tour d'Auvergne*'. This famed and valiant officer always refused promotion so that he could stay with his grenadier company, and despite long and distinguished service and his appointment as a Deputy to the Senate, he continued in the army until slain at Oberhausen on 27 June 1800, aged 57. General Moreau ordered that his place should never be filled and his name kept upon the regimental establishment and an-

Drummers in 1812 regulation dress, from a print by Carle Vernet. The figure on the left wears the all-green undress uniform with *pokalem* forage-cap bearing the number of the 10th Line. The right-hand figure in full uniform has the pointed cuffs usually associated with light infantry.

nounced at roll-call, whereupon the senior grenadier *fourrier* was to reply: 'Dead upon the field of honour.' La Tour d'Auvergne's heart was preserved in a silver casket, strapped to a velvet pad worn upon the breast of the 1st Battalion's senior grenadier sergeant, until deposited at Les Invalides in 1904; his name was still called on the roll more than a century after his death.

D1: Grenadier, 15th Line, 1807

This figure wears the white uniform and 1806 shako as originally issued, minus chinscales.

The 15th Line bore upon its Colours a unique inscription, awarded for outstanding service: '*Le 15ᵉ est couvert de la Gloire*'.

D2: Voltigeur Cornet, 18th Line, 1809

This figure wears *voltigeur* distinctions, with the regimental crimson facings and tricolour lace.

The 18th was one of the most distinguished regiments in the army, bearing upon its colours a motto bestowed by Bonaparte for gallantry at Rivoli: '*Brave 18ᵉ, je vous connais. L'ennemi ne tiendra pas devant vous*' ('I know you, brave 18th; the enemy never stands before you'). This reputation was maintained at Fribourg on 2 March 1798 when Sgt.

Musicians in the green 'Imperial Livery' of the 1812 regulations; print by Carle Vernet.

Barbe, *Fourrier* Troch and 13 men scaled the wall, despatched the guard and let in the French army.

D3: Voltigeur, 3rd Line, 1809
The *voltigeur* illustrated wears the 'sunburst' shako plate shown by Martinet c. 1808–09, though the regiment is also believed to have worn other non-regulation plates of eagle-on-crescent form.

E1: Caporal-Tambour, 67th Line, 1808
The 'drum-corporal' illustrated wears a uniform not unlike that of the drum major, with a simpler mace. The diagonal shako cords were a regimental peculiarity, believed not to have continued beyond 1809.

E2: Musician, 9th Line, 1809
A similarly magnificent light cavalry-style uniform, including czapka, was also worn by the musicians of the 17th Light Infantry.

The 9th features in a number of heroic exploits, as at Vitebsk in 1812 when 300 *voltigeurs*, isolated from the army by the River Dvina, stood off a Russian cavalry attack until the dead were piled around their square; Napoleon said every one deserved the Légion d'Honneur for so amazing an exploit. One of the 9th's hard-bitten veterans was Charles

François, who wrote an entertaining memoir: at Acre he stood on top of the French earthworks firing at the enemy with muskets passed up by his comrades, expending 17 packs of cartridges in 75 minutes, during which time eight balls passed through his clothes, but escaping with no more than a bruise. Though wounded, François saved the regiment's 'Eagle', retrieving it from the body of its bearer and carrying it hidden throughout the retreat from Moscow, for which he received the Légion d'Honneur. Medals were not the only rewards obtainable on campaign; when the 9th's paymaster died in January 1813, he was found to have 182,000 francs hidden on his person, as perquisites of his office!

E3: Grenadier drummer, 57th Line, 1809
This figure wears company distinctions with musicians' sky-blue facings and orange lace.

The 57th was nicknamed *Le Terrible* from Bonaparte's remark inscribed on their colours after Rivoli: '*Le Terrible 57ᵉ qui rien n'arrête*' ('which sticks at nothing'). A unique award for gallantry at Borodino was the badge of the Légion d'Honneur affixed to the 'Eagle' and stamped on the regimental buttons. Heroism even extended to the female members of this superb corps: *cantinière* Madame Cazajus was cited in the order of the day following Guttstadt (1807) for braving heavy fire to distribute two barrels of brandy, gratis, to the regiment, while another lady, the widow Brulon, actually served in the ranks under the name of Liberté until wounded in Corsica; she lived until 1863, an honorary *sous-lieutenant* and member of the Légion d'Honneur.

F1: Voltigeur, 88th Line, campaign dress; Spain, 1811
This figure wears typical Peninsular campaign dress, including covered shako with painted insignia, the waistcoat worn as a jacket, and trousers made from local cloth.

F2: Fusilier officer, 34th Line; Spain, 1810
Another Peninsular uniform, showing typical officers' service dress including the *surtout*, which was commonly cut so high at the front to expose a considerable part of the waistcoat; note the regimental tricolour cockade worn instead of a shako-plate.

F3: Grenadier, 65th Line; Spain, 1810

A third Peninsular uniform, with regimental distinctions in the blue cuffs with red flaps, cap badge, and white trimming to epaulettes and sword knot.

The 65th's most celebrated exploit was the defence of the Danube bridge at Ratisbon in April 1809 against two Austrian Corps. It expended all its ammunition before Col. Coutard capitulated, saving the 'Eagle' by burying it with three captured Austrian flags; it was recovered when the prisoners were released a few days later by the recapture of Ratisbon. Marbot is critical of Coutard's defence, claiming that he was only charged with the task so that, as a relative of Davoût, he could cover himself with glory, and when surrendering arranged for the 65th's officers to return home immediately, abandoning their men; but the regiment's casualties (265 killed alone, out of 2,087 engaged between 16 and 22 April) testify to the stubbornness of their defence of a hopeless position.

G1: Major, 100th Line, 1809

This figure shows majors' rank distinctions, silver epaulette-straps and a silver band below the upper shako band, riding boots, and a white plume (red-over-white was specified for majors in November 1810), with the regimental shako plate.

The 100th won fame at Dürrenstein in the advance on Vienna after Ulm. Overwhelmed by Russians, the 100th's battalion 'Eagles' were rescued by Maj. Henriot, who tried to cut his way through the enemy and rejoin the main French army. Addressing his men, he is reported to have said: 'Comrades, we must break through. They are more than we, but you are Frenchmen: you don't count numbers!' The shout came back: 'We are all grenadiers! *Pas de charge!*' The 'Eagles' were later recovered from beneath the bodies of Henriot's party, where they had fallen in their hopeless attempt to reach safety. Napoleon's 22nd Bulletin reported that 'the action at Dürrenstein will forever be remembered', and the 100th 'se sont couverts de gloire'.

Infantry escorting Russian prisoners, 1812; print by Faber du Faur. Note the use of the 1812-pattern shako with the previous *habit*, **a mixture of styles probably not uncommon; and the covered shako and plain** *surtout* **worn by the officer.**

G2: Fusilier sergeant, 30th Line, 1811

Though a fusilier, élite-style equipment is worn, to support the sabre.

In 1815 the 30th was cursed with a martinet in Col. Ramaud, who treated his veterans like recruits, making them drill for hours in deep snow. This caused much resentment, and there was delight when Ramaud pleaded ill-health to escape the 1815 campaign. More laudable members of the 30th were those like *Fourrier* Morin, who saved the 'Eagle' at Eylau by covering it with his body; with his last breath he indicated where it was hidden on the following morning.

G3: Officer, 125th Line, 1811

This figure wears the uniform of the old 4th Dutch Line, as noted in the main text, with a French shako plate replacing the white metal numeral worn in Dutch service.

G4: Voltigeur, 14th Line, 1811

This figure wears the *bonnet de police* and greatcoat; on campaign the shako plume was commonly carried in a waterproof cover, tied to the scabbard by the shako cords.

The 14th was known as an unlucky regiment; when Col. Savary was lanced by a cossack in December 1806, he was their fifth colonel killed in action. At Eylau the 14th defended a hillock assigned them by Napoleon, waving their 'Eagle' to

38

show they still held, though surrounded. By the time Marbot (Augereau's ADC) was able to reach them with orders to retire, the survivors were too few to attempt a breakout, so sent a message via Marbot bidding Napoleon 'farewell from the 14th of the Line, which has faithfully executed his orders'; they were submerged under a host of Russians. Thirty-six of the 14th's officers were buried in a mass grave, and about 590 other ranks.

H1: Fusilier, 70th Line, 1813

This illustrates 'Bardin' uniform of 1812.

Most renowned of the 70th was Lt. Poiret, alias 'the saviour of France', who shielded Bonaparte from attack during the coup d'état of *18 Brumaire*. The 70th in the Waterloo campaign, mainly conscripts, hardly emulated him; they broke at Ligny and again at Wavre, whereupon Col. Maury snatched the 'Eagle' and shouted: 'What, you scoundrels? You disgraced me two days ago, and again today! Forward! Follow me!' Their brief rally ended and they fled when Maury fell, leaving the 22nd Line to recover the 'Eagle' from across poor Maury's body.

H2: Grenadier, 3rd Line, 1813

This figure wears regulation dress, plus shako cords, and a plume including the regimental sky-blue colour.

H3: 'Marie-Louise', 82nd Line, 1814

Based upon pictures by Johann Adam Klein, this figure shows the wretched clothing and equipment of the often unwilling teenaged conscripts of 1813–14. Both single- and double-breasted great-coats are recorded, some with red collar-patches of varying styles.

The 82nd had been the centre of a plot to overthrow Napoleon when First Consul, which failed when their Col. Pinoteau, preparing to lead a revolt at Rennes, delayed in order to make his *toilette*. While his regiment waited impatiently, Bonapartist gendarmes arrested Pinoteau in the act of shaving; for such a trivial reason, perhaps, was the course of history changed!

H4: Drummer, 96th Line, 1814

This figure wears 'Imperial Livery' with the shorter, bushier plume introduced in 1812 but never adopted universally.

Best known of the 96th was Jean-Roch Coignet, author of an entertaining reminiscence. Enlisting in the 96th Demi-Brigade in 1798, he gained great distinction at Montebello by single-handedly capturing a fieldpiece in 'a bloody affair of bayonets' in which he slew all five of the crew. His reward for this exceptional gallantry was immediate: Berthier presented him with a piece of bread!

Sources

Apart from contemporary illustrations and extant items of uniform, the work of several later artists has been studied and is recommended, including Lucien Rousselot (*L'Armée Française*), Albert Rigondaud ('Rigo'), J. Onfroy de Bréville ('Job') and the illustrators of the Bucquoy cards, some of which are reproduced in *Les Uniformes du Premier Empire: l'Infanterie (*Cdt. E.-L. Bucquoy, ed. Lt.Col. L.-Y. Bucquoy and G. Devatour, Paris 1979). Examples of 'dress regulations' are catalogued in *Guide à l'usage des Artistes et Costumiers . . . Uniformes de l'armée française* (H. Malibran, Paris 1904, reprinted Krefeld 1972), while examples of unofficial insignia are recorded in *Aigles et Shakos du Premier Empire* (C. Blondieau, Paris 1980). Details of weaponry and tactics may be found in *Weapons and Equipment of the Napoleonic Wars* (P. J. Haythornthwaite, Poole 1979), *The Art of Warfare in the Age of Napoleon* (G. E. Rothenberg, London 1977) and *The Campaigns of Napoleon* (D. G. Chandler, London 1967).

'Tête de Colonne': the Premier Porte-Aigle flanked by the two 'Eagle-guards', c. 1813. The 'Eagle' is carried without the flag attached, as was common on campaign. The 1812-regulation uniform is worn. Illustration from a print by Job.

Notes sur les planches en couleurs

A1 L'un des '*Blancs*' portant l'uniforme réglementaire de 1791 avec le casque appelé '*Tarleton*' dans l'armée anglaise. En 1791, ce numéro de régiment fut attribué à l'ancien *Régiment Royal Vaisseaux*. **A2** '*Un bleu*' reproduit d'un dessin par Benjamin Zix mettant en évidence le détérioration de l'uniforme en campagne; en fait, Zix représente un habit à manchettes simples et jambes nues des genoux aux pieds. **A3** Les unités du cadre de la Garde Nationale de Paris se distinguaient par des panaches de différentes couleurs, et même dans certains cas par différentes couleurs de parements sur l'habit—par exemple: parements rouges pour Versailles.

B1 Le style d'uniforme dit 'Ordonnance *Kléber*' dans différentes couleurs de régiments, tel que porté en Egypte. Plusieurs années plus tard, ce régiment se distingua admirablement à Borodino, à l'attaque de la redoute *Shevardino*. **B2** Uniforme entièrement règlementaire à l'époque, reproduit d'un tableau contemporain. **B3** D'un uniforme qui a survécu: des variantes types de la tenue réglementaire comportaient le passe-poil rouge et blanc sur le parement, et le port de basques sans pans fixés à l'arrière en permanence. **B4** Tenue presque réglementaire: mais noter que, comme la plupart des grenadiers, il porte un bonnet à pièce supérieure en toile rouge ordinaire au lieu des quartiers réglementaires rouges et bleus.

C1 La dentelle orange sur la coiffure constituait un trait distinctif du 4ème Régiment de Ligne. L'aigle du 4ème a été perdu à Austerlitz malgré l'héroïsme du Sergent Major St. Cyr. **C2** Le 'garde-aigle' se distingue par son ceinturon porte-pistolet et ses quatre chevrons de manche (devenus deux depuis le règlement de mars 1811). **C3** Uniforme habituel de *sapeur* avec les distinctions de l'uniforme de grenadier ou, par régiment, des parements bleu ciel.

D1 Uniforme blanc livré à certains régiments avec distinctions sous forme de couleurs de parements appropriées au groupe dans lequel le régiment est classé; et le shako de 1806. **D2** Les distinctions de *Voltigeur* sont portées et noter les revêtements pourpres du régiment et la dentelle tricolore. **D3** A part la plaque de shako à 'rayons de soleil' le régiment est censé également avoir porté des exemples du motif aigle-et-croissant.

E1 Un uniforme analogue à celui du tambour major mais plus simple; les cordons de shako en diagonale sont un trait particulier du régiment de la période avant 1809. **E2** Noter le style 'cavalerie légère' de la tenue des musiciens y compris la coiffure *czapka*. **E3** Parements bleu ciel et dentelle orange identifient les musiciens et les tambours de cette unité. Les distinctions du style grenadier identifient la compagnie.

F1 Tenue de campagne typique comprenant un couvre-shako avec insigne peinte et le gilet porté comme une jaquette. **F2** Le *surtout* était un vêtement de campagne commun pour les officiers; noter également la cocarde tricolore régimentale portée au lieu de la plaque de shako. **F3** Les particularités du régiment sont la patte de parement rouge sur la manchette bleue, la garniture blanche des épaulettes et la dragonne, ainsi que la forme de la plaque de bonnet.

G1 Les distinctions de ce grade sont les pattes d'épaulettes argent et la bande de shako ainsi que le panache blanc d'un officier d'état-major de régiment. **G2** Bien qu'il soit un *fusilier*, il porte le style d'équipement personnel relatif aux compagnies d'élite de façon à pouvoir recevoir le sabre de son grade de sous-officier. **G3** Mis à part la plaque de shako, ceci est l'uniforme du quatrième régiment de ligne Hollandaise. **G4** Noter le bonnet de police et la capote. En campagne, le panache de shako est porté dans une enveloppe attachée au fourreau. Ce régiment s'est bien distingué à Eylau.

H1 L'uniforme réglementaire 'Bardin' de 1812. **H2** Tenue réglementaire plus cordons, et panache de shako y compris les distinctions bleu ciel du régiment. **H3** D'après une image de Johann Adam Klein représentant l'aspect malheureux du conscrit de 1813-14. **H4** La 'livrée impériale' des tambours introduite en 1812.

Farbtafeln

A1 Einer der *Les Blancs* in regulärer Uniform aus dem Jahre 1791 mit einem Helm, der in der britischen Armee als *Tarleton* bekannt ist. 1791 wurde diese Regimentszahl dem alten *Régiment Royal Vaisseaux* zuteil. **A2** *Un Bleu* nach einer Zeichnung von Benjamin Zix; hier sieht man deutlich den schlechten Zustand der Uniform nach einem Feldzug: Oftmals, Mantel mit einfachem Ärmelaufschlag und nackte Beine bis hoch zum Knie. **A3** Eigentümlich für die Einheiten der Pariser Nationalgarde waren unterschiedliche Federfarben und manchmal auch Mantelbesätze in verschiedenen Farben, z.B. rote Ärmelaufschläge für Versailles.

B1 Uniform im Stil der sogenannten *Kléber Ordinance* in verschiedenen Regimentsfarben; sie wurde in Ägypten getragen. Jahre später zeichnete dieses Regiment sich bei Borodino beim Angriff auf die *Shevardino*-Redoute aus. **B2** Die reguläre Uniform dieser Zeit nach einem zeitgenössischen Gemälde. **B3** Von einer späteren Uniform; zu den typischen Variationen der regulären Ausstattung zählten rote und weisse Ärmelumrandungen sowie Rockschösse ohne permanent befestigten Schoss. **B4** Fast die reguläre Uniform; beachten Sie, dass dieser wie die meisten Grenadiere eine Mütze mit Besatz aus rotem Stoff anstelle der roten und blauen Viertel trägt.

C1 Eigentümlich für das 4. Linienregiment war die orangene Spitze auf der Mütze. Den Adler verlor das 4. Regiment bei Austerlitz trotz der heroischen Taten des Hauptfeldwebels S. Cyr. **C2** Die 'Adlerwache' zeichnete sich durch den Pistolengürtel und durch die vier Winkel auf dem Ärmel aus; durch eine Bestimmung im März 1811 wurden die Winkel auf zwei beschränkt. **C3** Eine übliche *Sapeur*-Uniform mit Kennzeichen einer Grenadieruniform und dem himmelblauen Besatz des Regimentes.

D1 Die weisse Uniform die an bestimmte Regimenter ausgegeben wurde mit farbigem Besatz entsprechend der Regimentsgruppe und mit dem Tschako aus dem Jahre 1806. **D2** Er trägt *Voltigeur*-Auszeichnungen; beachten Sie den hochroten Besatz des Regiments und die Trikolorspitze. **D3** Man vermutet, dass das Regiment ausser diesem 'Sonnenstrahlen'-Plättchen am Tschako auch Muster mit Adler und Halbmond trug.

E1 Diese Uniform ist ähnlich der des Tambour-Majors nur etwas einfacher. Die diagonalen Bänder am Tschako sind charakteristisch für dieses Regiment vor 1809. **E2** Beachten Sie die leichte Kavallerieausführung der Musikeruniform mit der *Czapka*-Kopfbedeckung. **E3** Der himmelblaue Besatz und die orangefarbene Spitze kennzeichnen Musiker und Trommler dieser Einheit. Die Kompanie erkennt man an den Grenadiermerkmalen.

F1 Zur typischen Feldzugausrüstung gehören ein Tschako-Überzug mit aufgemalten Insignien sowie die als Jacke getragene Weste. **F2** Offiziere trugen in den Feldzügen häufig, einen *Surtout*. Beachten Sie die Trikolorkokarde anstelle des Tschakoplättchens. **F3** Eigentümlich für dieses Regiment waren bei blauen Ärmeln rote Ärmelaufschläge sowie weisse Epaulettenumrandung und Säbelquaste und die Form des Tschakoplättchens.

G1 Kennzeichnend für diesen Rang sind silberne Epaulettenstreifen und ein silbernes Tschakoband sowie die weisse Feder beim Stabsoffizier des Regiments. **G2** Obgleich er ein *Fusilier* ist, ist seine Ausrüstung ähnlich der von Elitekompanien, damit er als Unteroffizier seinen Säbel unterbringen kann. **G3** Abgesehen vom Tschakoplättchen ist dies die Uniform des alten 4. holländischen Linien-regiments. **G4** Beachten Sie den *Bonnet de Police* und den Mantel. Während des Feldzuges trug man die Tschakofeder eingewickelt an der Degenscheide. Dieses Regiment zeichnete sich besonders bei Eylau aus.

H1 Die reguläre 'Bardin'-Uniform im Jahre 1812. **H2** Reguläres Gewand mit Tschakobändern und Feder sowie den hellblauen Kennzeichen des Regiments. **H3** Von einem Bild von Johann Adam Klein: der dürftige Anblick eines Wehrpflichtigen im Jahre 1812-14. **H4** Die 'Kaiserliche Tracht' der Trommler sein 1812.

MEN-AT-ARMS SERIES

EDITOR: MARTIN WINDROW

Wellington's Generals

Text by

MICHAEL BARTHORP

Colour plates by

RICHARD HOOK

OSPREY PUBLISHING LONDON

Published in 1978 by
Osprey Publishing Ltd
Member company of the George Philip Group
12–14 Long Acre, London WC2E 9LP
© Copyright 1978 Osprey Publishing Ltd

ISBN 0 85045 299 6

Filmset by BAS Printers Limited,
Over Wallop, Hampshire
Printed in Hong Kong

The Command and Staff System of Wellington's Army

Up to the outbreak of the Napoleonic Wars the most usual, though not the only, method of obtaining a commission in the British army was by purchase. Thereafter, further promotion was either by purchase of the next step in rank, by seniority without purchase, or by the patronage of the commander-in-chief. This applied up to and including the rank of lieutenant-colonel. Above that rank, promotion was entirely by seniority, the date on which an officer achieved his lieutenant-colonelcy determining his seniority for life. In theory any lieutenant-colonel could expect, in due course of time, to attain the rank of general, quite regardless of whether he was ever employed in any of the intervening ranks; he only had to live long enough. In 1811 three major-generals were promoted lieutenant-general, none of whom had seen any service since the American Revolution! The officer would only receive pay for the higher ranks, however, if he was actually employed as a colonel or a general officer, and then only for the duration of that employment. Once he ceased to be so employed, his pay reverted to that of his regimental rank.

Ludicrous though the system sounds, it had advantages in that there was no limit to the number of generals in the army, and there was no obligation

Wellington and generals at the Battle of Nivelle, 1813. Above his right hand is Beresford, on his left is Cotton, above whose left shoulder are Colville, Dalhousie and Picton. Cole and Hill are looking towards the pointing hussar officer on the right. After Heaphy. (National Army Museum)

to employ those who had reached that rank. Thus, if it was desired to promote a promising younger officer, all that was required was to raise all those senior to him to the next higher rank, however aged or useless they may have been. In 1813, eighty-one colonels were promoted major-general in order that the 82nd in seniority could be appointed to a major-general's command in the field, and, in 1814, ninety-one lieutenant-generals and major-generals were promoted to the next higher rank, so that Major-General Charles Stewart could be advanced to lieutenant-general. The only exception to this ponderous system was the promotion, in 1813, of Wellington himself to field-marshal, when, at the age of forty-four, he jumped ahead of some one hundred and forty officers senior to him to a rank in which none of the previous incumbents, other than Royal dukes, had been less than sixty-one years old on appointment.

Front and rear of the embroidered coat of a lieutenant-general. Note the buttons in threes. (National Army Museum)

Sir John Hope (1765–1823), 3rd Earl of Hopetoun, in the undress uniform of a lieutenant-general, c. 1814. Adjutant-General to Abercromby in Egypt, 1801; brigade commander in the Hanover expedition, 1805; lieutenant-general in Moore's Corunna campaign, 1808–09; divisional commander at Walcheren, 1809; commanded the 1st Division of the Peninsular army in 1813 and the left wing of the army in 1814. After Raeburn. (National Army Museum)

The system resulted in a serious dearth of senior officers who were both young and competent enough to take command of Wellington's brigades and divisions in the field. The provision of officers for these appointments was the responsibility of the Military Secretary at the Horse Guards in London, and, as a general rule, Wellington, as commander in the field, had to make do with what he was sent. While the Military Secretary, Colonel Torrens, did his best to select suitable officers, Wellington also found himself saddled with the likes of the short-sighted and drunken Sir William Erskine. When Wellington remonstrated against Erskine's appointment on the grounds that he was 'generally understood to be a madman', Torrens replied: 'No doubt he is sometimes a little mad, but in his lucid

Staff officers, c. 1813. Adjutant-General or Quartermaster-General (mounted) and Assistant AG or QMG. Soldiers of the Royal Staff Corps in the background. After Hamilton Smith. (National Army Museum)

intervals he is an uncommonly clever fellow; and I trust he will have no fit during the campaign, though he looked a little wild as he embarked'. It is small wonder that Wellington felt constrained to write: 'Really when I reflect upon the character and attainments of some of the General officers of this army, I tremble'.

Wellington had little say in the appointment of general officers, and of the eighty-five officers who served in the field as commanders or on the staff, in the rank of major-general and above between 1809 and 1815, only Beresford, Hill, Picton, Craufurd, Graham, Houston, Leith and Nightingall were men whom he had particularly requested. All these, with the exception of Nightingall, turned out successfully, within their own limitations. However, it was these limitations, particularly when commanding formations larger than a brigade, that caused Wellington most concern. Almost all were brave, but what was most lacking was 'a cool, discriminating judgement in action' and the ability 'to convey their orders, and act with vigour and decision, that the soldiers will look up to them with confidence, in the moment of action, and obey

them with alacrity'. The lack of these qualities, even among his better commanders, caused him to write: 'They are really heroes when I am on the spot to direct them, but when I am obliged to quit them they are children.'

With the exception of Graham, who as will be seen did not join the army until he was forty-five, Wellington's senior officers were all, good or bad, comparatively young. On average they had received their ensign's commissions at the age of seventeen, reaching lieutenant-colonel at around twenty-eight, and major-general at forty. One of the most senior and most competent, Edward Paget, had been a lieutenant-colonel at eighteen and a major-general at thirty. This does not include general officers of the Royal Artillery and Royal Engineers, whose promotion from first commissioning was entirely by seniority and consequently much slower.

Of the eighty-five general officers who served Wellington, three were peers in their own right while twenty-one were the sons of peers or baronets. The remainder had either legal, clerical or service backgrounds or came from the country gentry. Twenty-two had been to public schools but most had been educated privately and only seven had attended university. A mere twelve had received any military education before joining the army, either at the Royal Military College or continental military academies. This, however, was balanced by the practical experience gained by many on active service since 1793 in the Low Countries, the West Indies, India, the Mediterranean and Egypt.

Whatever their failings as commanders or senior staff officers, lack of courage was not among them. Casualties from death, wounds, or being taken prisoner were quite common among formation commanders, and indeed this readiness to lead from the front, and show unconcern in the face of danger, could on occasion prove detrimental to the proper performance of their duties. The incompetent Skerrett, briefly and disastrously in command of the Light Division, was observed by an officer, 'standing in the most exposed spot under the enemy's fire as stupidly composed for himself as inactive for the welfare of his command'. Only in three cases was the courage of Wellington's generals suspect: Long, whose poor showing may have been more inspired by his revulsion with war than want of bravery; Slade, like Long a cavalry commander; and Hay, of whom it was said: 'That he is a paltry, plundering old wretch is established beyond doubt. That he is no officer is as clear, and that he wants spirit is firmly believed'.

The formations entrusted to these general officers were initially, for Wellington's Oporto operations in 1809, eight British and one King's German Legion infantry brigades, each being a major-general's command, and comprising between two and four battalions, a company of the 5th (Rifle) Battalion 60th Foot and, in five brigades, a Portuguese battalion. The cavalry was formed in a division of two brigades. The Talavera campaign of the same year saw the first divisional organization of the infantry. The 1st Division had four brigades, one Guards, one Line and two K.G.L., each of two battalions, while the 2nd, 3rd and 4th had two brigades, each of two or three battalions. Wellington envisaged the divisions being commanded by lieutenant-generals, but as he only had two, the senior major-general of brigade was to take temporary command.

Early in 1810 Wellington began attaching Portuguese brigades, each of one *Caçador* (rifle) and two Line battalions, to his existing British divisions, and at the same time created the Light Division, formed of Craufurd's Light Brigade (43rd, 52nd and 95th) and two Portuguese *Caçador* battalions. He visualized this formation providing the same service for the army as a whole, as the rifle companies of the 5th/60th performed for the brigades. In August 1810 the 5th Division was formed and, in the winter of 1810–11, with the arrival of fresh battalions from home, he was able to form the 6th and 7th Divisions. Thereafter no new divisions were formed, and from 1811 the infantry organization remained largely as follows: the Light Division as before but with the addition of two, later three, battalions; the 1st Division with two British and one K.G.L. brigades; the 2nd with three British brigades and Hamilton's Portuguese division attached to it, forming a small corps; and the remainder, 3rd–7th, having two British and one Portuguese brigades. A British brigade usually had three battalions and a company of riflemen, a Portuguese five battalions and a company of *caçadores*. To make each division self-contained with its own artillery, one field battery, either British or Portuguese, was attached from 1811, increasing to two batteries in 1812. A horse artillery battery was attached to the Light Division.

Apart from the Light Division, which had the 1st K.G.L. Hussars almost permanently attached, the infantry divisions had no cavalry. This remained organized in one division of three, later seven, brigades, each of two regiments, except for a period between 1811 and 1813 when it was split into two divisions, one of four brigades, the other of two. However, the cavalry was seldom used in mass under its own commander, Cotton, but was deployed by brigades under the direct orders of Wellington.

Up to Vittoria in 1813, Wellington exercised direct control over his divisional commanders with no intermediate level of command, except for the force in Estramadura, the 2nd Division, Hamilton's Portuguese and two cavalry brigades, which formed a more or less independent corps under Hill. This direct control stemmed largely from Wellington having no senior officer of sufficient ability, other than Hill, whom he felt he could

Sabretache of general officer of hussars worn by Lord Uxbridge at Waterloo. (National Army Museum)

entrust with the command of a corps of two or more divisions. The officers appointed as his second-in-command between 1809 and 1813, Sherbrooke and then Brent Spencer, who in theory should have been able to undertake such a task, were quite unfitted for it. Spencer was 'exceedingly puzzle-headed' and always referred to the Tagus as the Thames. He was replaced in 1813 by Graham, an admirable officer in many ways, but lacking experience with a large command and suffering from increasing blindness.

After Vittoria, owing to the difficulty of exercising personal command over eight divisions in the broken country and wide frontages of the Pyrenees, Wellington organized the army into three almost permanent corps, or rather a centre and two wings: the left under Graham, until ill-health forced him to return home, when he was replaced by the able Hope, the right under Hill, while the centre, as strong as the two wings combined, Wellington kept under his direct control, with Beresford acting as his second-in-command and occasionally commanding half of it.

In the Waterloo campaign the Allied army was organized thus: two corps, commanded respectively by the Prince of Orange and Hill, the former having four infantry and one Dutch cavalry divisions, the latter three divisions; a reserve of two British divisions and two Allied contingents under Wellington's direct control; and the Anglo-German cavalry of eight brigades under Uxbridge. Apart from the 1st (Guards) Division, the British divisions consisted of two British or K.G.L. brigades and one Hanoverian brigade, although the 6th Division had only one of each; each division had two field batteries. The British brigades had between two and four battalions, the Hanoverian between four and six. The cavalry brigades had, on average, three regiments. At Waterloo itself, the corps organization was not really of much consequence, since Wellington exercised complete control over the whole army, at times giving orders direct to brigades and even to battalions.

To assist commanders at each level in the execution of their duties were the members of the staff. These fell into three categories: personal staff; the officers of the Adjutant-General's and Quartermaster-General's Departments; and the staff of the civil departments—Commissary-General's, Paymaster-General's and Medical. The first category included aides-de-camp and brigade-majors. The former were all young men, chosen by the general they served to perform such duties as writing letters, carrying messages and organizing the general's personal establishment. In an age when all orders had to be passed by word of mouth or in writing, the ADC was a vital link in the chain of command. Brigade-majors were concerned with the daily routine of their brigades and implementing the orders of the brigade commander, who had no other military staff officer, unless he was entitled to an ADC. Lieutenant-generals were allowed two ADCs and Wellington himself seldom had less than six. The Adjutant-General's and Quartermaster-General's Departments provided the channels through which commanders, above brigade level, issued their orders, and arranged for the daily management of the formation they served. Under Wellington, due to the proven reliability of George Murray, who served as Quartermaster-General throughout the Peninsular War with only one break, that department became pre-eminent, while the Adjutant-General's remained largely concerned with routine matters such as discipline, strength returns, supervision of clothing and armaments and the issue of regulations. The Quartermaster-General's work was involved with the conduct of operations and posed problems that changed daily—the quartering and movement of the army, allocation of transport, acquisition of intelligence about the countryside and the enemy, and the maintenance of communications.

At Wellington's own headquarters, apart from his personal staff of ADCs and his Military Secretary, who was responsible, *inter alia*, for his financial business and all matters regarding officers' appointments, there would be the Adjutant-General, with perhaps two Assistant AGs (lieutenant-colonels or majors) and two Deputy Assistant AGs (captains or subalterns), and the Quartermaster-General with a similar staff, both departments having their own quota of clerks, orderlies and servants. At a divisional headquarters there might be only one Assistant AG and an Assistant QMG with a deputy.

The civil departments would all be represented at the main headquarters, and in the case of the Commissary-General's, responsible for the procuring, storing and issuing of all manner of stores and

Sir Thomas Graham, Baron Lynedoch of Balgowan, in the
embroidered uniform of a lieutenant-general, c. 1814. After
Lawrence. (National Army Museum)

Henry Paget, Earl of Uxbridge, later Marquess of Anglesey, in the uniform of colonel of the 7th Hussars. (National Army Museum)

supplies, there would be officials at both divisional and brigade level.

Apart from these three categories of staff, there were also to be found at Wellington's headquarters his Commanders Royal Artillery and Royal Engineers with their staffs, the Provost-Marshal and his assistants, also represented at divisional headquarters, and the Deputy-Judge-Advocate-General.

Henry Paget, Earl of Uxbridge

Henry Paget was born on 17 May 1768, the eldest son of the Earl of Uxbridge. After being educated at Westminster and Christ Church, Oxford, he served briefly in the regiment of Staffordshire Militia commanded by his father. The outbreak of war with revolutionary France in 1793 required the expansion of the army, so Paget raised the 80th Foot, chiefly from among his father's tenantry, and

at the age of twenty-five, with no proper military experience, was granted the temporary rank of lieutenant-colonel in command of the 80th. He took his regiment to join the Duke of York's army for the unfortunate campaign in Flanders in 1794 and soon found himself commanding a brigade. His real wish, however, was to transfer to the cavalry: 'I own I am disgusted with the Infantry and the 80th and think Cavalry so infinitely preferable.' Eventually, through lobbying his father, he obtained a permanent lieutenant-colonelcy in the 16th Light Dragoons, after receiving regular commissions for all the lower ranks over a space of three months. On 6 April 1797 he obtained command of the 7th Light Dragoons and over the next four years made it one of the finest regiments in the army. He distinguished himself in the disastrous 1799 campaign in Holland, where, in command of a brigade consisting of the 7th and 15th Light Dragoons, he routed a superior force of French cavalry. In 1802 he was promoted major-general and in 1808, after only fifteen years' service, lieutenant-general.

Later that year he was given command of the cavalry division in Sir John Moore's army in Portugal, joining Moore in late November after the latter had advanced to Salamanca to threaten the French lines of communication. When the advance continued, Paget was sent ahead towards Sahagun with the 10th and 15th Hussars. Arriving there before daylight he found it occupied by the French, so, leaving the 10th to advance upon the town, he led the 15th round to its rear to cut off the enemy's retreat. However, the alarm was given and Paget found himself confronted by 600 dragoons. Though the 15th only mustered 400 sabres and the 10th had not yet come up, Paget immediately charged, routing the dragoons and taking 167 prisoners. Moore called the action 'a handsome thing and well done'. Two days later Moore learned that Napoleon himself was advancing upon him from Madrid so, rather than risk the loss of the only army England had in the field, he ordered a retreat. During the terrible retreat to Corunna Paget earned high praise for his handling of the cavalry, which kept the French horse from the heels of the infantry, particularly with a dashing charge at Benavente on 29 December.

Paget was not to serve in the Peninsula again, for, shortly after his return from Corunna, he chose to desert his wife and elope with Lady Charlotte Wellesley, Wellington's sister-in-law. With Wellington now in command in Portugal, there was no place for Paget in his army. Though given an infantry division in the Walcheren Expedition, his undoubted talents as a cavalry leader were wasted until 1815.

He succeeded his father in 1812 and on 2 January 1815 was made G.C.B. In the spring he was appointed to command all the cavalry and horse artillery of the army Wellington was then assembling in Flanders, following Napoleon's return from Elba. On 17 June he covered, with his cavalry, the withdrawal from Quatre Bras to Waterloo, bringing the French advance guard to a halt at Genappe by his handling of his own regiment, the 7th, now hussars, and two squadrons of the 1st Life Guards, supported by horse artillery.

At Waterloo he ordered the Union Brigade to charge D'Erlon's corps when it attacked the British left. He himself led forward the Household Cavalry against Milhaud's cuirassiers, but was unable to prevent them or the Union Brigade from charging too far. He went back to bring forward his second line to cover the retirement of the heavy cavalry, but it was too far to the rear and the heavies, though successful in their charge, suffered severe casualties. In the closing stages of the battle he was wounded in the knee and his leg had to be amputated.

On 4 July 1815 he was created Marquess of Anglesey and in 1818 was made a Knight of the Garter. In later life he served as Master-General of the Ordnance and proved a very popular Lord-Lieutenant of Ireland. He was promoted field-marshal in 1846 and died in 1854, aged eighty-six.

Thomas Graham

Graham was unique among Wellington's commanders in that he did not begin his military career until middle age. He was born on 19 October 1748, the third son of Thomas Graham, Laird of Balgowan in Perthshire, and was educated privately and at Christ Church, Oxford. In 1774 he married Lord Cathcart's beautiful daughter, Mary, who was subsequently painted four times by Gainsborough. The couple lived abroad for some

years on account of Mrs Graham's poor health, but on returning home he purchased an estate in Perthshire to which, being a keen agriculturalist and sportsman, he devoted close attention. In 1790 they again went abroad, but Mrs Graham died in southern France in 1792. When Graham was bringing her body home for burial, the coffin was opened at Toulouse by revolutionary officials in search of contraband. Appalled by this incident, Graham decided to devote his life to fighting the excesses of the French Revolution.

In July 1793 he got himself attached as unofficial ADC to Lord Mulgrave during the operations at Toulon, and on his return home he raised, at his own expense, the 90th Foot. For this he was granted a temporary lieutenant-colonelcy on 10 February 1794. He served with his regiment during the Quiberon Bay expedition and in 1796 was appointed British Military Commissioner to the Austrian Army in Italy. Besieged with Wurmser in Mantua, he escaped in a snowstorm, taking news of the garrison's plight to the Austrian headquarters. From 1798 he served in the Mediterranean until the Peace of Amiens. He accompanied Moore to Sweden in 1808 and to Spain, where he was present

Lieutenant-General of Cavalry, c. 1812. The hat bore a gilt star loop, not visible in the illustration. After Hamilton Smith. (National Army Museum)

at the latter's death at Corunna. Though he had tried for some years to have his military rank made permanent, it was only as a result of Moore's dying request that this was granted, with seniority from the date of his temporary lieutenant-colonelcy in 1794.

Now aged fifty, he was officially promoted major-general and commanded a brigade at Walcheren, but had to be invalided home. In 1810 he was sent to command the garrison at Cadiz with the rank of lieutenant-general. From here, in February 1811, he launched an attack against the rear of the French force blockading him, and a month later won a victory at Barrosa. In June he joined Wellington's main army and was given the 1st Division. To this command were added the 6th and 7th Divisions, thus forming a corps, with which he provided part of the covering force for the final siege and capture of Badajoz the following January. During the advance to Salamanca he commanded the same force with two brigades of cavalry added, but an eye infection forced his return to England twelve days before the battle of 22 July.

He was back in the Peninsula by early 1813 in time for the Vittoria campaign. Wellington sent Graham with a corps of 20,000, including the 1st and 5th Divisions, two Portuguese brigades and a Spanish force, on a wide sweep round the French army at Vittoria to cut the main road to France in their rear. This manoeuvre, which was to prove fatal to French morale, was completely successful and, after blocking the road, Graham attacked the French from the rear as Wellington broke through the centre. Only the mass of plunder left by the French, which distracted Wellington's troops from pursuit, enabled the remains of King Joseph's army to escape by side roads.

After Vittoria Graham was sent on after the French rearguards towards St Sebastian, round which he threw a blockade on 28 June. While the rest of the army engaged Soult in the Pyrenees, Graham besieged St Sebastian with the 5th Division and a Portuguese brigade, but it was not until September, when Wellington was able to release further troops after defeating Soult, that the town fell. The success of the final assault was largely due to Graham's bold decision, unusual at that time, to order his artillery to fire over the heads of the attacking infantry. Graham commanded the left wing at the crossing of the Bidassoa, but his recurring eye trouble and failing health compelled him to hand over to Sir John Hope.

He took the field again in November when he was sent with a force to capture Antwerp in conjunction with the Prussians, but his failure to take Bergen-op-Zoom in February 1814 was an unhappy end to an otherwise distinguished military career.

Graham was greatly respected by all ranks and his popularity rivalled Hill's in the Peninsular army. He had been made a Knight of the Bath in March 1812, and in May 1814 was created Baron Lynedoch of Balgowan, subsequently receiving the G.C.B. and G.C.M.G. In later life he founded the United Services Club as a meeting place for officers and devoted himself to agriculture, sport and politics, until he died at the great age of ninety-five on 18 December 1843.

Edward Paget

A younger brother of Henry Paget, Edward was born on 3 November 1775 and educated at Westminster. Receiving a cornetcy in the Life Guards in March 1792, nine months later he was a captain in the 54th Foot and by April 1794, at the age of only eighteen, he was lieutenant-colonel commanding the 28th Foot. Despite his youth, he had a flair for command and led his regiment with great confidence in the Flanders campaign of 1794–95. His elder brother wrote of him: 'I am told he has a very fine Regiment and is everything he ought to be'. In 1797 he was at the Battle of Cape St Vincent and the following year was made a colonel in the army and an ADC to the King. He fought throughout the Egyptian campaign of 1801, being wounded at the Battle of Alexandria, where the 28th particularly distinguished themselves under his leadership. In October 1803 he was made a brigadier-general and, on 1 January 1805, a major-general.

From 1806 he served in the Mediterranean and in January 1808 went with Moore's expedition to Sweden in command of the Reserve, the picked troops of the army. Later that year he was in the

The capture of Sir Edward Paget by French cavalry, 1812, when he was a lieutenant-general and second-in-command to Wellington. After Atkinson. (National Army Museum)

Corunna campaign, commanding the rearguard with great skill during the retreat. At the Battle of Corunna his handling of his brigade was responsible for the defeat of Soult's flank attack against the British right. He was a handsome man with a commanding presence and Blakeney of the 28th said that when Paget 'gave an order, there was something peculiar in his glance, impressive in his tone of voice, and decisive in his manner. The order was clear. The execution must be prompt'.

Under Wellington he was promoted local lieutenant-general and commanded the left wing of the army during the advance from Coimbra to Oporto in 1809. He led the attack across the Douro above Oporto on 12 May, and held the seminary against French counter-attacks with only 600 men while the main force crossed, being wounded in the arm, which had to be amputated.

He had to return to England to recover from this wound, thus missing the campaigns of 1810–11. He was made lieutenant-general in the army on 4 June 1811, now aged thirty-five, and received the K.B. on 12 June 1812. In the autumn of that year he

returned to the Peninsula as Wellington's second-in-command, but, during the retreat of the army from Burgos, while trying to close a gap between the 5th and 7th Divisions, he was surprised by three French cavalrymen on 17 November. Being unable to defend himself with only one arm and escorted by a single Spanish orderly, he was taken prisoner. His capture lost to the army a brave and talented commander, whose only defect was shortsightedness, which Wellington believed 'was the immediate cause of his being taken'.

In January 1815 he was made G.C.B. but took no part in the Waterloo campaign. In 1822 he went out to India as Commander-in-Chief and was responsible for the operations of the Burma War of 1824–25. In 1825 he was promoted general and subsequently became Governor of Chelsea Hospital, a post he held until his death on 13 May 1849. With his brilliant early career and his undoubted competence, Edward Paget should have become

John Gaspard Le Marchant (1766–1812) in light dragoon uniform. He served in the 16th, 29th and 7th Light Dragoons and the 2nd Dragoon Guards. Founder and Lieutenant-Governor of the Royal Military College, 1801–10. Major-general, 1810. Commanded the heavy cavalry brigade in the Peninsula from 1810 until his death in action at Salamanca. Author of a number of books on military subjects. (National Army Museum)

Sir Stapleton Cotton, later Viscount Combermere, in the uniform of a general officer of hussars. After Heaphy. (National Portrait Gallery)

one of Wellington's most distinguished commanders, but the wound he received at Oporto and his capture prevented him from achieving the fame which otherwise should have attended him.

Stapleton Cotton

Born on 14 November 1773, the second son of Sir Robert Cotton, Bt., Stapleton Cotton was educated at Westminster and a military academy in London, receiving his first commission in the 23rd Royal Welch Fusiliers in 1790. He transferred to the cavalry, in which he was to make his name, as captain in the 6th Dragoons in 1793, serving in the Flanders campaign of 1793–94. At the age of twenty he obtained the lieutenant-colonelcy of the 25th Light Dragoons, which he commanded at the Cape and in the Seringapatam campaign in India in 1799, where he first met Wellington. Transferring to the 16th Light Dragoons in 1800, he was promoted colonel the same year and major-general five years later. In 1808 he commanded a brigade of the 14th and 16th Light Dragoons on the Portuguese frontier during the Corunna campaign and

later at Oporto and Talavera.

Having become his father's heir on the death of his elder brother in 1800, he succeeded to the title in January 1810 and had to go home on family business. Despite these new responsibilities, he chose to return to the Peninsula and, as a local lieutenant-general, was given command of all Wellington's cavalry. In this capacity he covered the retreat to the Lines of Torres Vedras without, it is said, losing a single baggage wagon.

Until 1813 Wellington was always weak in cavalry and those regiments he had were seldom used in mass, as was the French practice, so purely cavalry encounters were few. However, in April 1812, Cotton, having been promoted lieutenant-general in the army in January, fought a well-organized little battle at Llerena with two brigades against Soult's rearguard cavalry, forcing the French marshal to withdraw. Just before Salamanca he was in command of Wellington's rearguard, and his handling of this force, consisting of the 14th Light Dragoons and the 4th and Light Divisions, in the face of Marmont's army which had suddenly changed direction on 18 July, enabled Wellington to regroup his forces successfully. At Salamanca itself the decisive cavalry charge against Maucune's division, led by Le Marchant's heavy brigade, inspired Wellington to exclaim: 'By God, Cotton, I never saw anything so beautiful in my life; the day is *yours*'.

Cotton was wounded in the right arm by a shot from a Portuguese picquet after Salamanca and had to go home, where he was awarded the Order of the Bath. He returned to the army in 1813 three days after Vittoria and commanded the cavalry all through the closing stages of the Peninsular War.

Cotton was an excellent horseman and was noted for the magnificent appearance of his uniform and horse furniture, which was reputed to be worth 500 guineas. He was brave, and was known as the 'Lion d'Or'. Despite his own love of finery, he had a keen eye for serviceability rather than mere smartness among his cavalrymen, and he never tired men or

Rowland Hill

Sir Rowland Hill, later Viscount Hill, in the undress uniform of a lieutenant-general, 1819. After Dawe. (National Army Museum)

Of all Wellington's senior officers, Hill was not only the most dependable, he was also the most popular with all ranks. Born on 11 August 1772, the second son of a Shropshire gentleman, he joined the army in 1790 as an ensign in the 38th Foot, transferring to the 53rd a year later but spending two years at the military school in Strasbourg. In 1793 he earned 'golden opinions' while serving as an ADC at the siege of Toulon, where he was noticed by Graham, who had him appointed to a majority in the latter's new regiment, the 90th. In May 1794 he became lieutenant-colonel in the 90th, which he made into a fine regiment, and commanded it during the Egyptian campaign of 1801. By 1805 he was a major-general commanding a brigade in the Hanover expedition, and three years later he was present at the first British victories in the Peninsula, Rolica and Vimiero. He led a brigade in the Corunna campaign and also, after returning to Portugal, during the Oporto operations of 1809. Later that year he was given the 2nd Division, with which he held the important Cerro de Medellin feature at Talavera.

During 1810 Wellington entrusted him with the independent command of a small corps in defence of the Portuguese frontier between the Rivers Gaudiana and Tagus. This, in view of Wellington's preference for keeping a tight control over his subordinates, shows the faith the commander had in Hill's reliability. In the winter he had to go home with malaria, handing over his command to Beresford, under whom it suffered heavily at Albuera. Hill returned in May and was ordered to take command of the force in Estramadura, 10,000 strong including the 2nd and 4th Divisions, watching Wellington's right flank as he besieged Badajoz. After the main army began the blockade of Ciudad Rodrigo in August, Hill made a masterly surprise attack at Arroyo dos Molinos, completely routing the force opposing him and taking 1,300 prisoners for the loss of only 7 killed and 64 wounded.

On 1 January 1812 he was promoted lieutenant-general and two months later was admitted to the Order of the Bath. His corps and Graham's formed the covering force in southern and eastern Estra-

horses unnecessarily. His ability as a cavalry commander has been accorded mixed judgements, but Wellington thought 'he commands our cavalry very well'.

In 1814 he was raised to the peerage as Baron Combermere. Although Wellington hoped to have him commanding the cavalry for the Waterloo campaign, the post went to Uxbridge, but Cotton joined the army in Paris, where he commanded the cavalry of the army of occupation.

After serving consecutively as Governor of Barbados and Commander-in-Chief in Ireland, he was appointed to the chief command in India from 1825–30, where he led the successful operations against the Jats, culminating in the taking of the great fortress of Bhurtpore. He became a viscount in 1827 and a field-marshal in 1855. He spent the last thirty years of his life attending to his estates and parliamentary duties until he died on 21 February 1865, aged ninety-one.

madura while Wellington began the final siege of Badajoz, and in May he conducted another fine operation which resulted in the destruction of the French forts and bridge at Almaraz. When the Salamanca campaign began, Hill was again left to protect the rear of the main army against any attack from Soult in Andalusia and later, when Wellington was at Burgos, he carried out the same protective role against three French armies.

Throughout the final campaigns of 1813–14 Hill commanded a corps the strength of which varied, but which included British, Spanish and Portuguese divisions with, as its permanent backbone, his old 2nd Division. He began the attack on the right at Vittoria; he prevented any relief of, or break out from, Pamplona during Soult's counter-offensive at Sorauren; and of St Pierre, near Bayonne, where he was attacked by Soult with a force twice his strength, Wellington said that he, Hill, had given the French 'the soundest thrashing they had ever had'. St Pierre was said to be only the second occasion when Hill had been heard to swear! Intelligent, energetic, ever thoughtful and considerate for the needs of his men, he was above all entirely trustworthy, and Wellington always knew that any task given to Hill would be planned and carried out with care, foresight and drive. No man, be he exhausted British private, wounded French prisoner, or dispossessed Spanish peasant, was beneath Hill's charitable attentions, and it is little wonder that he was known affectionately by his troops as 'Daddy Hill'.

After the Peninsular War he was created Baron Hill of Almaraz and Hardwicke. As soon as news of Napoleon's escape from Elba reached London, he was sent to Brussels to supervise the preparations made for war by the young Prince of Orange. For the Waterloo campaign he was given a corps consisting of the 2nd and 4th Divisions and various allied formations. In the closing stages of the battle he rode to the head of Adam's brigade (52nd, 71st and 95th) to lead the counter-attack on the Imperial Guard. His horse was shot and, seeing him fall, his staff thought he had been killed, but found that he was only severely concussed.

Hill accompanied the army to Paris and served as second-in-command of the army of occupation until 1818. Thereafter he retired to his estate in Shropshire and, refusing all important offices

Sir Edward Barnes (1776–1838). Staff officer in the Peninsula, 1812. Major-General, 1813. Commanded a brigade at Vittoria, Pyrenees, Nivelle, Nive and Orthes. Appointed Adjutant-General for the Waterloo campaign and severely wounded on 18 June 1815. After Heaphy. (National Portrait Gallery)

offered to him, devoted himself to the pursuits of the country gentleman, the best type of which he so clearly typified. When Wellington became Prime Minister in 1828, he accepted the post of Commander-in-Chief of the Army, which he held for fourteen years. He was made a general in 1825, a viscount in 1842 and died on 10 December of that year.

William Beresford

Beresford was born on 2 October 1768, the illegitimate son of the Earl of Tyrone, later the first Marquess of Waterford, a nobleman from whom he was never to lack patronage. He was sent to the military school at Strasbourg and in August 1785 was given an ensigncy in the 6th Foot. By 1793 he was captain in the 69th, then serving as marines aboard the Mediterranean fleet, and, after the siege of Toulon, he first attracted attention during operations in Corsica, for which he was granted a brevet-majority. He was promoted lieutenant-

Sir William Beresford, later Viscount Beresford, in the uniform of a marshal of the Portuguese army. After Lawrence. (National Army Museum)

officers. With the aid of a few British officers, he set about converting what was little more than an unwieldy, chaotic rabble into a small disciplined force. Many of the existing officers he sacked as worthless, replacing them by younger men of ability, rather than position; the conscription laws were rigidly enforced, deserters were shot, and the best material was all grouped into the regiments singled out for the field army, while the remainder was formed into a militia. Picked men were chosen to form the *Caçador* battalions. Infringements of the stern discipline he imposed were ruthlessly punished but good conduct was suitably rewarded. Many of his measures earned him enormous unpopularity in Portugal, but within a year the effectiveness of his endeavours began to be demonstrated by the performance of Portuguese regiments at Busaco.

He held no field command with the Portuguese Army, his task being organization, administration and training, and in any case, although some Portuguese divisions were formed, Wellington was convinced that they were best employed in separate brigades incorporated into British divisions. Beresford's first big command in the field, that of Hill's corps during the latter's absence in England, was an unhappy experience and resulted in the bloody and ill-fought Battle of Albuera in 1811, where his inept handling of his force was redeemed by the gallantry of the British infantry. Thereafter he returned to his work with the Portuguese and, though he was present with the main army in the 1812 campaign and was wounded at Salamanca, he held no command and merely exercised a general supervision over the Portuguese troops.

After continuing in much the same capacity during the Battles of Vittoria and the Pyrenees, he was given the occasional command of a corps during the fighting in southern France, but always under Wellington's close watch. Following the Battle of Orthes, he was sent with a force of just over two divisions to support a royalist uprising in Bordeaux, but as no opposition was encountered,

colonel in August 1794, taking the 88th Foot to India in 1799 and commanding it during the Egyptian expedition. As a brigade commander he took part in the recapture of the Cape of Good Hope in 1806, and later the same year took Buenos Aires with only two battalions. However, he was not reinforced and, following a mass uprising, he was compelled to surrender after some hard fighting. Whitelocke's expedition failed to relieve him and Beresford remained in prison for six months, until he escaped and returned to England. At the end of 1807 he was sent to occupy Madeira, where he learned Portuguese, which was to stand him in good stead later on.

He was promoted major-general in April 1808 and, after fighting in the Corunna campaign, was given the task of reorganizing the Portuguese Army with the rank of marshal and local lieutenant-general in the British army in Portugal, a step which placed him above several more senior

Sir Denis Pack (1772–1823) in the embroidered uniform of a major-general, with lapels buttoned back. Commanded 71st Foot at Rolica and Vimiero, 1808, and a Portuguese brigade from 1810–13. Major-General, 1813. Commanded a British brigade in the 6th Division from 1813–14 and the Division itself at Sorauren. Eight wounds in the Peninsula. At Waterloo in command of a brigade in the 5th Division and again wounded. (National Army Museum)

19

Wellington and staff officers at the Battle of Fuentes d'Onoro, 1811. Note the party of light infantry escorting two French officer prisoners into headquarters. After Major St Clair (detail). (National Army Museum)

Thomas Picton

his competence was not greatly tested. At Toulouse Wellington ordered him to turn the French flank with the 4th and 6th Divisions, a task he completed with energy and efficiency.

Beresford was a man of great height and strength—his one-armed feat of unhorsing the Polish lancer at Albuera is famous—and his discoloured left eye, injured in a shooting accident, gave him a somewhat disconcerting appearance. Despite his failure in independent command, Wellington seems to have thought highly of him, saying he was the man with 'the largest view' among general officers, and that since only Beresford would know how to feed an army, he was Wellington's most suitable successor.

After the Peninsular War he was made a baron and returned to Portugal, where he stayed until he left for England in 1822 to go into politics. He became a viscount in 1823, a general in 1825 and served in Wellington's first cabinet in 1828. He died on 8 January 1854.

Born in 1758, the son of a Welsh country gentleman, Picton received an ensigncy in the 12th Foot at the age of thirteen. After reaching the rank of captain seven years later, he was placed on half-pay for the next twelve years and spent his time in Pembrokeshire studying his profession. In 1794, still without employment, he sailed on his own initiative for the West Indies where he was taken on the staff of the general in command. He stayed there until 1803, proving his ability as a soldier and reaching the rank of lieutenant-colonel, but his robust and vigorous rule as Governor of Trinidad brought him to trial on charges of cruelty in 1806. He was found guilty but was cleared at a second trial.

In 1808 he was promoted major-general and two years later was appointed to the 3rd Division in Portugal. He commanded this division throughout the Peninsular War except for a short break when wounded, showing himself to be a stern disciplinarian and a courageous, determined and farsighted commander. Too cold and blunt ever to be loved like Hill, he was always respected and made the 3rd Division one of the finest fighting formations in the army.

His first major action was Busaco in 1810, when his strong, tough personality and speed of decision defeated a major French attack. When Wellington advanced from the Lines of Torres Vedras in 1811 in pursuit of Massena, Picton's division played an important part in the operations, culminating in the Battle of Fuentes d'Onoro. In September Picton again displayed his skill and coolness in action when his division was attacked on the march at El Bodon by fifteen squadrons of cavalry, supported by horse artillery. Rather than halt the whole division and form square, he continued the march, protecting his flanks and rear by a series of leap-frogging battalion squares.

He was made a local lieutenant-general at this time, a rank which was confirmed in June 1813. In January 1812 he led the 3rd Division to the assault of Ciudad Rodrigo, storming the main breach, while the Light Division attacked the other. Wellington wrote: 'The conduct of the 3rd Division in the operations which they performed with so much gallantry affords the strongest proof of the abilities of Lt-Gen Picton'. Two months later, at the fierce and bloody siege of Badajoz, Picton personally led the storming of the castle. Though wounded and lying disabled in a ditch, he continued to urge his men on with his great voice until victory was theirs.

He was invalided home, created a Knight of the Bath in February 1813, and returned to Spain in time for the great victory at Vittoria. Impatient with waiting for the 7th Division, with whom he was to advance, he led the 3rd to a surprise attack on the French right flank, roaring at his men: 'Come on ye damned rascals, come on ye fighting villains!' Though he suffered nearly 2,000 casualties, he caused the collapse of the French right. On over the Pyrenees and into France he led his fighting division until the Battle of Toulouse concluded the campaign.

When the peerages were awarded after the war, for Picton, who was only a divisional commander, there was none, only the G.C.B. He said: 'If the coronet was lying at the crown of a breach, I should have as good a chance as any of them'. Neverthe-

Sir Thomas Picton in the pre-1812 uniform of a lieutenant-general with the lapels buttoned across and wearing the Star of the Order of the Bath, awarded in 1813. After Shee. (National Army Museum)

Picton's round hat and spurs. (National Army Museum)

Major-General of Infantry, c. 1812. Note the aiguillette which replaced the epaulettes in late 1811. Brigade-major in undress uniform in background. After Hamilton Smith. (National Army Museum)

less, when Wellington summoned him for the Waterloo campaign, he came, though he had a presentiment it would be his last. Now aged fifty-six and in command of the 5th Division, he fought the long and desperate day at Quatre Bras, defending the vital cross-roads against infantry and cavalry attacks. Though badly wounded in the ribs, he remained in command, holding his men together by dint of his powerful personality. He concealed his wound from all but his servant, who bound him up, and though in considerable pain the next day, he took up position with his division in the centre of the line near La Haye Sainte. When D'Erlon's corps attacked that sector, Picton kept his men out of sight below the ridge until the division opposing him was only forty yards away. Then he brought his men to their feet, fired a massive volley which

stopped the French infantry dead, and ordered them forward in the counter-attack, shouting: 'Charge! Hurrah! Hurrah!' A bullet struck him in the head and tumbled him dead from his saddle.

Galbraith Lowry Cole

Cole was born in Dublin on 1 May 1772, the second son of the first Earl of Enniskillen. He obtained a cornetcy in the 12th Light Dragoons in 1787, subsequently serving with various regiments and as ADC to Sir Charles Grey in the West Indies campaign of 1794, until he reached the rank of lieutenant-colonel in November of that year. He went through the Egyptian campaign as Military Secretary to Sir John Hely-Hutchinson, was made colonel in 1801, and in 1805 took command of the 27th Foot at Malta. He led this regiment in the Italian campaign of 1806, in which he was appointed to a brigade consisting of his own regiment and a composite battalion of grenadier companies, and acted as second-in-command to Sir John Stuart at the Battle of Maida.

Promoted major-general in 1808, he joined the Peninsular army the following year as commander of the 4th Division. At Busaco his division saw little action, but after Massena's withdrawal from before Torres Vedras, the 2nd and 4th Divisions were despatched under Beresford to besiege Badajoz. Hearing of Soult's approach, Beresford advanced to meet him, leaving Cole to cover his rear and destroy the accumulated siege material. Soult attacked Beresford at Albuera on 16 May 1811, Cole meanwhile having made a forced march by night to reach Albuera on the morning of the attack. At the critical moment of the battle, Cole, who had been in reserve, advanced on his own initiative to relieve Hoghton's hard-pressed brigade by attacking the French left. With his three Fusilier battalions and five Portuguese, he launched the famous and decisive counter-stroke which, though attacked by cavalry and infantry supported by artillery, swept the French from the field, but at heavy cost, Cole himself being among the wounded.

After going home in late 1811 to take his seat in the Commons as M.P. for Fermanagh, he rejoined

Sir Galbraith Lowry Cole in the uniform of a lieutenant-general, c. 1814. The badge round his neck and the lower star on the left breast are of the Portuguese Order of the Tower and Sword; the upper star is the Bath. The cross and ribbon is the Army Gold Cross awarded for service at four battles with clasps for further battles. After Lawrence. (National Army Museum)

facing vastly superior numbers at Roncesvalles in the Pyrenees. Like many of the divisional commanders, Cole found himself at a loss without Wellington's supervision and, though he fought a hard delaying action, he decided to withdraw to Sorauren, despite orders to the contrary. However, Wellington's arrival restored the situation and Cole redeemed himself in the following two days' fighting, in which two of his battalions, his old 27th and the 48th, made a magnificent counter-attack against four French battalions.

At the Battle of Nivelle the 4th Division carried the important fortified village of Sare, and at Orthes Cole attacked the village of St Boes, the key to the French position. A month later, at Toulouse, when the sudden flight of a Spanish division left a dangerous gap, the 4th and 6th Divisions stormed the commanding height of Calvinet, thus restoring the position.

If lacking the ability for an independent command, Cole was a popular and competent divisional commander, who was noted for his good nature and kindness to all ranks. Wellington, whose hospitality was always a little spartan, observed that the best dinners were to be had at Cole's headquarters.

In 1815 Wellington asked for him as a divisional commander, but, having only just married, Cole said he would join as soon as his honeymoon was over. However, Waterloo was fought before he could do so. He served with the army of occupation until 1818, and in later life, from 1828–33, was a popular and successful Governor of the Cape. He died on 4 October 1842.

Robert Craufurd

Born on 5 May 1764, the third son of a Scottish baronet, Craufurd received his first commission in 1779 as ensign in the 25th Foot. From 1783, as a captain on half-pay, he spent four years on the Continent studying the Prussian and other European armies. In 1787 he returned to England and transferred to the 75th Foot, a regiment newly raised for service in India against Tippoo Sahib. His superiors in the regiment being absent, the task of preparing it for war fell almost entirely on Craufurd as the senior captain, and he continued to

the army in time for Salamanca. The 4th Division was in the centre of the British line facing the French-held hills, the Arapiles. Supported on the left by Pack's Portuguese brigade, Cole attacked two French divisions, but, when Pack was thrown back, Cole's seven battalions became greatly outnumbered and outgunned. He had to retreat, but a crucial situation was saved by the 6th Division blocking the French counter-attack. Cole was again wounded but was able to rejoin his division in time to cover the retreat from Burgos.

In March 1813 he was invested with the Order of the Bath and in June promoted lieutenant-general. He continued in command of the 4th Division during the Vittoria campaign, and in July found himself detached from Wellington's command and

Robert Craufurd in the embroidered uniform of a major-general, c. 1812. (National Army Museum)

command it in the campaign against Tippoo, which lasted until 1792. He proved himself a stern disciplinarian and a most able commander in the field, but despite this and representations made by his brother on his behalf, the authorities were unwilling to grant him a majority. In 1793 he therefore resigned his commission, a step which lost him considerable seniority later. As a civilian, he joined his brother, who was British liaison officer with the Austrians in the Netherlands in 1793, thereafter obtaining commissions in two foreign regiments, Waldstein's and Hompesch's (later in British pay), between 1795 and 1797. He acted as British Military Attaché with the Austrians in Italy, subsequently being gazetted lieutenant-colonel in the 60th. After serving on the staff in the Irish Rebellion of 1798 and in Holland in 1799, he was sent to Switzerland to raise troops for British service. His study of his profession and his experience of foreign troops made him one of the best qualified officers in the army, but his advancement was slow, due, perhaps, to his violent temper.

In 1807, now a full colonel, he commanded a brigade of light troops during Whitelocke's hopeless expedition to Buenos Aires, and though compelled to surrender through no fault of his own, he established a reputation as a leader of light infantry. In late 1808 he joined Sir John Moore's army as commander of the brigade trained by Moore himself at Shorncliffe, the 43rd and 52nd Light Infantry and 95th Rifles. With this force Craufurd protected the rear of Moore's army during the initial stages of the retreat to Corunna. A rifleman wrote: 'General Craufurd was indeed one of the few men who was apparently created for command during such dreadful scenes as we were familiar with in this retreat. He seemed an iron man; nothing daunted him, nothing turned him from his purpose'.

Craufurd and his light brigade returned to the Peninsula later in 1809, joining the army just after Talavera, having made his celebrated forced march of forty-two miles in twenty-six hours. The brigade was immediately pushed forward on outpost duty and covered the subsequent retreat of the army to Portugal. Early in 1810 the Light Brigade was expanded into a division by the addition of two Portuguese *caçador* battalions and Craufurd, though still only a comparatively junior brigadier-general, was placed in command of it.

His finest achievement with the Light Division was his guarding of the forty-mile stretch of the River Agueda in north-east Portugal during the first five months of 1810, against a force six times his strength. His line was never pierced, his troops were never surprised, and the French were denied any intelligence of what was going on in Craufurd's rear. Sadly he marred this splendid record by choosing to engage Ney's entire corps on the wrong side of the River Coa in July 1810, thus disobeying his orders and risking his division. Nevertheless he held the bridge across the Coa and extricated his division with minimum loss.

He showed his best talents again at Busaco by a masterly delaying action against Ney's corps, followed by a decisive counter-stroke at precisely the right moment. He went home on leave in the winter of 1810, returning for Fuentes d'Onoro in May 1811, when the Light Division was sent out to rescue and cover the retreat of the almost sur-

Major-General Hill

RICHARD HOOK

A

Brigadier-General Craufurd

B

RICHARD HOOK

Major-General Picton

RICHARD HOOK

C

Major-General Lowry Cole

D

Lieutenant-General Beresford

RICHARD HOOK

Lieutenant-General Stapleton Cotton

F

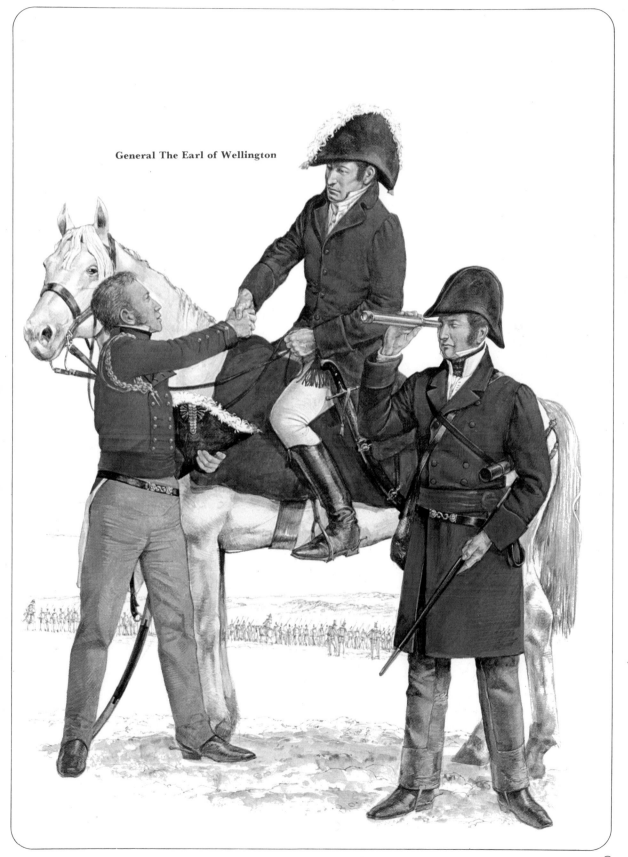

General The Earl of Wellington

Lieutenant-General The Earl of Uxbridge

H

RICHARD HOOK

rounded 7th Division. Craufurd carried out the task with great skill, and then withdrew his own men across two miles of open ground under constant attack by French cavalry with the loss of only fifty men. He was promoted major-general in June 1811. On 24 January 1812 the Light Division suffered a great loss when their commander died of his wounds received during the assault on the breach at Ciudad Rodrigo. A short, dark man with flashing eyes and fiery disposition, Craufurd made many enemies, never suffering fools gladly; but he also had his admirers, particularly among the rank and file, and he was, without doubt, one of Wellington's most brilliant officers.

Charles von Alten

Of a number of Hanoverians who achieved general officer's rank in Wellington's armies, probably the best known—and the only one to command a British, as opposed to a King's German Legion, formation—was Charles von Alten. A member of an ancient Protestant family, he was born on 12 October 1764, the youngest son of Baron Alten. Appointed to a commission in the Hanoverian Foot Guards in 1781, he fought in the Hanoverian service during the Duke of York's campaign in the Low Countries between 1793 and 1795. Here he made a name as a commander of light troops when in charge of a line of outposts along the River Lys.

After Napoleon's conquest of Hanover in 1803, its army was disbanded, but the officers and men were permitted to go where they chose. Many went to England to form the King's German Legion, a force of all arms which, in January 1805, included two light battalions. Command of these was given to Alten, who led them during Lord Cathcart's expedition to Hanover in November, and in the Copenhagen operations of 1807. He accompanied Sir John Moore to Sweden in 1808 and later to Spain, where his battalions formed the 2nd Flank Brigade of Paget's Reserve. He served at Walcheren in 1809 and, after being promoted major-general on 25 July 1810, returned to the Peninsula, where he commanded an independent K.G.L. brigade at Albuera. This brigade subsequently joined the newly formed 7th Division, which was commanded by Alten from October 1811.

Sir Charles von Alten, later Count von Alten, as a major-general, c. 1813. After Heaphy. (National Portrait Gallery)

After Craufurd was killed at Ciudad Rodrigo in 1812, the Light Division was temporarily under Barnard, one of its brigadiers, and then Vandeleur, but on 2 May this important and élite formation was given to Alten, who was to command it until the end of the Peninsular War. Though lacking Craufurd's brilliance, he was a competent and conscientious officer who, unlike Craufurd, could be relied upon to obey Wellington's orders implicitly. Under him the Light Division maintained the very high standard it had achieved previously, both in the performance of outpost duties and on the field of battle. It led the advance to Salamanca in mid-1812, and in 1813, with the 4th Division, it formed the right centre of the British attack at Vittoria, quickly carrying its objectives. In these operations Alten was working under Wellington's eye, but during the battles in the Pyrenees he was on his own and, despite a great feat of marching and counter-marching for nineteen consecutive hours over mountain tracks, culminating in a brisk engagement, he just failed to cut off Soult's retreat

25

from Sorauren at the Yanci bridge. At the Battle of Vera on 7 October 1813, fought in support of the crossing of the Bidassoa, Alten led his division in a very rapid attack up the Great Rhune. A month later, at the Nivelle, he made another fine attack on the Lesser Rhune, rolling up the French defences from a flank of this very rugged feature. At the Nive, he was attacked by four French divisions, but made an orderly retreat to a stronger position in rear, where he held firm. Wellington thought the Light Division under Alten was 'the flower of the army, the finest infantry in the world', and when the Peninsular army broke up, Alten was presented with a sword of honour subscribed for by the officers of the division as a mark of their respect. He was made a K.C.B. on 2 January 1815.

In the Waterloo campaign Alten was given the 3rd Division of three brigades, one British (C. Halkett), one K.G.L. (Ompteda), and one Han-

overian (Kielmansegge). After fighting at Quatre Bras, his division was placed in the right centre of Wellington's line, just behind La Haye Sainte. Though he held this position throughout the day, he made one bad mistake by ordering two of Ompteda's battalions to counter-attack in line in the presence of French cavalry, just after the loss of La Haye Sainte. They were badly cut up, and Alten himself was severely wounded and had to leave the field.

He was made a count after Waterloo and, when the K.G.L. was disbanded in 1816, was given command of the Hanoverian contingent of the Allied army of occupation in Paris. In 1818 he returned to Hanover as Minister of War and

Wellington and ADCs in the Pyrenees, 1813. The soldier behind the horse possibly represents his orderly, Corporal Baeckefeld, 1st Hussars, King's German Legion. After Atkinson. (National Army Museum)

Foreign Affairs, and Inspector-General of the Hanoverian Army, in which he became a field-marshal. He was made a G.C.B. on 12 August 1820 and died in the Tyrol on 20 April 1840.

Edward Pakenham

Born in 1778, the second son of Baron Longford, Pakenham entered the army at the age of sixteen. He served as a major in the 23rd Light Dragoons in the Irish Rebellion of 1798, obtaining the lieutenant-colonelcy of the 64th Foot a year later and serving with that regiment in campaigns in the West Indies from 1801–03. He exchanged to the 7th Royal Fusiliers in 1805, and commanded its first battalion at Copenhagen in 1807 and in Martinique in 1809. Later that year he joined the Peninsular army as a staff officer, soon becoming Deputy-Adjutant-General at Wellington's headquarters.

At Busaco he commanded a brigade of the 1st Division, later transferring to the 4th Division but retaining his brigade until January 1811. He then reverted to the staff but took over the brigade again later in the year. He was made a local major-general in 1811 and received that rank in the army a year after.

When Picton was wounded at Badajoz, Pakenham took over the 3rd Division. At Salamanca he was ordered by Wellington to attack the leading division of Marmont's army, while the other divisions attacked the French in flank. This Pakenham did brilliantly, completely routing Thomières' division and pressing on to drive back the next. After the battle Wellington wrote of him: 'He made the movement with a celerity and accuracy which I doubt if there are very many capable, and without both it would not have answered its end. Pakenham may not be the brightest genius but my partiality for him does not lead me astray when I tell you that he is one of the best we have'.

Pakenham remained in command of the 3rd

Division until the end of the year, and early in 1813 was given the 6th Division. He was appointed Wellington's Adjutant-General in June, but had to take over the 6th again in the closing stages of the Battle of Sorauren, when its temporary commander, Pack, was wounded. In the final attack on 30 July Pakenham led his division in the assault on the village of Sorauren itself and, notwithstanding its heavy fortifications, he inflicted heavy losses on the French division opposing him, which ceased to exist as an effective force. In September he was made a Knight of the Bath. He returned to his post of Adjutant-General in August and continued in that capacity until the end of the Peninsular War.

Pakenham himself disliked staff work, referring to it as 'this insignificant clerking business', and much preferred being in command of troops. Nevertheless he performed the duties of Adjutant-General effectively and to Wellington's great satisfaction. He enjoyed a good and close relationship with his chief, being not only devoted to him but also his brother-in-law.

In the closing stages of the war with America (1812–15) Pakenham was appointed to the command, after his predecessor, Ross, was killed at Bladensburg. Arriving in December 1814, he found his troops had been landed in a most unsatisfactory position before New Orleans. Unable to rectify this deployment, he ordered an unimaginative assault for 8 January 1815. It was beaten back with disastrous loss and Pakenham himself was killed. Four days before his death he had been made a G.C.B.

George Murray

Murray differed from the other generals in this book in that the whole of his service under Wellington's command was spent on the staff, rather than in command of troops. He became Wellington's most trusted staff officer and developed a very close working relationship with his chief.

He was born in 1772, the second son of a Scottish baronet, Sir William Murray of Ochtertyre, and was educated at the High School and University of Edinburgh. His military career started as an ensign in the 71st Foot in 1789, transferring to the 3rd Foot

Sir Edward Pakenham in the embroidered uniform of a lieutenant-general, c. 1814. After Heaphy. (National Army Museum)

Guards in 1790. He served with his regiment in Flanders from 1793–95 and received his first staff appointment in 1796 as ADC to Major-General Campbell in the expedition to Quiberon Bay. He was on the Quartermaster-General's staff in the Netherlands in 1799 and was wounded. After going through the Egyptian campaign in the same capacity, he attended a course of study at the Senior Department at the Royal Military College at High Wycombe, and afterwards went as Adjutant-General to the West Indies. He returned to the Quartermaster-General's department for the expeditions to Hanover and Copenhagen. In 1808 he was appointed Quartermaster-General to Moore's Swedish expedition and subsequently accompanied Moore in the Corunna campaign.

In March 1809, by now a brevet-colonel, he became Wellington's Quartermaster-General in the Peninsula, a post he continued to hold, except for a gap in 1812, until the end of the war. He was promoted brigadier-general on 4 June 1811 and major-general on 1 January 1812.

Murray was ideally suited to this work. He was calm, methodical, well-mannered, with an excellent memory, an aptitude for history and geography, and had behind him staff experience in all the most important campaigns of the French wars. He was both quick and accurate in interpreting Wellington's wishes and transmitting his orders to the component parts of the army. Wellington exercised very close supervision over his army, much closer than many commanders, and though he trusted Murray completely and had him constantly in attendance, listening to his views and recommendations, he allowed him only limited powers of decision. Nevertheless, he relied on him greatly, and when, in 1812, Murray applied to go home for private reasons, Wellington wrote: 'I acknowledge that when I first heard of your intention to quit us, my sentiments were not confined to concern and regret.' After the Peninsular War, he pronounced Murray to be 'a very able man and an admirable Quartermaster-General'. One of the most valuable of Murray's many duties was his control of a network of agents and observing officers, who provided intelligence about the enemy and topography. For his work Murray was made a Knight of the Bath.

At the end of 1814 he was appointed to the staff of

Sir George Murray as a major-general, c. 1813. After Heaphy. (National Portrait Gallery)

the army in America with the local rank of lieutenant-general. When Napoleon escaped from Elba he was recalled to Europe, and though arriving too late for Waterloo, was subsequently Chief of Staff to the Allied army of occupation and Quartermaster-General of the British contingent, a post he held until 1818.

In later life he acted as Governor of the Royal Military College at Sandhurst (1819–24), Lieutenant-General of the Ordnance (1824), Commander-in-Chief in Ireland (1825–28), Colonial Secretary and a Privy Councillor (1828–30), and twice as Master-General of the Ordnance (1834–35 and 1841–46). He also served as M.P. for Perthshire. He became a general in 1841 and died in 1846.

The Plates

The Uniform of General and Staff Officers

The uniform for general officers according to the Clothing Regulations in force in 1802 was as follows. The black cocked hat, increasingly worn fore-and-aft instead of athwart, had a black cockade and a gilt scale loop with button, surmounted by a white feather with red at the base. At each corner were crimson and gold tassels. Their scarlet coats had blue patches at either end of the collar, small indented blue cuffs, and blue lapels down to the waist which could either be buttoned back to show the blue and fastened in front with hooks and eyes or buttoned across the body making the coat double-breasted. The long skirts were lined with white cassimere and hooked back, being fastened at the bottom with a gold-embroidered scarlet ornament. There was a gilt button on the blue collar patches, nine or ten down each lapel, three or four set vertically on each skirt and cuff, and two at the back at hip level. Generals had their buttons at equal distances, lieutenant-generals in threes, major-generals and brigadier-generals in pairs, except the latter had their skirt and cuff buttons set two over one. On each shoulder was worn an epaulette of gold embroidery on scarlet cloth with gold bullion fringe. There were two types of coat: the embroidered version, which had gold-embroidered loops on all the buttonholes, including the collar, cuffs and skirts, and the plain or undress coat which was without embroidery, but normally had the buttonholes marked by loops of narrow twist the same colour as the cloth.

White cloth or cassimere breeches with black-topped boots were to be worn with either coat, and the dress was completed by a crimson sash worn round the waist with the knot and ends at the left side. The sword was suspended by a white waist belt with slings and fastened by a snake clasp between two lions' heads.

Following a General Order dated 24 December 1811, certain alterations were made which will be noted in the relevant plate notes.

Senior staff officers wore the same uniform as general officers but with silver lace. The uniform of Adjutant- and Quartermaster-Generals corresponded to that of a lieutenant-general, and Deputy AGs and QMGs to a major-general. Assistant and Deputy Assistant AGs and QMGs, Brigade-Majors and ADCs had single-breasted coats without lapels and with all-blue collars, ADCs having gold lace embroidery, the others silver.

In the field, following the example of Wellington himself, the dress of generals and staff officers often diverged from that prescribed by regulations, and some examples will be found in the individual plates.

(Readers requiring further details are directed to the *Journal of the Society for Army Historical Research*, Vol. XIX, p. 200, Vol. XXII, p. 339, Vol. XXXI, pp. 64 and 96.)

A Major-General Hill

This plate shows Hill at Talavera on the evening of 27 July 1809, just before the French made a surprise

General and field officers' Army Gold Medal for distinguished service, 1810–13. This example was awarded for an action in the East Indies. The ribbon was crimson, edged blue. (National Army Museum)

attack on the Cerro de Medellin hill, held by his division, when, in his own words, he 'was with the 48th Regiment in conversation with Colonel Donellan'. It also illustrates his never-failing kindness to ordinary soldiers, in this case Donellan's orderly drummer. Hill's 2nd Division contained two battalions of the 48th, which played a prominent part in the battle, and Donellan's counter-attack on the 28th earned Wellington's commendation that 'the battle was certainly saved by the advance, position and steady conduct of the 48th Regiment'.

Hill wears the embroidered coat of a major-general with the lapels buttoned across except at the top, showing the gold embroidery on the buttonholes. Dark tight-fitting pantaloons and hessian boots are worn in preference to the regulation lower garments. According to the 1802 Regulations, generals were to have a straight sword of the 1796 infantry pattern, although another type with a gilt boat-shell, similar to the heavy cavalry officers' 1796 sword, was also used. In 1803 a new pattern with a lion's head pommel was introduced for general officers, but the former types continued to be carried, and many officers, particularly those like Hill who had served in Egypt, preferred the mameluke sabre.

Lieutenant-Colonel Donellan of the 1st/48th, though an efficient and much-loved commanding officer, indulged in certain eccentricities of appearance, which gave him the nickname of 'the last of the powderers'. Though the practice of powdering the hair had been abolished in 1795 and the queue discontinued in 1808, Donellan ignored both changes and was also well known for his habit of wearing the cocked hat, breeches and top boots in the fashion of the previous decade. In accordance with the regulations for regiments with buff facings, his breeches and sword belt are of that colour and, as a field officer, he wears epaulettes on both shoulders. The lapels of his coat are buttoned across. He was mortally wounded at Talavera while leading his battalion to the attack.

His orderly drummer wears a shako instead of the full dress bearskin cap and his jacket is in reversed colours as authorized for drummers. His breeches are covered by white overalls and he is armed with a short sword with a twenty-four-inch blade.

B Brigadier-General Craufurd

Craufurd is represented here shortly after taking command of the newly formed Light Division in early 1810, discussing outpost positions along the River Agueda with officers of the 95th Rifles and Ross's Troop, Royal Horse Artillery. The Rifles performed for the Light Division what the Division performed for the Peninsular army and were highly skilled at outpost duties, earning a special commendation from Craufurd, who was never lavish with praise, for their night action at the bridge of Barba del Puerco in March 1810. Ross's Troop was the only horse artillery attached to an infantry division and, with the 1st Hussars, King's German Legion, gave invaluable support to Craufurd's 'Light Bobs'.

Craufurd wears the plain or undress coat of a brigadier-general, as he then was, with overalls. He is armed with the 1803-pattern sword, suspended from an undress waist belt of black leather.

The Rifleman is based on a contemporary drawing made by an officer of the regiment in the Peninsula and shows the light cavalry style affected by its officers. Although the rifle-green jacket had three rows of silver buttons, the pelisse, which is, rather curiously, half worn and half slung, had black olivets instead of buttons. The jacket is faced black and the pelisse trimmed with brown fur. His grey overalls are reinforced with brown leather in a decorative fashion and have black braid down the outside seams. His shako is similar to the watering caps worn by cavalry officers, tapering towards the top and with a folding peak. A whistle is attached to the silver lion's head fitted to the black leather pouch belt. The sabre is also of light cavalry pattern.

The R.H.A. officer's dress also emulates the light cavalry, including the light dragoon helmet of black leather with fur crest, and, except for the colours, is very similar to the 95th officer's dress.

Wellington and staff at Waterloo. Uxbridge can be seen galloping towards Wellington and the dying figure in the right centre foreground is probably Picton. The mounted figure on the grey behind may be Hill. After Atkinson. (National Army Museum)

C Major-General Picton

The incident depicted in this plate occurred at Busaco in 1810, when, according to Oman, 'the light companies of the 45th and 88th ... were rallied by Picton in person, and brought up along the plateau to the right of the 8th Portuguese'.

Picton was notorious for his indifference to regulation dress and his example was followed by his staff, resulting in their being known in the Peninsular army as 'the bear and ragged staff', an allusion to the arms of the Earl of Warwick. He usually wore a blue military frock coat or a civilian coat. At Vittoria he was seen in a broad-brimmed beaver hat to protect his eyes and in the Waterloo campaign he appeared entirely in civilian clothes. He usually carried a stick or an umbrella. However, his great frame and bellowing voice, 'with the power of twenty trumpets', was so well known in the army that he needed none of the trappings of a general officer to distinguish himself. When the French attacked up the Busaco ridge at dawn,

Picton sprang straight from his bed into action, forgetting to remove his red night cap, in which he is shown here, and doubtless putting on the first coat that came to hand.

The Light Company soldier of the 88th Connaught Rangers recalls the long-standing feud between Picton and that regiment, which served in his division throughout the war. Though he admired the 88th's great fighting qualities, he deplored their indiscipline out of action. The soldier wears the felt, 1805 version of the 'stove-pipe' shako, originally introduced in 1800, with the green tuft of the light infantry companies. His red jacket has the wings of a flank company. Trousers, usually white, grey or blue were taken into regular use during the Peninsular War, often being worn over the regulation white breeches. He is accoutred with his pouch, knapsack with greatcoat rolled on top, haversack and water bottle.

The third figure is an officer of the 8th Portuguese Regiment of the Line, whose conduct at Busaco proved the increasing effectiveness of Beresford's reforms of the Portuguese army. Although officially in Leith's 5th Division, the regiment served under Picton's command at

Busaco. He wears the 1806 uniform with the blue collar and yellow cuffs, piped red, of the 8th. He is shown in the 1806-pattern shako, but this was being replaced from 1810 by a 'stove-pipe' shape, resembling the British infantry headdress. The brass plate bears the arms of the House of Braganza, a motif that is repeated on the gorget and shoulder belt plate. He wears a captain's epaulettes, consisting of shoulder straps covered in metal scales and terminating in short fringes.

D Major-General Lowry Cole

George Napier of the 52nd said of Lowry Cole, commanding the 4th Division, 'he is as kind and generous as he is brave'. This plate represents an incident during the retreat to Torres Vedras after Busaco, when Cole gave shelter and rest to the wounded Napier, an officer of another division, who had been abandoned by the Portuguese driver of the cart in which he had been travelling.

Cole is dressed as he might have been for dinner at his headquarters, wearing his major-general's embroidered coat with the lapels buttoned back and unhooked to show the white waistcoat, dark blue pantaloons and hessian boots.

Napier wears the scarlet jacket with buff facings, silver lace and buttons in pairs of the 52nd Light Infantry, serving in the Light Division. His grey overalls are reinforced round the bottom with leather. Light infantry officers carried sabres instead of the straight infantry sword, and wore them suspended from a shoulder belt with slings instead of the more usual frog.

The sentry at Cole's door is from one of the regiments of his division, the 7th Royal Fusiliers. In action fusilier regiments wore the shako like other Line regiments, but here he is wearing his full dress bearskin cap, and to further smarten himself up for this duty has removed his trousers to reveal the regulation white breeches and black gaiters. It was two battalions of this regiment and one of the 23rd

Front and rear views of a major-general's embroidered coat, post-1811, with aiguillette. The latter was looped up to the buttons on the right lapel. (National Army Museum)

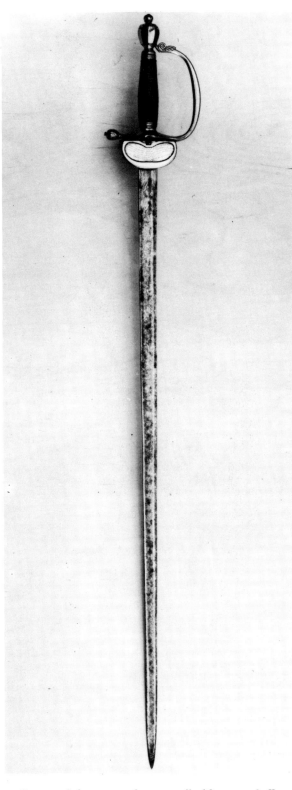

1796-pattern infantry sword, as prescribed for general officers by the 1802 regulations. The guard was brass and the grip bound with silver wire. The sword knot was crimson and gold and the scabbard black leather with gilt mounts. (National Army Museum)

Royal Welch Fusiliers that formed Myers' Fusilier brigade of Cole's division, which delivered the decisive counter-stroke at Albuera.

E Lieutenant-General Beresford

Though Beresford's chief role in the Peninsula was the reorganization of the Portuguese army, he fought at Albuera in 1811 as a lieutenant-general in the British army while temporarily in command of Hill's corps. During the height of the battle he personally tried to bring forward Carlos de España's Spanish brigade to support Hoghton's hard-pressed British brigade (29th, 48th, and 57th). Although some Spanish formations fought well at Albuera, this was not one of them, and they refused to advance, despite Beresford dragging forward one of the Spanish colonels by his epaulettes—the incident depicted here.

Beresford is wearing the cocked hat of a British general but with the red and blue cockade of Portugal added to the black British one. As shown in a contemporary print, he is dressed in a pelisse-coat with black frogging, strictly speaking an unofficial undress of light cavalry officers, but also popular with senior and staff officers. His sash and sword belt are of regulation British pattern.

The ADC helping Beresford to rally the Spaniards has an oilskin cover over his hat and, although on service blue frock coats were often worn by staff officers, he is shown here in the plain, single-breasted coat of his appointment in order to illustrate its details. Being an undress garment it lacks the tasselled, foliate gold lace loops (silver for brigade-majors) worn on the embroidered coat, and has the buttons in pairs down the front and set two over one on the cuffs and skirts. The single epaulette of gold (or silver) embroidery on blue cloth was worn on the right shoulder by infantry ADCs and brigade-majors, and on the left by those attached to cavalry commanders. Brigade-majors retained silver embroidery on the collar and cuffs of their undress coats. The ADC shown here wears a regulation staff sword belt and the 1796-pattern infantry sword.

Carlos de España's brigade included the regiments 'Rey', 'Zamora' and 'Volontarios de Navarra' and had been severely handled by the French earlier in the year. The Spanish field officer in the plate wears the white uniform with violet facings of the first-named regiment. This was the 1805 uniform which, by 1811, was soon to be replaced by a more practical dress, predominantly blue in colour. His cocked hat bears the red cockade of Spain.

F Lieutenant-General Stapleton Cotton

On 11 April 1812 Cotton, in command of the Cavalry Division, conducted a masterly action at Llerena against Soult's rearguard corps with W. Ponsonby's light cavalry brigade (12th, 14th, and 16th Light Dragoons) and Le Marchant's heavy brigade (5th Dragoon Guards, 3rd and 4th Dragoons). The plate shows Cotton as he might have appeared on this occasion, with an orderly dragoon of the 4th, giving an order to an officer of the 14th Light Dragoons attached to his staff.

Cotton was famous for his splendid appearance and is wearing the magnificent scarlet uniform with blue facings of a general officer of hussars, in which he is shown in Heaphy's paintings. Here he wears dark blue overalls, but on more ceremonial occasions these were replaced by scarlet breeches and hessian boots, and a white over red plume was fitted to the busby.

At this time the dress of the heavy and light cavalry was being changed in accordance with the new regulations of 1811–12, but it was some time before regiments in the Peninsula were re-equipped. The officer of the 14th Light Dragoons wears the old uniform of crested helmet and laced jacket, and is based on a portrait of an officer of that regiment painted in 1812. The 14th did not receive the new clothing until 1813 and an officer noted that he was still wearing the old helmet as late as May 1814. A blue pelisse trimmed with black fur and black braiding was also worn sometimes by officers of the 14th, but is not shown here. Officially the regiment's facings were orange, but in practice were almost scarlet. In the field, grey overalls with the double orange stripe were worn instead of the full dress white buckskin breeches.

The 4th Dragoons received their new clothing, with the exception of the helmet with horse-hair mane, about two weeks after the action at Llerena, so it must have been almost the last occasion the old dress was worn in action by this regiment. The old heavy cavalry headdress was still officially the cocked hat worn athwart, but in the field felt

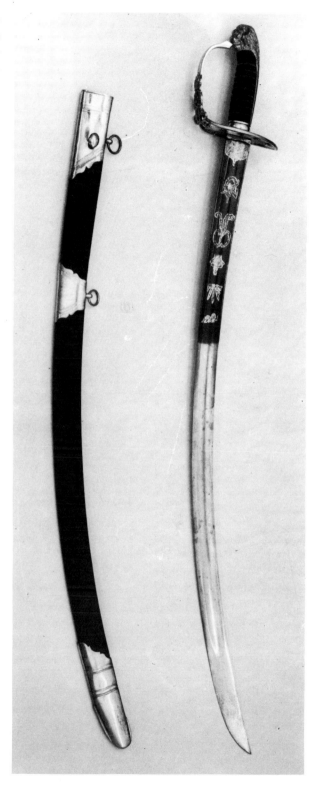

1803-pattern general officers' sword with scabbard. The guard and scabbard mounts were gilt brass and the grip was bound with brass wire. The Royal Cypher with crown above was inset in the guard. (National Army Museum)

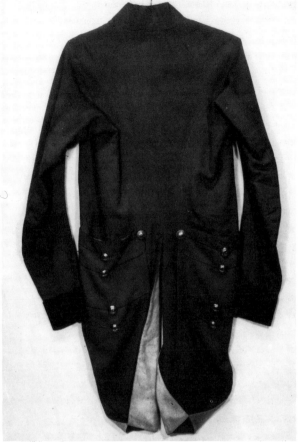

Front and rear views of a major-general's plain or undress coat. This example is buttoned across on the wrong side and the epaulettes or aiguillette are missing. (National Army Museum)

watering caps with a movable peak were more usually worn, as shown in the plate, and overalls replaced the white leather breeches and jacked boots. The dragoon is armed with the heavy cavalry 1796-pattern carbine and straight sword and, in addition to his pouch belt, carries a haversack and water bottle over the right shoulder.

G General The Earl of Wellington

The incident depicted in this plate shows Wellington, accompanied by his Military Secretary, Lord Fitzroy Somerset, ordering Major-General Pakenham, commanding the 3rd Division in Picton's absence, to attack the French left at the Battle of Salamanca, 22 July 1812. According to Lady Longford, *Wellington—The Years of the Sword*, the following exchange took place:

'Ned, d'ye see those fellows on the hill?',

Wellington said, tapping Pakenham on the shoulder, 'Throw your division into column; at them; and drive them to the devil'.

'I will, my lord, if you will give me your hand', replied Pakenham.

With his well-known campaigning costume of plain frock coat, white breeches and hessian boots, Wellington wears a low cocked hat, often encased in an oilskin cover, but here displaying the white ostrich feathers round the brim, as prescribed exclusively for general officers by General Order dated 24 December 1811. His sword belt and crimson sash are worn under his coat, as was his practice. Later in 1812, after being made *Generalissimo* of the Spanish forces, he took to wearing the red and gold sash of a Spanish general and added the cockades of Spain and Portugal to the black cockade of England in his hat. Under his coat he wears a white waistcoat and a white stock in preference to the more usual black. Sometimes his clothes might be grey and overalls would replace the breeches, but although he would don his general's, and later field-marshal's, scarlet coat for ceremonial occasions, his field dress always made a neat and restrained contrast to the showy attire of his opponents.

Pakenham wears the plain coat of a major-general. In accordance with the above-mentioned order of 1811, general's epaulettes were abolished in favour of an aiguillette worn on the right shoulder only; this was arranged differently according to the rank of the general officer. Besides adding the ostrich feathers to the hat, the 1811 order retained the scale loop for infantry generals but prescribed a star loop for those of the cavalry.

Somerset is dressed very similarly to his chief, except that his frock coat is double-breasted and he wears overalls reinforced with leather, a costume based on a description of Wellington's 'blue-coated staff' and a contemporary print by Atkinson of Wellington and staff at Salamanca. He carries a telescope in a leather case and a haversack covered in black oilskin to hold any writing materials, maps, etc., that his chief may require. Though only in his early twenties, Somerset served Wellington with devoted efficiency all through the Peninsular War and afterwards until Wellington's death in 1852, when as Lord Raglan he became Commander-in-Chief of the Army and held the chief command in the Crimea.

H Lieutenant-General The Earl of Uxbridge

This shows Lord Uxbridge, in command of the Allied cavalry during the Waterloo campaign, accompanied by an ADC from the 2nd Hussars, King's German Legion, giving orders to an officer of the 1st Life Guards, as they might have appeared at Genappe during the retreat from Quatre Bras.

The figure of Uxbridge is based on the Denis Dighton painting of Waterloo in the Royal Collection, which shows him in the uniform of a general officer of light cavalry. His shako, of the 1812 light dragoon pattern, bears a triple row of gold gimp, denoting his rank. He wears the fur-trimmed dark blue pelisse, with five rows of gilt buttons, over his jacket, though whether the latter was the scarlet pattern worn by general officers of hussars or the dark blue he was entitled to wear as colonel of the 7th Hussars is not known. Another painting by Dighton of the same incident shows him in light blue overalls cut in the cossack style,

but this cannot be correct as the actual overalls he wore, now in the possession of the Marquess of Anglesey, are dark blue. In full dress, general officers of hussars carried a mameluke sabre, but in the Waterloo campaign Uxbridge appears to have used the light cavalry pattern sabre with stirrup hilt.

Serving as an extra ADC was Captain von Streerwitz of the 2nd K.G.L. Hussars. The figure is shown in his regimental uniform with a forage cap covered in oilskin. In the plate he is wearing his pelisse slung, in order to show the details of the jacket, but in view of the weather on 17 June he would probably have been wearing it over the jacket, like Uxbridge.

The officer of the 1st Life Guards is dressed in

Embroidered coat of an ADC, c. 1815. Scarlet, faced blue, with gold lace. A brigade-major's coat was similar but with silver lace. The epaulette is missing. From late 1811 ADCs and brigade-majors attached to cavalry commanders wore an aiguillette instead of an epaulette, infantry staff keeping the latter. (National Army Museum)

accordance with the uniform changes of 1812. The black leather helmet with gilt fittings was surmounted by a crimson and blue silk 'chenille'. He wears the undress jacket, or frock collett, instead of the laced dress jacket, and cloth overalls. His belts and sabretache are all of the undress pattern. On service, officers of the Household Cavalry carried the ordinary heavy cavalry officer's sword as opposed to their more ornate parade sword with half-basket hilt.

(The author acknowledges with gratitude the help given by the Marquess of Anglesey in the preparation of this plate and by Mr John Mollo with this and other plates.)

Notes sur les planches en couleur

A Major-General Hill à la bataille de Talavera, le 27 juillet 1809. Il porte la tunique brodée d'un général de brigade avec les revers boutonnés sur la poitrine à l'exception du haut de revers; comme beaucoup d'officiers qui étaient au service en Egypte il porte un sabre mameluke en préférence à l'epée réglementaire. Avec lui sont un tambour du 48th Foot et Lieutenant-Colonel Donellan du même régiment qui continua à porter les cheveux en le style poudré démodé en dépit de consignes contres.

B Brigadier-General Craufurd visitant avant-postes de sa Division Légère au bord du fleuve Agueda en 1810. Il porte la tunique *undress* de ce grade. Avec lui sont un officier du 95th Regiment mis en la tenue verte typique des Chasseurs à Pied; et un officier du Royal Horse Artillery.

C Major-General Picton, un excentrique gallois grossier et intrépide, fut souvent vu en champ de bataille mis en vêtements civils. A Busaco en 1810 il fut réveillé de son lit à la bataille et il porta le bonnet de nuit rouge illustré. Il est illustré avec un soldat de la Compagnie Légère, 88th Foot, et un officier du 8eme Infanterie de Ligne de l'armée Portugaise, qui furent au service sous le commandement de lui avec distinction.

D Les mémoires de George Napier font mention de l'incident quand Napier, blessé, chercha l'abri chex le logement de Major-General Lowry Cole. Cette planche illustre Cole, mis en la tunique brodée de son grade, saluant à Napier, mis en la tenue d'un officier de la 52nd Light Infantry. Le sentinelle à la porte du général porte la grande tenue de la 7th Royal Fusiliers.

E A la bataille d'Albuera en 1811 Lieutenant-General Beresford essaya à amener la brigade espagnole de Carlos de España pour appuyer l'infanterie Brittanique aux abois mais il échoua à persuader les Espagnols d'attaquer quand même il tira un de leur colonels vers lui par ses épaulettes! Nous illustrons Beresford mis en une *pelisse-coat*, avec cocardes brittanique et portugaise dans son chapeau mis de coté. Le colonel est mis en la tenue du Régiment del Rey. Dans le fond est un aide de camp brittanique mis en tunique *undress*.

F Lieutenant-General Stapleton Cotton commandant la Division de Cavalerie à Llerena en avril 1812, mis en la tenue d'un général d'Hussars. Avec lui sont un planton de la 4th Dragoons et un officier de la 14th Light Dragoons.

G General The Earl of Wellington comme il fut en juillet 1812, à la bataille de Salamanca (Los Arapiles). Il est mis en civil de campagne ordinaire. Il est accompagné de son secrétaire militaire Lord Fitzroy Somerset, et son beau-frère, Major-General Pakenham, commandant la 3rd Division. Pakenham porte la tunique ordinaire de son grade avec l'aiguilette que remplaça les épaulettes de grade de général en 1811. Somerset porte un costume similaire à son commandant en chef.

H Lieutenant-General The Earl of Uxbridge mis en la tenue d'un général de la Cavalerie Légère, ordonnant la retraite de l'armée alliée de Quatre Bras à Waterloo le 17 juin 1815. Avec lui est un aide, Captain von Streerwitz de la 2nd Hussars, King's German Legion, est un officier de la 1st Life Guards mis en tenue *undress*.

Farbtafeln

A Major-General Hill am 27 Juli 1809 an der Schlacht bei Talavera. Er trägt die bestickte Jacke eines Generalmajor mit den Aufschlägen über der Brust zugenknöpft bis auf den Oberteil; wie viele Offiziere, die in Ägypten dienten, trägt er einen mameluke Säbel lieber als ein Kommisssschwert. Mit ihm sind ein Trommler des 48th Foot, und Lieutenant-Colonel Donellan des gleichen Regiments, der die altmodische gepuderte Haarmode weiter trug trotz Befehlen dagegen.

B Brigadier-General Craufurd besichtigend in 1810 Vorposten seiner Leichtdivision an dem Agueda Fluss. Er trägt die *undress* Jacke dieses Dienstgrads. Mit ihm sin ein Offizier des 95ten Regiments in der typischen grünen Uniform der Schützenregimenter; und ein Offizier der Royal Horse Artillery.

C Major-General Picton, ein furchtloser walisischer exzentrischer Mensch, der ein loses Maul hatte, wurde oft in Zivilkleidern auf dem Schlachtfeld gesehen. In 1810 in Busaco wurde er aus seinem Bett zu der Schlacht aufgeboten und er trug die rote Schlafmütze, die hier illustriert wird. Er wird mit einem Soldat der Leichtkompagnie, 88th Foot, und einem Offizier der 8ten Linieninfanterie portugiesischer Armee, gesehen, die Dienst mit Auszeichnung unter seinem Befehl taten.

D Die Memoiren George Napier erwähnen den Zwischenfall, als Napier, verwundet, Obdach bei dem Quartier Major-General Lowry Coles suchte. Diese Farbtafel illustriert Cole, in der bestickte Jacke seines Dienstgrads, grüssend an Napier in der Uniform eines Offiziers der 52nd Light Infantry. Der Posten an der Tür des Generals trägt die Galauniform des 7th Royal Fusiliers.

E In 1811 an der Schlacht bei Albuera versuchte Lieutenant-General Beresford die spanische Brigade Carlos de Españas anzuführen, um die hart bedrängte britische Infanterie zu unterstützen aber er verfehlte die Spaniers zu überfallen bereden, selbst, als er einen ihrer Obersten an seinen Epauletten herbeizog! Wir illustrieren Beresford in einer *pelisse-coat* mit britischen und portugiesischen Kokarden in seinem Hut. Der Oberst ist in der Uniform des Regiments del Rey. In dem Hintergrund ist ein britischer Adjutant in *undress* jacke.

F Lieutenant-General Stapleton Cotton in April 1812 in Befehl der Kavallereidivision in Llerena und er trägt die Uniform eines Generals Husars. Mit ihm sind ein Ordonanz des 4th Dragoons und ein Offizier des 14th Light Dragoons.

G General The Earl of Wellington, als er in Juli 1812 an der Schlacht bei Salamanca (Los Arapiles) war. Er trägt seinen gewöhnlichen Zivilfeldanzug. Er ist mit seinem Militärsekretar, Lord Fitzroy Somerset, und seinem Schwager, Major-General Pakenham, in Befehl der 3ten Division, begleitet. Pakenham trägt die ungemusterte Jacke seines Dienstgrads, mit der Achselschnur, die in 1811 die Epauletten Generalsdienstgrads ersassen. Somerset trägt ein gleiches Kostüm als das von seinem Oberbefehlshaber.

H Lieutenant-General The Earl of Uxbridge in der Uniform eines Generals Leichtkavallerie, am 17 Juni 1815 in Befehl von dem Rückzug der verbudeten Armee von Quatre-Bras nach Waterloo. Mit ihm ist ein Adjutant, Captain von Streerwitz des 2nd Hussars, King's German Legion; und ein Offizier des 1st Life Guards in *undress* uniform.

Men-at-Arms Series

* cased edition also available

ISBN 0 85045 299 6

Avec annotations en français sur les planches en couleur
Mit Aufzeichnungen auf deutsch über die Farbtafeln